Weird

HIKES

HIKES

A Collection of Bizarre, Funny,
and Absolutely True Hiking Stories

SECOND EDITION

Art Bernstein

FALCONGUIDES

GUILFORD, CONNECTICUT
HELENA, MONTANA

AN IMPRINT OF GLOBE PEQUOT PRESS

This book, like me, is dedicated to Lynn Bernstein, my wife, whom I love with a never before experienced fervor and who has read and enjoyed every word I've ever written. That's one of the things wives do, after all.

FALCONGUIDES®

Copyright © 2003, 2011 by Art Bernstein

FalconGuides is an imprint of Globe Pequot Press.

Falcon, FalconGuides, and Outfit Your Mind are registered trademarks of Morris Book Publishing, LLC.

Project editor: David Legere
Text design: Sheryl Kober
Layout artist: Kevin Mak

All interior photos by Art Bernstein except where otherwise noted.

Library of Congress Cataloging-in-Publication Data is available on file.

ISBN 978-0-7627-6386-3

Printed in the United States of America
10 9 8 7 6 5 4 3 2 1

Contents

Acknowledgments

The following people helped make this book possible: Lynn Bernstein, Jessica Haberman (editor at Globe Pequot Press), David Pitt, Marcia Ruff (Roeper School), Crater Lake Search and Rescue, Anna Bernstein, Sara Bernstein, Brandon Bremer, David Robbins, Mrs. Shotka, Jon Emanual, Monty Elliott, Sharon Kleyne, Calvin Kennedy, Brian Boothby, Stacey Elam, Chuck Smith (Klamath National Forest/retired), Linda Drescher, Laurie Lerner, Mikki Dolgin, Old Augie Atteberry, George Roeper, Terri Dworkin, Nick and Monique, Leelyn Pritchett, Natalie and Larry Katkowski, Thelma and Henry Bernstein, Zaydie and Dora, Barbara Gornowich, Jerry Bernstein, Paul Bernstein, Steve Bernstein, Ross Tocher, Bev Driver, Tonya Ozone, Georgia O'Keeffe, Ansel Adams, and Santa Claus.

Introduction

I'm excited about the second edition of *Weird Hikes,* especially the five new stories included in this fully revised edition. The new stories, like the original stories, all involve weird incidents that happened to me while hiking. However, in the new stories, the weird incidents also represent major turning points in my life. They range from my first hike at age seven, when I wandered away from school in the snow and had a remarkable experience in which I first learned to value my personal eccentricities, to a dramatic broken leg and wilderness rescue when I was sixty-two, when a strange event removed my lifelong fear of death. As for the original fourteen stories, the editors and I revisited all of them, making this a better, weirder, and more exciting book.

Readers will note that there are no demon-possessed dogs or cars in any of my stories (although there are some rather frightening nocturnal deer and at least one seemingly demon-possessed trail). That's because every one of the stories is essentially true. Therefore, even though each story involves a weird or bizarre event, they truly could happen to anybody.

I have no special psychic talents or paranormal abilities whatsoever. Weird things do not usually happen to me . . . except once in a very great while and, for some reason, almost always while hiking. As a writer, I am well aware that certain basic elements are critical to any good story. This includes things like establishing a connection between the climactic weird event and a need or desire of the main character (who is almost always me). Without good story elements, even the most bizarre event just doesn't make very good reading. In a few cases, turning an isolated event into a cohesive, readable story took a little ingenuity. But aside from that, the stories are all based on true events. If you have doubts, I encourage you to experience the weirdness for yourself—all the stories include information on how to get to each hike, for those that are still accessible.

1

The First Hike

PART 1

I went on my very first hike in 1950, when I was just seven years old. And I did it alone. My parents certainly did not take me on any hikes because they were sedentary big-city types who never, to my recollection, took me, my sister, or my brother on so much as a walk in the park. Later on, when our family visited places like the Grand Canyon and Yellowstone, I still rarely saw them engage in anything that approached hiking.

In the 1950 hike, therefore, I was completely on my own, sneaking off into the "wild" with no adult supervision or permission. It was a perfect setup for disaster. But in the end it proved to be a grand adventure, and it forever changed me in many ways.

You have to understand that in 1950, I was considered a "problem child." The concepts of ADHD and Asperger's syndrome were completely unknown in those days. Also, "Talented and Gifted" programs in public schools were years in the future. So children who fell into one of those categories were simply out of luck. I had the misfortune to fall into all three categories (although the Asperger's was very slight).

It is not surprising that when I was seven, I felt a yearning to get away from adult supervision, especially teachers. Nor is it surprising that I acted on it.

PART 2

As a small child, the one person in the world able to look beyond my various behavioral quirks was my mother. She mostly enjoyed my curiosity and imagination, although when the ADHD kicked in, which was frequently, I could be a bit of a handful. Nevertheless, even at my most mischievous, my mother was always patient with me and always took me seriously.

A good example was the time in 1948, when I was five, that she took me shopping at Federal's department store. I remember it because it was also my first encounter with a department store Santa Claus, and I did not react like most other children. In the days before K-Mart and Walmart, Federal's was way less expensive than, say, J. L. Hudson, Detroit's "big" department store.

In a place like Federal's, I had a tendency to wander off and investigate whatever attracted my curiosity, which was just about everything. I still do. My mother, despite staggering under an armload of bags and boxes, calmly, patiently, and repeatedly dragged me back to reality, usually by the collar. At one point, I disappeared under a clothing rack, and without breaking stride, she grabbed my foot and yanked me back out.

"No fair," I complained. "I was exploring the Lost Cave of the Aztecs. I coulda found some hidden treasure."

"You can look for hidden treasure when we get home."

"You never let me do anything," I pouted.

"Life is hard," said my mother, giving me a kiss on the head, which I ignored.

And then, rounding a corner, there it was! I'd never seen anything so enchanting. Right smack in the middle of Federal's, there was a genuine fairyland with a golden, jewel-covered throne attended by magical-looking elves and surrounded by sparkling, multicolored Christmas trees, papier-mâché statues of reindeer, and giant, gaily wrapped presents. Sitting on the throne was none other than Santa Claus himself.

I stopped and stared in awe and wonder.

"I wanna see Santa," I announced.

"But Sweetie, our family doesn't believe in Santa." My mother grabbed my hand and attempted to drag me on past.

"I don't care," I whined, tugging back. "I wanna see Santa."

With a patient sigh, my mother set down her packages and crouched so that we were at eye level.

"That's not really Santa, just a person dressed like Santa. And he's not going to bring you any gifts. The presents you get for Christmas will be from your dad and me."

"I don't care. I want to see Santa. Just this once. Pleeeeeeeeease!"

"All right. Just this once."

As soon as I got in line, reality set in. Close up, the setting, the elves, and especially Santa began to look run-down and fake. As I moved toward the head of the line, and I got a closer and closer look at Santa, or whoever he was, I could see the stubble of his black beard underneath his fake white beard. I found it repulsive. And his eyes just didn't look like Santa Claus eyes. They didn't twinkle, and they definitely weren't merry.

As I stood in line staring at the guy in the Santa suit, I was reminded of Black Pete, a recurring villain in the *Mickey Mouse* comic books that I faithfully purchased each month for 10 cents. Black Pete was a burly, stubble-bearded pirate with a huge mouth and jaw and little furry cat ears. I suddenly got all scared, as though it really was Black Pete, and not Santa Claus, sitting up there.

"I think I changed my mind," I quietly announced to my mother.

"After all that fuss? I don't think so."

When I reluctantly climbed aboard Santa's lap, I found myself not only frightened but also tongue-tied. Santa, or Black Pete, kept asking what I wanted for Christmas, and all I could think of was that he probably had a sword hidden under his suit and was going to kill me. I could not imagine letting that awful person into our house.

"Come on, kid," he kept saying in a loud and impatient voice, "what da yez want from Santa?"

"Surprise me," I finally blurted out. "In fact, why don't you just drop the present down the chimney so you won't have to bother coming in?"

When I said that, everybody around me started laughing, including Santa and my mother. It was loud and embarrassing. I was just trying to be helpful, and as a result everybody was laughing at me. To make matters worse, Santa's laugh was not the traditional "ho-ho-ho" but a high-pitched "hee-hee-hee." I put my hands over my ears to shut out the noise.

Some Santa.

"I told you he's not the real Santa," said my mother as we walked away.

"I hope not. But does that mean that somewhere, there *is* a real Santa?"

PART 3

The worst results of my impulsiveness, curiosity, and overly active imagination came at school, James Vernor Elementary, named for some guy who started a ginger ale factory in Detroit in 1865. In 1949, of course, I was unfamiliar with terms like "impulsiveness" and "overly active imagination." All I knew was that even though I tried my best to "be good," I kept getting into trouble. On the rare occasion when something at school truly interested me, it only meant I would get into even more trouble. It didn't help that at Vernor School, students were forced to walk through the halls in absolutely straight, lock-step lines, with eyes forward. And to rub it in, the corridors were lined with enticing, gaily decorated display windows that students weren't allowed to look at.

In first grade, I was bored most of the time and constantly squirming at my desk. My teacher, Miss Grunderson, sometimes reminded me of Miss Grundy from the *Archie* comics, which I regularly read in addition to *Mickey Mouse.* I don't think Miss Grunderson was too smart, and any questions I asked in class always seemed to make her mad because she usually couldn't answer them. She frequently ended up yelling at me and accusing me of purposely being "disruptive." At the time, I didn't even know what disruptive meant.

I remember a class where she tried to teach us about flying saucers because they had been in the news a lot. She asked what we would do if we met a person from another planet. All the other kids sat there with blank expressions. All except me. My hand immediately shot up with an excited, "Ooh, ooh, ooh." There was no way the teacher could avoid calling on me.

"Yes, Artie," she said. "What would you do?"

"I'd introduce him to Harry."

"Harry?"

"Yes, Harry," I replied, pleased with my brilliance.

"And just who is Harry?"

"The president of the United States. You've never heard of Harry Truman?"

"Oh. That Harry. Yes. Does anyone else have an answer?"

I spent the next few minutes fantasizing about meeting an alien, taking off with him in his flying saucer, and zapping the school with a disintegrating ray, causing the building and everything in it, including Miss Grunderson, to immediately vanish.

Another time, when Miss Grunderson told the class that "a noun refers to a person, place, or thing," I raised my hand and pointed out that people and places *are* things. Another time, when she was showing us how to plant a seed in a flowerpot full of earth, I asked her whether, if we did the same thing on Mars, we would fill the flowerpot with "mars."

Those are just a few examples. There are dozens more. Were it not for Miss Grunderson getting mad at me, I would have raised my hand a lot more, although even when I did raise my hand, she rarely called on me. And when she called on me, I invariably ended up being ridiculed, accused of something terrible, or being sent to the office. Just for asking a question.

Every time I asked a question and Miss Grunderson got mad, she reminded me of the Queen of Hearts from *Alice in Wonderland,* the first full-length novel I ever read and still my favorite book sixty years later. The Queen of Hearts was sweet and pleasant as cherry pie—until you got her angry, which didn't take much. Then she would turn into an evil monster who thought nothing of having peoples' heads chopped off.

The biggest difference between Miss Grunderson and the Queen of Hearts was that the queen wanted to chop off *everybody's* head. Miss Grunderson, for some reason, only seemed interested in my head.

I was terrified of Miss Grunderson and, as I had done in the Black Pete/Santa Claus situation, I reacted to her as though she really was the Queen of Hearts, prepared to chop off my head at any time.

No wonder I didn't like school. I never told my parents about my problem, about not being allowed to ask questions, about being sent to the office all the time, or about the other kids laughing at me whenever I got into trouble. It simply never occurred to me that I could or should. And in 1950 seven-year-olds just did not question the behavior of teachers.

Miss Grunderson was by no means the only teacher with whom I had a problem in first grade. One of the most frustrating incidents at Vernor School in first grade occurred toward the end of the school year, during gym class. The boys, including myself, were on the baseball field that day and the girls were off playing field hockey. I remember the boys all having a great time laughing and shouting at one another. None of them talked to me, and whenever my side was at bat, I would sit down by myself against the fence and read a book.

I'd been reading since I was four and did pretty well for a first grader. While everyone else in my class was still working on *Fun with Dick and Jane,* I was reading *Shanghai Passage* by Howard Pease, a children's adventure novel the school librarian told me about.

"Hey, Artie," said Mr. Spafford, the gym teacher, as I sat by the fence. He was a tall, muscular man with a jutting lower jaw. "You're not supposed to have your nose in a book; you're supposed to be playing ball."

Mr. Spafford reminded me of Reggie, also from the *Archie* comics, except twenty years older. He was tall, naturally good at sports, and regarded himself as God's gift to something or other. He tended to look down his nose at kids who were bad at sports. He regarded me as completely hopeless and a little strange, and he didn't hesitate to let me know it. Some teacher.

"I'm waiting to bat," I said in reply to Mr. Spafford's question. "And it's a really good book. It's all about this orphan kid who stows away on a cargo ship and gets to visit Tahiti, Pago Pago, and Shanghai. Someday I'm going to do all those things."

"Well, you'd better not do it now because you're up to bat next. Don't worry, though. If I know you, you'll be back in about thirty seconds. Then you can go to Tahiti."

Sure enough, I walked to the batter's box, lunged awkwardly at three straight pitches nowhere near home plate, and struck out. I was a terrible athlete. Whenever I struck out, which was all the time, the other kids always laughed at me. Mr. Spafford never once stopped them or made any attempt to teach me to throw or hit.

The most frustrating incident of the school year occurred a few minutes later, as my class was walking in line back to the school building. I brought up the rear, as always. And, as always, we walked past a large, windowless brick building immediately next to the school, with all sorts of ducts coming out of the roof. I'd always wondered what was inside, but the heavy iron door was always tightly shut.

To my amazement, on that day the door was slightly ajar. Nobody noticed when I quickly stepped out of line, walked to the door, and peeked in. I was peering into the school's boiler room, which supplied heat to the classrooms. The interior contained two growling, glowing cast-iron boilers and reeked of burning coal and oil. A man, stripped to the waist, shoveled coal into one of the giant, flaming maws.

I knew about boiler rooms from the book I was reading. I pretended it was the cargo ship's boiler room. I imagined myself walking in, grabbing a shovel, and going to work. When my shift was over, I would go upstairs to the gently rocking deck, look out over the railing, and enjoy the ocean breeze and endless horizon.

"Hey, kid," an angry voice shouted from inside the boiler room. And I was suddenly, once again, a small child peeking through the doorway. "You're not supposed to be here. Now scram!"

Getting to see the inside of the boiler room was by far the most interesting thing that happened at school that year. And it touched off a fantasy that I didn't want to end.

When the big iron door slammed in my face, I shrugged and walked sadly away, as I always did. In my limited experience, adults in authority were simply not supposed to be nice to small children. It never crossed my mind to expect otherwise.

PART 4

Oddly enough, things started changing for the better at school because of a visit at home from my grandfather and his girlfriend. My grandfather, my mother's father, lived six blocks away and came over all the time, but this was the first time he brought one of his "lady friends." My grandmother had passed away before I was born.

My sister, Barbara, and I were playing together behind the sofa that night, pretending to be deep-sea divers. Barbara was ten, my brother, Paul, was four, and I was seven. We heard the doorbell ring and adult conversation in the distance, then my parents and grandfather came into the living room accompanied by Rifka Fiddler. She was an elegant woman in her late sixties with a mink stole, dyed black hair, too much makeup, high heels, and rimless glasses. My grandfather was a short, smiling, well-dressed, gray-haired gentleman in his mid-seventies.

After Rifka and my grandfather were seated in the living room, Barbara and I were summoned from behind the sofa and, joined by our brother, Paul, lined up in front of them.

"This is Grandpa's friend, Rifka," said my mother. "Say hello."

"Hello," we recited in unison.

"Would you children like to see a funny trick?" asked Rifka.

"Yes, ma'am," we replied, again in unison.

Suddenly, Rifka's teeth shot forward in her mouth, hideously distorting her face until she looked to me like a snarling demon baring its fangs. Barbara covered her mouth and giggled. Paul didn't seem to care. I ran into the kitchen shrieking.

My mother followed, knelt down beside me, and hugged me.

"She turned into a monster," I sobbed.

"No she didn't. She just pushed her false teeth forward with her tongue. I understand why you got scared though. You've never seen anything like that before, and it did look pretty strange. But trust me, there's nothing to be afraid of. Rifka is a very nice lady and I'm sure she didn't mean to frighten you. Now please come back to the living room."

"No! She's going to get me."

"She's not going to get you."

"She is so. First Miss Grunderson wants to chop my head off, and now Rifka turns into a monster and wants to eat me."

"Miss Grunderson wants to chop your head off?"

"All the time. She turns into the Queen of Hearts."

My choice of words, here, can only be described as "unfortunate." But what did I know? I was only seven, and I used the vocabulary at my disposal. I had so closely associated Miss Grunderson with the Queen of Hearts, and I was so frightened of her, that I mistakenly gave my mother the impression that I actually believed I *was* in physical danger of being beheaded by my teacher.

"Does she really turn into the Queen of Hearts, or does she just act like the Queen of Hearts?" asked my mother, who could be pretty perceptive.

"I don't know. All I know is that when I ask questions, she gets mad and yells at me like she wants to chop my head off. I try real hard not to ask questions so she won't get mad, but sometimes I can't help it."

My mother gave me another hug but was apparently still not completely convinced that I wasn't hallucinating. Either way, she definitely did not like what she'd just heard. And my mother was not a person to stand around and allow bad things to happen to her children.

"I promise," she said, "that Rifka will not hurt you. As for Miss Grunderson, we'll just see about *that*."

I was not there for my mother's conference with Miss Grunderson. It wasn't until many years later, after I'd grown up, that she described the conversation, and the other interviews that resulted in my going to a private school for one year.

"My son tells me he's afraid of you," said my mother to Miss Grunderson.

"I'm sorry to hear that, but he can be disruptive. We can't just let him do whatever he wants or there would be complete chaos and nobody would learn."

"What exactly does he do that's so awful?"

"He asks questions all the time."

"He asks questions? Aren't students supposed to ask questions? For this you punish him? What kind of school are you running?"

"A school where children whose parents fail to discipline them at home aren't allowed to run wild."

"And in my son's case, that means he's not allowed to ask questions?"

"Of course he is. It's the questions he asks that causes problems."

"What kind of questions does he ask?"

"Questions nobody can answer. I'm positive he only asks them to make me look foolish and get a rise out of the class."

"It would appear that making you look foolish is not that difficult," said my mother. "Besides, that sounds like your problem, not his. How does he get along with the other children?"

"Fine, I guess."

"Very interesting. He claims that nobody at school likes him or talks to him very much. Not his classmates or his teachers."

"I was unaware of that. I'm sorry."

"I don't suppose you have any special programs or supplemental material to keep Artie occupied so he doesn't get quite so bored?"

"I've given him all that. But he can do in ten minutes what takes everyone else an hour. And then he's back to squirming in his chair, yawning, looking bored, and asking impossible questions. I wish I had an answer. If you had the financial means, you could send him to the Country Day School or maybe the Roepers' school out in Bloomfield Hills. I think it's called the City and Country School. They only have ten or fifteen students in each class, so there's far more individual attention."

"The Roepers, huh? You know, I just might have a connection there. Thank you, Miss Grunderson. And please try to ease up on Artie. He's really very sweet."

My mother's connection was Dr. Morris Raskin, a noted child psychiatrist who was also an art patron of my father's and a family friend.

"So anyhow, Morrie," said my mother, sitting on a leather chair in front of the doctor's immense mahogany desk, "what can you tell me about the Roepers?"

"George and Annemarie? They're two of the finest people I've ever met. Why?"

"It's about Artie. He's a wonderful student and his grades are fantastic, but public school just does not seem right for him. They can't keep him occupied, and he's not allowed to ask questions because they make the teacher feel stupid. He also keeps talking about his teacher turning into the Queen of Hearts from *Alice in Wonderland*. I'm pretty sure he's not actually hallucinating, but I can't be positive. In any case, I was thinking that a more progressive school with much smaller class sizes might be better for him. There's no question that he's unhappy."

Dr. Raskin smiled. "I doubt if he's hallucinating. He's just a very bright child with an exceptionally vivid imagination."

"Could the Roepers' school help him?"

"It might be just the thing. It's expensive, though."

"So there's nothing to be done?"

"I didn't say that. George Roeper is reluctant to just hand out scholarships, but he's been known to let parents work off the tuition. Shall I talk to him?"

"I would be grateful beyond words. I hear that the Roepers are from Germany and originally came to Detroit to escape the Nazis."

"That's right. Annmarie studied psychoanalysis in Vienna under Anna Freud, Sigmund's daughter, and they ran a school in Germany until the Nazis shut it down because Annemarie's family was Jewish. They started the Michigan school in 1941. It's located in a beautiful mansion on the highest hill in the town of Bloomfield Hills, surrounded by hundreds of acres of farm and forest land."

My mother's subsequent interview with George Roeper took place in George's modest and cluttered office at the school. Mr. Roeper, as I recall, spoke with a slight German accent that was very cultured and tinged with British.

"It seems to me," said Mr. Roeper, "that Artie is behaving like a normal, active, inquisitive little boy. Even under ideal circumstances, however, inquisitive little boys can demand a lot of attention, from both parents and teachers. But he scored amazingly well on our aptitude test. He tested at fifth grade level in verbal and reading, which is incredible for a first grader."

"Can you do anything for him?"

"Perhaps. I'm willing to give him a year in exchange for a little work on your part."

"Will a year be enough?"

"I hope so. If we can build up his self-confidence and social skills during the year so he's able to satisfy his intellectual curiosity without being disruptive or inappropriate, he should be able to return to public school and thrive. If not, we'll decide where to go from there. Personally, I'd be optimistic."

"What would I have to do?"

"Well, we run three school buses every day from Detroit. Because our kids come from all over the city, most don't live near our bus stops.

Usually the parents drive them to the bus every morning, but a few can't because both parents work. If you could pick up four children every morning and drive them to the bus stop, I'd call us even."

"That's all? An hour a day? Five hours a week? I'll take it."

"Wonderful. I'll see you and Artie in the fall."

PART 5

On the first day at City and Country School, my mother dropped off her four assigned kids and gave me a hug good-bye. The Bernstein family car was a green 1946 Plymouth that I remember very well. The bus, like all school buses in 1950, was red, white, and blue.

"I still don't see why I have to go to that stupid school," I said to my mother. "I don't know anybody, and I'll have to make all new friends."

"All new friends, huh? Trust me, you'll like City and Country a lot better than Vernor."

"No I won't."

"I know you're frightened. Just be brave and things will work out."

"I am brave; I just don't want to go."

"Well, you have to."

On the bus, nobody talked to me and I made no effort to talk to anybody. I just sat and read my latest book, another Howard Pease saga called *Secret Cargo.* Nobody sat next to me.

At the school, after the other students had gone to their classroom and met their new teacher, Mr. Roeper had all the new kids, about fifteen of us, come down to the lobby. Following a little welcoming speech, he took us on a tour of the school and grounds. I brought my book, just in case.

I remember Mr. Roeper wearing a brown suit and standing in the middle of the playground explaining the school's boundaries and the concept of being "out of bounds." He pointed to the boundary lines in each direction as he described them.

The playground sat at the foot of a large hill. On top of the hill was an impressive stucco mansion, the school building. On the other side of the playground there flowed a small creek lined with dense willow brush.

"You're free to go anywhere you want during recess," said Mr. Roeper, "or any other time you are outdoors, as long as you don't go out of bounds."

"What does 'out of bounds' mean," a little blond girl asked.

"It's an imaginary line you must never cross."

"What's an 'imaginary line'?" I asked.

"It means you must pretend there's a brick wall there, and act accordingly."

"What happens if you go out of bounds?" a little boy inquired.

"You might get talked to by a teacher or asked to stay inside at recess for a while. The worst punishment is that once you've violated our honor system, it becomes difficult to trust you."

To me, that didn't sound like much of a punishment, but apparently the approach almost always worked, even with the school's problem children. The last thing anybody wanted was to lose Mr. Roeper's trust.

Mr. Roeper pointed out three of the four boundaries, which were lines of trees to the south and west, and the fence along the front of the school to the east, where it faced Woodward Avenue.

As he talked, I found myself irresistibly drawn to the row of willow bushes and the creek, about fifteen feet away. I wandered over, started examining them, and quickly noticed a tunnel-like opening, formed by branches and leaves, which led inside the bushes. I ducked in and found myself in a fascinating maze of hidden paths and secret alcoves. It reminded me of the mysterious jewel mine of the seven dwarfs, from the movie *Snow White and the Seven Dwarfs,* which I'd seen a few months earlier.

When I reached the creek on the other side of the bushes, I looked across. On the out-of-bounds side—the forbidden side—an idyllic woods again reminded me of *Snow White.* This time, it was the scene where animals and birds were all coming up to Snow White and happy music was playing. I was just about to cross the creek, which was only a few inches deep, and visit the imaginary Snow White, when I heard Mr. Roeper's voice behind me. I turned and saw him peeking into bush-tunnel entrance.

"And these bushes, ladies and gentlemen, as Mr. Bernstein is about to discover, are the boundary on this side of the school. You're not allowed either in the bushes or across the creek. Now if you'd care to rejoin us, Mr. Bernstein."

"I'm sorry," I said, with profound disappointment.

"No need to be. I was informed that you are a very curious fellow. Most of the time, that's a good thing. But I hope you will respect our boundaries just as we, in turn, promise to respect yours."

"I don't see why we can't go out of bounds," I said.

"For two reasons. First, it's a discipline. There are no fences, and although we have teachers keeping an eye on you, it's ultimately your choice to do what is right. Second, we would be very unhappy, and probably get into serious trouble, if one of our students was to vanish because they decided to wander off."

"Too bad," I said. "Out of bounds looks like a very nice place."

"It certainly does. For now, however, I'm afraid you're going to have to admire it from afar."

As the group made its way to the other side of the hill, I concluded that while the City and Country School may be fancier than public school, it had just as many rules, nobody talked to you here either, and the most interesting places were still off-limits.

Some of that changed about five minutes later when a little boy actually started a conversation with me. I'd first seen him on the bus and again when we'd assembled in my classroom. He was taller than I, blond, and looked like an athlete. I was kind of short at the time, had dark hair with bangs, and was a little bit chubby.

"What are you reading?" asked the boy, who had dropped back from the main group to walk beside me.

"It's called *Secret Cargo*."

"What's it about?"

"Cargo ships that go to the South Seas."

"Really? I like books about ships too. I've been reading *Treasure Island*. It's all about old-time sailing ships and pirates."

"Pirates? Really? Like Black Pete?"

"I guess," said the little boy, whose name was Jeff and who had just become my best friend. I got the impression that he'd never heard of Black Pete.

Mr. Roeper then led us around to the other side of the hill, stopping at an old rickety-looking wooden door built into the hillside.

"This is the entrance to the woodshop," said Mr. Roeper. "Everybody loves woodshop, and they especially love Mr. Heilig, the teacher. He's an expert toy maker from Germany, just like I'm from Germany. His first name is Klaus, which is very German indeed. Klaus Heilig. He's going to show you some of the basics of German toy making. I'm sure you'll all find him fascinating and great fun."

The woodshop room was small and rustic and lit by flickering old lanterns. It was dark, dusty, windowless, and very spooky, like a gnome house, and smelled of kerosene and wood shavings. Mr. Heilig was about seventy-five, short and plump with a red face, a short white beard, and white hair. He wore red suspenders and a flannel shirt. Before he could say anything, one of the kids raised her hand.

"Ja?" said Mr. Heilig.

"Are you Santa Claus?" said the little girl. Everyone giggled.

"To some people, maybe. To most, probably not."

"He ain't Santa," Jeff whispered to me. "Santa lives at the North Pole. What would he be doing here?"

"You're absolutely right," said Mr. Heilig to Jeff, having overheard our whispered exchange. "Vot's your name, young man?"

"Jeff," said Jeff, looking embarrassed. Mr. Heilig held out a hand for Jeff to shake, which Jeff did. I quickly noticed that Mr. Heilig's outstretched hand was immense and covered with peeling calluses and scabs, probably from using all those tools for so many years. Also, his fingernails were thickened, yellow, misshapen, and overly long, reminding me of eagle talons or pterodactyl claws. I couldn't help staring at the hand, even though I really did not want to look at it.

"Pleased to meet you, Jeff. And you," he said, turning to me, "who are you?"

"Artie."

"I'm pleased to meet you too, Artie."

Mr. Heilig again held out his hand but I wanted no part of it and quickly hid my own hands behind my back. Then I stared up at the teacher, terrified that he would force me to touch him and prepared to make an awful scene if he did.

Mr. Heilig, still smiling, shrugged, withdrew the hand, turned away, and continued talking to the class. I breathed a sigh of relief.

When I got off the bus that day, my mother was waiting.

"See you tomorrow, Artie," Jeff shouted out the bus window.

"So how did your first day go?" asked my mother.

"OK. I made a friend, but a teacher's hand was a monster claw."

"Just his hand, huh? I guess that's better than the whole teacher being a monster. So we're making progress."

"I guess."

"But you made a friend. That's good news."

"Yeah. But so far, I don't think City and Country is much different from my old school."

"Well, like I said, give it time."

My class, I had to admit, was a lot better than the one at Vernor. The teacher, Mrs. Shotka, was a motherly gray-haired woman who usually wore an apron. I liked that we could get up and walk around any time we wanted, which meant I didn't squirm nearly as much. Also, Mrs. Shotka took every question anybody asked very seriously.

A turning point in my year at City and Country came the day I finished a math assignment early and went to my locker and got out my *Secret Cargo* book.

"Still reading Howard Pease, eh?" said Mrs. Shotka. "His stories are very exciting, aren't they? Is it OK if I tell the class a little about Howard Pease?"

"I guess."

"This might be a little advanced for second grade, so if you have any questions, just ask. Does anybody know what a novel is?"

Nobody answered.

"A novel is a long, made-up story in the form of a book. Artie's book is what they call a 'children's novel.' The first children's novels were written one hundred years ago, mostly by women for little girls. How many have heard of books called *The Secret Garden* or *Little Women*?"

Three children raised their hand, including Jeff. I did not.

"In those early books, boy characters were usually shown as rich and weak, and not very boylike or adventurous. *Little Lord Fauntleroy* is a perfect example. How many have heard of *Little Lord Fauntleroy*?"

Five children raised their hands, including Jeff and myself.

"Excellent. Because of books like *The Secret Garden, Little Women,* and *Little Lord Fauntleroy,* it came to be that nearly all books with young boys as main characters did not show them as strong and adventurous but as very weak and not in control of their own destiny. David Copperfield is a perfect example."

The class looked confused. I immediately raised my hand.

"What does 'in control of their own destiny' mean?"

"It means that they, and nobody else, are in charge of their life. It means that they make things happen themselves rather than allowing others to make things happen for them. Does that make sense?"

Her statement smashed into my brain like a shotgun blast. It explained everything I'd been feeling—everything, in my mind, that was wrong with school.

"I want to control *my* own destiny," I said.

"Don't we all," said Mrs. Shotka. "It's almost impossible at age seven—almost but not completely. The good news is that the older you get, the easier it becomes. But even as an adult, controlling your own destiny can be a challenge."

"I still want to control my own destiny," I said. "But what does that have to do with Howard Pease?"

"I was getting to that. In the late 1800s and early 1900s, there was a movement to make boys in literature more boylike. That's exactly why Mark Twain wrote *Tom Sawyer* and *Huckleberry Finn*. How many have heard of *Tom Sawyer*?"

Everybody raised their hand.

"Howard Pease agreed with Mark Twain. The boys in his books go on high-seas adventures and definitely control their own destinies. These days, of course, you have characters like Nancy Drew and Andy Hardy, who very much control their own destinies and have great adventures all the time. Any more questions?"

"Nancy Drew? Does that mean that girls can also control their own destiny?" a little girl asked.

"Of course. *Alice in Wonderland* is an excellent example. It was her choice and hers alone to crawl into the rabbit hole and to taste the 'eat me' cookies. And to stand up to the tyranny of the Queen of Hearts."

At the bus stop later that day, my mother asked how things went.

"Good," I announced. "I learned what 'control your own destiny' means."

"Really? What does it mean?"

City and Country School, circa 1950
Photo courtesy of the Roeper School (c) Roeper City and Country School, Inc.

PART 6

In early October, everyone at the school was excited about "Fall Field Day." On and around the playground, areas were set up for track and field events. Mrs. Shotka had explained Field Day to the class, but none of what she said registered in my brain.

"What's going on?" I asked Jeff when the big day arrived.

"It's a bunch of sports contests," he said. "They give a blue ribbon for first place, a red for second, and a white for third."

"I can tell you right now," I said, feeling dubious about the whole business, "you're going to win everything, and I'm going to finish last in everything."

"Maybe," said Jeff with a modest smile. "And maybe not."

The first contest was the softball throw. The event leader was a pleasant young man dressed as a gym coach, with a whistle around his neck. When my turn came, I closed my eyes and let loose feebly with no shoulder action whatsoever. The ball went sideways and landed after about four feet. Several children watching the event laughed at me. Until the teacher spoke up.

"At this school," he announced, "we don't laugh at people who try their best. We encourage them to do better. Do I make myself clear?"

And to me, he said, gently, "Can I make some suggestions? Keep your eyes open, look in the direction you want to throw, and be sure to follow through."

"What does 'follow through' mean?"

"It means you move your shoulder back when you start the throw, and move it forward as you move your arm. Like this. It gives you a lot more power and control."

He demonstrated the follow-through motion and had me practice it a couple of times. Until that moment, I had never been taught how to throw a ball. I tried again, and this time the ball went forward instead of sideways and landed after about fifteen feet. It was much better but still not very good. Nevertheless, the onlookers shouted encouragement at my improvement, which made me happy.

"One more time," said the leader. This time, the ball went about thirty feet. Jeff's first throw, of course, went about eighty feet.

"At least you didn't finish last," said Jeff as we walked to the next event.

"Yeah, I finished second from last. Big deal."

As the day wore on, I did finish last in several events. Jeff, meanwhile, had two blues and a red ribbon pinned to his shirt. He was doing well but had definitely not won every event. Together, we walked to the final contest, the standing broad jump (now called the long jump). The person in charge was none other than Mr. Heilig.

"You vant to try za broadyoomp, Artie?" asked Mr. Heilig.

"Do I have to? I'll just finish last again." I was careful to keep my distance, lest Mr. Heilig touch me.

"Maybe you do better zis time."

"I doubt it."

"You go first. I sink you do gut."

Reluctantly, I stood at the line. After a couple words of instruction from a crouching Mr. Heilig, I jumped across the pit. To my surprise, I found myself sailing gracefully though the air, as though held aloft and propelled by some magical force. It was a perfect, amazing jump, the kind I could not have ever imagined making. I was stunned, especially when all the onlookers cheered and Mr. Heilig got out the tape measure.

"Sixteen feet tree inches. Maybe a school record. You vant to try again?"

"No. I'm satisfied." And to Jeff, I said, "Think you can beat that?"

"I'll try," said Jeff.

"You go last," said Mr. Heilig to Jeff. "Make a little excitement."

All the other kids tried to beat my mark, but nobody came anywhere near it. Then it was Jeff's turn. His first jump missed by three feet. His second missed by a foot. His third missed by two inches. And I got the blue ribbon, with Jeff getting the red. Mr. Heilig pinned the ribbon on my shirt and I wore it proudly every day for six months, until my mother made me take it off.

"Congratulations," said Mr. Heilig, extending his hand for me to shake. I took a step backwards and put my hands behind my back. But I managed, at least, to smile at him.

A couple weeks after Field Day, with the aroma of crisp autumn leaves in the air, Jeff and I, as always, were playing in the bushes by the creek during recess. We always seemed to end up there, even though it was out of bounds.

"You still reading that pirate book?" I asked.

"Nah. I'm reading *Tom Sawyer* now. You still reading that South Seas book?"

"Nope. I'm reading *Through the Looking Glass,* by the same guy that wrote *Alice in Wonderland.* I especially like this poem where a little boy hunts down and kills a terrible monster called the jabberwock."

"Jabberwock? That's a funny word."

"Yeah. The poem goes, 'Beware the Jabberwock, my son, the jaws that bite, the claws that catch. Beware the jubjub bird, and shun the frumious Bandersnatch.'"

"That doesn't make any sense," said Jeff, with a laugh. "But it sounds really scary."

When the teacher rousted us out of the bushes at the end of recess, I stayed behind for a second, as I often did, and gazed longingly across the creek. Not crossing it was getting harder and harder. As I watched, I pretended that a cartoon white rabbit, wearing a waistcoat and looking at a pocket watch, was scurrying past on two feet.

I watched for a minute, debating whether or not to follow the pretend rabbit, as Alice had done in the book. Then it occurred to me: If Alice's white rabbit is across the creek, there might also be a jabberwock lurking in the out-of-bounds woods.

I headed back to school.

PART 7

When I got off the bus on the day I finally "controlled my own destiny," it was sunny out and warm for Michigan in winter—the mid-30s—even though four inches of glistening new snow had fallen over the weekend and still covered the ground.

I was wearing a heavy coat, a knitted scarf, a hat with turned-down earflaps, and galoshes. The outside of the school building was trimmed with brightly colored Christmas lights. The school's lobby was decorated with a large, gaily decorated Christmas tree, wreaths, and more Christmas lights. A fire in the immense fireplace radiated cheerful warmth and an aroma of charcoal.

Arriving in my classroom, I hung up my hat, coat, and scarf and took off my galoshes. Then I walked to the window and looked out at the panorama of snow-covered woods and fields. I found myself wanting more than anything to see it all up close. I imagined myself as Admiral Byrd, the famous polar explorer, speeding across the frozen expanse on a dogsled. I stood there until Mrs. Shotka called the class to order and the other children were seated. Then I took my seat. But I continued glancing out the window whenever I got the chance.

Later that day, in the lunchroom with Jeff and two other little boys, amid the warming aroma of vegetable soup, I unveiled my plan. It wasn't much, but at least it would get me out into the snow.

"I'm going outside for recess today," I announced.

"Not me," said Jeff. "I'd rather stay inside where it's warm."

"We haven't been outside at recess since before Thanksgiving," I said. "That's almost a month. I think we should go out. I want to play in the snow."

"I don't know," said Jeff. "I guess I'll go if you do."

"Me too," said the other two boys.

In the snow-covered playground, a lone teacher, huddled in an overcoat, felt hat, earmuffs, and rubbers, kept watch on the smattering of children who dared brave the winter weather. In addition to my friends and I, there were maybe three others, all playing on the swings—although less enthusiastically than they would have in spring or fall. In better weather, all two hundred students would normally be outdoors at recess. My group, bundled in winter attire, made a beeline for the bushes by the creek, but we quickly discovered that without leaves, the secret passageways through the willows didn't amount to much. Also, the teacher could see us perfectly.

"You know that's out of bounds," the teacher hollered to us.

"We know," said Jeff. "We'll be out in a minute."

"Just don't cross or fall into the creek," said the teacher, who then walked away to check on the other children.

We played along the edge of the frozen creek, taking a cautious step or two onto the edge of the ice until it cracked. The creek was only three or four inches deep, so there wasn't much danger.

"I wonder where the creek starts," I said.

"Who knows?" said Jeff. "That way." He pointed upstream. "In the other direction it goes under the highway through a big pipe and probably ends up in the ocean, like *Scuffy the Tugboat.*"

"Does the creek have a name?" somebody asked.

"Probably not," said Jeff.

Chatting among ourselves, and paying no attention to the rest of the world, the four of us slowly worked our way upstream, stopping frequently to examine dead twigs and fallen leaves and to throw snowballs (my throwing had greatly improved). Then a bell rang in the distance and the teacher could be heard calling everyone back. The other boys responded immediately, but I was not quite ready to return.

"Hurry up," Jeff urged. "You'll get in trouble."

"You go ahead. I'll catch up in a minute."

The boys went away, and I was alone. I wanted more than anything to stay outside and continue exploring, but I knew I couldn't. I was within one second of returning to the school when something caught my eye.

On the other side of the creek, a large white rabbit ran past, heading upstream and leaving deep tracks in the snow. At first I thought it was my imagination again, like the cartoon white rabbit I pretended to see from *Alice in Wonderland* a couple months earlier. But this seemed to be a genuine flesh-and-blood rabbit. And I was positive that, like Alice's rabbit, it wanted me to follow it.

How could I refuse?

To follow the rabbit, I had to cross over to the forbidden, out-of-bounds side of the creek. With a single giant step, after all those months of standing and looking, there I was. The rabbit quickly disappeared, but the tracks were easy to follow. I started walking, with my booted feet crunching into the snow.

"I guess I'm in charge of my own destiny now," I said out loud.

After a while I drew parallel to the line of trees that was the school's northern out-of-bounds limit, which meant I was now out of bounds in two directions, north and east. There were woods all around me, but it was a hardwood forest and all the trees had lost their leaves for the winter. They looked very desolate.

After a while I lost the tracks, stopped, and looked around. It was only then that I began worrying about what might be lurking behind the trees, waiting to get me. Like a bear, a mountain lion . . . or the jabberwock. Out of the corner of my eye, I thought I saw the shadow of an imaginary, dragonlike beast. Or I pretended to see it. Either way, it was pretty scary.

"The jabberwock," I recited, "with eyes of flame, came whiffling through the tulgey wood, and burbled as it came."

I stopped, picked up a stick, and held it like a sword, executing a few practice parries and thrusts. Then, sword at the ready, I continued on. I knew that a pretend sword wouldn't help much against a real beast or monster. But against a pretend jabberwock, it made me practically invincible. In any case, it was important to pretend to be brave.

After a while I emerged from the woods into a field, where dead wheat stalks poked up through the snow. It was beautiful but also very lonely. I could feel the wind and smell the snow and cold. I thought about turning back because it was the distant frozen fields, seen through the classroom window, which I'd longed to visit close up. So technically, I'd met my objective. But just then, the white rabbit showed up again, so I went back to following it upstream.

What the heck, I thought. I've come this far. How much more trouble could I get into?

Eventually I came to a barbed-wire fence. The rabbit tracks went under the fence and continued on the other side. I squeezed between two of the sagging, rusted wires, snagging my coat and ripping it slightly. I'd never seen barbed wire before.

"Now I'm really out of bounds," I muttered to myself.

I walked and walked, and the rabbit tracks and stream eventually left the field and went back into the woods. I heard a noise and imagined it was the jabberwock, so I raised my stick-sword and ran for a few dozen feet to get away, slipping and almost falling in the snow.

In the middle of a small clearing, the tracks disappeared again. I stopped and looked around, sword at the ready, and wondered whether this might be a good place to make my pretend stand against the pretend jabberwock.

Just then, to my relief, the white rabbit appeared again. I took off after it, heading back into the woods and still farther upstream. I soon arrived at another barbed-wire fence, this one much newer and better made. On the other side stood a cute little rustic farmhouse with a large barn and a frozen pond. I climbed over the fence, snagging and slightly ripping my pants. Curious but wary, I walked toward the pond, which covered about a half-acre. A concrete gate at the edge of the pond, full of iron wheels and valves, appeared be the creek's source. So at least that question was now answered.

And then the jabberwock attacked with full force and fury. I knew it wasn't real, but for a pretend monster, it fought surprisingly hard. I was scared but, like the kid in the poem, I was determined to defeat the beast once and for all. I slashed at it with the stick-sword, which only enraged it further. As I fought my life-and-death pretend fight, I failed to notice that I was being slowly driven backward onto the ice-covered pond.

When I was standing on the ice in the dead center of the pond, the ice broke, and I abruptly fell through with a huge splash, ending up in water up to my chest. The jabberwock, which weighed far less than I did, paced back and forth on the unbroken part of the ice, looking irate and suddenly all too real. I didn't know what to do. If I somehow managed to climb out, shivering and defenseless, it might eat me. If I stayed where I was, I could freeze to death.

In a panic, I did the only logical thing. "HELP!" I screamed, as loudly as I could.

PART 8

The wet ice around me was very slippery, and whenever I tried to put weight on it, it cracked into large plates that tipped and slid me back into the water. I was also shivering badly, having trouble moving my fingers, and my legs were starting to go numb.

And then I heard a shouted reply to my call for help.

"Yoost a minute. I get you out."

I turned around and there, near the barn, was Mr. Heilig running toward the pond. As he approached, the jabberwock attacked him. Since I'd assumed that the jabberwock existed only in my imagination, I was surprised and confused when the creature and Mr. Heilig started going at it. I tried my best to make the imaginary monster go away, but I couldn't. Worse, in a fight to the finish, I didn't give the poor old shop teacher, who was overweight and not very tall, much of a chance.

As it turned out, Mr. Heilig was an amazing monster fighter. He slashed at the jabberwock with his huge hand-claws, slowly driving it back. Finally, a vicious swipe from Mr. Heilig opened a deep bleeding gash on the jabberwock's chest. Then, with just a threatening glare from Mr. Heilig, the jabberwock turned and ran away like a frightened puppy.

Mr. Heilig immediately turned in my direction. He walked two or three steps onto the ice, then dropped onto his belly and slowly began making his way toward me. Had he stood up, the ice would have broken instantly.

He got to within a few feet of me, with the ice creaking ominously, and reached out in my direction.

"Hold out your arm," he said.

"No!" I shouted. I was terrified of Mr. Heilig's hand but even more frightened of drowning or freezing. The confusion touched off another flailing, screaming panic.

Somehow, despite it all, Mr. Heilig managed to grab my wrist, even though it was really too far away for him to reach. His awful claw hand locked on like a vice-grip pliers.

And suddenly, I had never felt so safe, calm, and peaceful—or so rescued—in my life.

Thirty-seconds later, Mr. Heilig was carrying me in his arms toward the barn.

"Was all that stuff real, about the jabberwock?" I asked.

"Don't vorry," Mr. Heilig whispered gently. "He no bozer you no more."

To be honest, I actually remember very little of what happened between falling through the ice and becoming aware of Mr. Heilig carrying me in his arms. All I really recall is being in a panic because I couldn't pull myself out of the water and my legs and hands were going numb. I vaguely recall Mr. Heilig battling the jabberwock and briefly turning into a giant, clawed Santa Claus but I couldn't swear to it.

As we walked, with Mr. Heilig carrying me, a sign over the barn doorway caught my attention. It said, KLAUS HEILIG—FINE HANDCRAFTED GERMAN TOYS.

"Ve go in barn, get you dried off. Quick before you catch cold. I got nice varm stove, towels, and blanket. Zen we go in house and I call school."

He set me on my feet so he could open the door, and I followed him into the barn. The inside was far beyond anything my imagination, active as it was, could ever conjure up. I stared open mouthed as Mr. Heilig led me to a glowing potbellied stove, wrapped a blanket around me right over my wet coat, sat me on an old wooden chair, and helped me off with my boots, pouring the water out of them.

I felt surprisingly and wonderfully warm inside the blanket, considering that my clothes were drenched.

"Vot you doing vay out here?" he asked.

"I went for a walk. I guess I'm in really bad trouble."

"Maybe yes, maybe no. Ve see." Mr. Heilig smiled, and I smiled back.

The inside of the barn smelled like burning wood from the stove. It was many times larger than the little woodshop at school. But like the woodshop, it contained a well-used workbench and a huge collection of antique hand tools.

Mostly, there were toys everywhere, one more fabulous than the next, sitting on dozens of hand-made shelves or dangling from wires. They filled every inch of free space. There were hand-carved marionettes, wooden toy trains, push toys, pull toys, tyke-bikes, hobbyhorses, and on and on, all brightly painted.

"You sure have lots of toys."

"Ja. It's almost Christmas. After Christmas, zey be mostly gone."

"Does that mean you really are Santa Claus, like everybody at school says? How can you be Santa and teach at the Roepers' school?"

"I sink any school would luff to hire Santa as teacher. But no, I'm not Santa. I liff here and vork at za school two days a veek. You za first City und Country kid to see my vorkshop."

After I had looked around for a while and examined many of the toys, Mr. Heilig asked if I minded going into the house with him so he could call the school. He started toward the barn door. I stood there, not sure what to say.

"If you don't mind, I'd rather walk back to school," I whispered finally.

"I dunno. Better I drive you."

"NO!" I shouted. I threw off the blanket, grabbed my galoshes, and ran out the door, back toward the fence. "No rides. I'm not done walking."

Mr. Heilig rushed after me.

"Artie, iss OK. I no make you stay here."

I stopped for a second and faced Mr. Heilig.

"I understand," he said. "You vant to control your own destiny. Zat's who you are, and you must always be true to yourself."

That was when I noticed that my coat and pants, incredibly, were completely dry. I put on the galoshes, walked to the fence, and climbed over it, with a boost from Mr. Heilig, who waved as I began my return trek.

"I call school," Mr. Heilig yelled. "Let zem know you OK. And you don't tell anyone about my vorkshop, ja?"

"I won't," I promised, waving one last time and wondering how the heck he knew about the "control your own destiny" thing.

PART 9

Back in the woods, it wasn't long before my path was again blocked by the jabberwock, now much smaller. This time, I wasn't afraid. I quickly raised my sword-stick.

"One, two! One, two! and through and through," I recited, waving the stick, "the vorpal blade went snicker-snack. He left it dead, and with its head, he went galumphing back."

Instead of striking the animal, however, I reached out with my other hand and petted it. It happily rubbed its face against my hand.

"Now shoo!" I said as the jabberwock scampered off.

After a while, just past the old rusty fence, I saw Mr. Roeper in the distance, walking toward me with a grin. A cloud of breath-mist surrounded his head and he wore an expensive looking overcoat with a velvet collar, a silk scarf, a homburg, and rubbers over his shoes.

"Ahh, the elusive Mr. Bernstein. Are you warm enough?"

"Yeah. I would like to get inside though."

"I think that can be arranged. How was your great adventure?"

"Good. I saw a white rabbit."

"A white rabbit, you say? Like Peter Cottontail?"

"More like *Alice in Wonderland*."

"I understand. And did you enjoy Mr. Heilig's workshop? He donates every one of those toys to charity, you know."

"It was good."

"He's certainly an excellent toy maker, isn't he?"

"He sure is. Just like Santa Claus."

"Funny you should say that. Did you know that 'Klaus Heilig' is German for 'Nicholas Saint'?"

"Honest? He said he wasn't the real Santa Claus."

"That's a matter of opinion. One person's real Santa is not necessarily somebody else's."

I thought about that a minute. "I'm pretty sure Mr. Heilig is *my* real Santa," I concluded.

"Excellent choice. Just remember that Klaus normally doesn't entertain visitors in his shop, so you might keep that to yourself. Otherwise, all the other children will want to go there too."

"I will."

We walked in silence for a minute.

"Are you aware, my young friend, that when we get back to the school, you will have walked two and a half miles? That's quite a trek for a little fellow, all by yourself."

"I'm not that little."

"Indeed not. You have a spirit of adventure that I find enviable. Nobody has ever gone that far out of bounds before. You, my friend, have set the all-time record."

"I'm sorry I was bad."

"Don't be. And you're not bad. But I do have a request. Don't do it again. Also, I think the teachers will rest easier at recess if you stay inside for a while. Is that agreeable?"

"I guess."

"Excellent. That's all anyone can ask."

PART 10

A few days later, as I was about to leave school on the bus, Mrs. Shotka ran out with a paper bag and handed it to me. I peeked into the bag and saw that it contained a gift-wrapped Christmas present.

"What's this?" I asked.

"I have no idea. I was told to tell you not to open it until Christmas morning, and not to show it or talk about it to any of the other students."

"OK."

As instructed, I opened the gift at home on Christmas morning. It was a polished wood carving of the jabberwock. Underneath, it said: "To Artie, my fellow jabberwock fighter. Always remember that you, and you alone, control you own destiny. Best wishes, Klaus Heilig."

I still can't figure out how he knew about the destiny thing. I guess the real Santa Claus just knows stuff like that.

EPILOGUE

As it turned out, that little escapade when I was seven was the first of many glorious and wonderful hikes, quests, and adventures. It's the nature of my personality to seek out such journeys. However, it was not until the hike at the City and Country School and my encounter with Klaus Heilig—Nicholas Saint—that I fully understood that my personality quirks were not terrible burdens but very good things, to be cherished, nurtured, and, if need be, defended.

That's why Klaus Heilig will always be my personal Santa Claus.

Because the truth about Santa Claus, as I learned when I was seven, is that he does not care in the least whether a child is "nice" or believes in him. The real Santa is far more concerned about whether a child believes in himself—or herself. The real Santa knows that some gifts are far more valuable than mere toys. And the real Santa, if he has to, will stand up and fight for a child. Even a "problem child."

TO VISIT

The trail wasn't really a trail to begin with, and in sixty years the area around the Roeper School (it's no longer called the City and Country School) has been built up so that there's not much left of my route. The school is still there, though, including the mansion on the hill. They changed it to a school for gifted children in 1956. It's in Bloomfield Hills, Michigan, ten miles up Woodward Avenue from Detroit's northern city limits, just past Opdyke Road.

2

The Grand Canyon and Other Great Leaps

PART 1

In the summer of 1953 in northwestern Detroit, every evening after dinner a bunch of kids in the neighborhood went outside and joined in a game of "street ball." There was me, Bernie Goldstein across the street, Wayne Cohen from the end of the block, Steve Solomon, who lived on the next street over, a skinny kid named Ronnie who appeared out of nowhere, and sometimes a pretty little girl named Jill, who lived on the opposite end of the block from Wayne. Bernie Goldberg and I lived in the middle of the block.

We usually did not use a bat because of the possibility of broken windows. Since my own special talent was tossing baseballs extremely high into the air, and since my throws were completely random because I had absolutely no control over where they landed, the game mostly consisted of me throwing the ball and the other kids catching it and throwing it back.

I was also better than the other kids at "calling" the game.

"Here's the pitch from Lary to Mantle," I would say. "Mantle swings." Then I would toss the ball into the air. "Fly ball to right field. Kaline goes back, back, back. And makes a spectacular one-handed catch on the warning track."

Frank Lary and Al Kaline played baseball for my beloved Detroit Tigers. Mickey Mantle, of course, was the big superstar on the hated New York Yankees.

Next door to Bernie Goldstein's house was the home of a Mr. Gannon. The only vacant lot on the block lay between Bernie's house and Mr. Gannon's house. Mr. Gannon owned the vacant lot and planted an elaborate, spectacular flower garden there each summer. He was retired, had no children, and spent nearly all his time tending his house and garden. Among neighborhood kids, Mr. Gannon had a reputation for being rather unfriendly.

Mr. Gannon lived in a neatly tended red brick house with white wooden window frames, black shutters, and a two-sided roof. Of course nearly every house in the neighborhood could be similarly described, except for a few that had white or dark blue shutters. The only house that differed substantially was my own family's house. It had a pyramidal roof, corner windows made of black-painted metal, and glass brick decorations. It bothered me that our house was different. Fortunately, none of the other kids seemed to notice.

On the day in question, one of my errant throws landed, you guessed it, smack in the middle of Mr. Gannon's garden. Bernie Goldstein started to run after it, and as he did I said something that I immediately regretted. I should have known better, but it just slipped out.

"Don't mess up old man Gannon's garden," I hollered. "He keeps it like a damned Monet painting, and he'll be pissed if anything happens to it."

"Like a what?" said Bernie, turning and walking over to me instead of continuing to the garden.

"Nothing."

"Come on, what did you say? Something about a painting."

"I said, 'He keeps his garden like a damned Monet painting.' Monet was a French artist who painted pictures of flower gardens."

"And just when did you become an expert on French artists?"

"I don't know. My parents like to go to museums. I also know the words to a bunch of Gilbert and Sullivan operettas that my parents play on the phonograph all the time. It's not my fault; I just have a really good memory."

"Operettas? Are you serious? What are you, a sissy?"

"What's that supposed to mean?"

"Only sissies talk about artists and operettas."

"My dad's an artist, and he's no sissy. He knows all about cars and baseball and fixing things and stuff, just like anyone else."

Bernie's dad owned a clothing store, Wayne's dad sold life insurance, and Steve's dad owned a hardware store. My dad, in stark contrast, was an artist, something I normally went to great lengths to keep to myself.

"Nah, your dad's a big sissy," said Bernie in a taunting voice.

"Take that back, or I'll kick your ass."

We ended up scuffling briefly, which all the other kids seemed to thoroughly enjoy. I'm pretty sure I won, although it was hard to say positively.

"My dad's no damned sissy, and neither am I," I mumbled as I walked back to my house. In any case, it was starting to get dark, so the game was pretty much over for that day. The following day it resumed and all seemed forgotten—until the next time my parents dragged me to an art museum.

PART 2

Eight months later, during spring break of 1954, my family drove to New York City to visit my Aunt Blanche, who was my mother's sister, and her husband, my Uncle Milton. After a day on the Pennsylvania Turnpike, we ended up at their elegant brownstone townhouse on West Seventieth and Central Park West.

The first thing my parents did, naturally, was haul the kids off to the Metropolitan Museum of Art, across Central Park and about ten blocks up from my aunt's. And there I was, yet again, on a forced death march through an art museum. Only this time, it was the largest art museum in the country. For some reason, my dad always stayed near me in museums, while my mother usually went off with my brother and sister. The arrangement might have been because I was more prone to acting up. Or it might have been because my father was the family art authority and knew that I alone, among my siblings, would remember everything he said, even if I wasn't interested.

"How come we always go to New York on spring break?" I asked as we entered the millionth gallery and my father spent twenty minutes examining the first painting, a Goya from the Baroque period. "All my friends get to go to Florida. Why don't we ever go to Florida?"

"We don't always go to New York. We've been to Chicago twice and Boston once. There aren't any good museums in Florida."

"You and your stupid museums. I hate museums."

"I'm sorry to hear that. But trust me, you'll eventually come to like them, and when you do, you'll be able to talk intelligently about them."

"I don't want to talk intelligently. I'd rather go to the Monkey Jungle or the Parrott Jungle, like all my friends."

"In the first place, not *all* your friends have been to Florida. Also, that's an awfully long way to go just to look at a bunch of monkeys and parrots."

At that moment, a minor miracle occurred, which created the first chink in my grand indifference to things artistic. Out of the corner of my eye, I noticed a painting in the next gallery room. It stopped me dead in my canvas-top Keds. I quit talking to my dad, walked to the next gallery as though being led by a dog leash, and stood there and stared. In all my previous museum trips, that had never happened before.

The painting was *Fur Traders on the Missouri River* by George Caleb Bingham, done in 1845. I found myself yearning to crawl inside the painting and become part of it. That had never happened before either.

The painting touched off an elaborate fantasy about living in the wilderness, trapping beavers, hauling the furs back in a canoe, and the way the world feels very early on a misty summer morning with a sense of complete and absolute tranquility.

That had never happened before either.

"You like that?" asked my dad, coming up behind me.

"Yeah."

"I like it too. It's one of the museum's masterpieces. So you like wilderness landscapes?"

"I don't know," I shrugged. I was beginning to regret saying anything, and I wished my dad would leave me alone. I like one painting, and suddenly he's all over me like dandruff.

"Maybe you'd also like the Hudson River School," he said. "Thomas Cole, Albert Bierstadt, and those guys. That's something this museum is big on." He led me to a nearby gallery, full of large old paintings of mountains and rivers and forests and pioneers on horses. They were pretty nice, but I wasn't going to tell my dad that.

"What do you think?"

"They're OK. Can we go now?"

"Sure. At least you didn't think they were awful. That's progress, I guess."

PART 3

Back at my aunt's house, my dad was still trying to push landscapes on me. Now it happens that my aunt and uncle, being art historians, had a library with five thousand books on art and art history. With my aunt's help, my dad pulled down an assortment of immense, coffee table art books for me to peruse—books on Albert Bierstadt, John Singleton Copley, George Caleb Bingham, Georgia O'Keeffe, Ansel Adams, and Margaret Bourke-White and one titled the *Family of Man*. The last three were photographic books. Boy, was I thrilled.

"This should get you started," they announced. I rolled my eyes and groaned. To shut them up, I spent a half hour leafing through the books and trying to look busy. Then I went outside onto the sidewalk, where my sister, Barbara, was jumping rope, and never looked at them again.

For some reason, they never bothered Barbara, who was fourteen, or my brother, Paul, who was eight, about that kind of thing.

"So the Bingham thing was a one-time fluke?" asked my dad the next day.

"I liked Ansel Adams," I said. "And I sort of liked Georgia O'Keeffe, even though she's a little weird."

"Interesting," said my dad. "It just so happens that Adams and O'Keeffe are best friends."

PART 4

A few weeks after that, back in Detroit, my parents announced to their three kids that we were all going on a vacation to California by car that summer and would be gone the entire month of July.

"That's even better than Florida," my dad suggested.

"No it isn't," I said. "You go to Florida so you can come back with a tan in the middle of winter or on spring break. We're going in summer, when you can get a tan in Detroit. So what good is it?"

"Most of your school friends who have been to Florida have never been to California," my mother pointed out. "You'll be the first."

"Big deal. Most of them have never been to Chicago either. We'll probably sit in the car most of the time and only get out when we come to a museum."

My parents laughed. "We'll see a couple of museums, but we'll also visit the great national parks, San Francisco, Los Angles, Las Vegas, and Hollywood! You'll remember it for the rest of your life. I promise."

"I guess," I grumbled. "Just try to go easy on the museums."

PART 5

We left Detroit in our brand new 1954 two-tone green Dodge, which was packed to the rafters with suitcases, laundry bags, picnic baskets, coolers, cardboard boxes, etc. For the trip's first leg, my parents sat in front and the three children rode in back. Later on, as I became fascinated with the *AAA TripTik*—a specially made book of strip maps that my parents inevitably carried with them on long journeys (not to be confused with a triptych, or three-paneled religious painting)—I spent considerable time riding shotgun and giving directions. I'm not sure whether my brother and sister, who remained in the backseat, were less interested in maps or if they simply fidgeted less than I and thus didn't need to be given tasks to keep them distracted.

We drove by day and spent the nights in wooden tourist cabins at a buck or two a night. Mostly following US 12, 20, 30, 101, and 40 (there were no interstates), we saw everything: the spectacularly tacky Corn Palace in Mitchell, South Dakota; the immense and carnival-like Wall Drug in Wall, South Dakota; the Badlands; Mount Rushmore (back then, only a dirt trail led to the small viewing platform); Yellowstone and Old Faithful (which my brother still calls "Old Face-Full"); Salt Lake City; Reno; Lake Tahoe; San Francisco; the Monterey Peninsula; Los Angeles (pre-Disneyland); Las Vegas (we didn't even bother with the Strip—in 1954 the Flamingo was eight years old, the Desert Inn was four years old, and the Sands was two years old); and Hoover Dam.

My parents, ever the culture mavens, even managed to throw in a couple of museums, including the San Francisco Palace of Fine Arts, where I found myself strangely attracted to Western artist Charles M. Russell, and the Los Angeles County Museum of Art. I mostly remember the La Brea Tar Pits behind the museum, with the saber-toothed tiger and woolly mammoth skeletons.

PART 6

And then we arrived at the Grand Canyon. We stopped and ate lunch at the North Rim's Grand Canyon Lodge then headed out a side road to see the actual canyon. The North Rim was supposed to be a little less touristy than the South Rim.

As much as I loved the Grand Canyon, my brother and I were starting to get antsy from three weeks of traveling. Any time we got out of the car, we both went wild and started running around, climbing up things and jumping off things. Remember that this was midsummer, and if you wanted your car to be air-conditioned, you had to purchase an immense, expensive aftermarket unit that attached to the outside of the window. Such items were far beyond my parents' modest, middle-class means.

Barbara remained pretty mellow—she always did—and if she too was falling victim to the vehicle equivalent of cabin fever, she never let on. Paul was a little easier to control than I. However, Paul usually took my lead in things, since I was his big brother, instigator, and co-conspirator.

The first thing my mother did when we pulled into the first turn-off on the Grand Canyon rim, on the way to Bright Angel Point, was warn us to stay away from the edge. I thought her warning was pretty silly because there were prominent split-rail barriers protecting the rim edge at all the viewing areas. But my mother worried that we'd somehow fall over the barrier and into the canyon to our death a mile below.

For bored and mischievous little boys, it was a perfect opportunity to drive their mother crazy. After three weeks cooped up in the car, there could be no more rewarding activity. We wouldn't dare do that with our father, because he spanked. Also, our father didn't give a rip if we stood near the edge or not. He was too busy taking overexposed 8-millimeter movies.

"Hey, Mom," I yelled shortly after we arrived at the second vista point. "Look at this."

I stood inches from the edge on the wrong side of the barrier, in a crouch with my arms forward, like a diver about to jump into a pool.

My mother shrieked and grabbed me, and everyone else laughed. Immediately after, Paul did exactly the same thing, with the exact same response. I was extremely pleased with myself. It wasn't often that I could frighten my mother half to death and get away with it.

Despite our antics, I actually was impressed with the Grand Canyon. It was beyond description, one of the greatest displays of natural beauty and wonder that I had ever seen in my life—or have ever seen since. Tier upon tier of red, brown, orange, purple, and white striped rock fanned out as far as the eye could see. In the middle of the canyon, huge striped sandstone mountains rose up thousands of feet. I was genuinely amazed.

The awe lasted about thirty seconds, which was my typical attention span in those days, especially when my parents were working their hardest to try to get me to appreciate something. In fact, the visit produced one of the greatest parental lines ever, fortunately directed at my brother for once and not me:

"Will you at least look at the Grand Canyon?"

To which he responded with an even better line:

"Do I have to?"

After Bright Angel Point, we drove out on the Cape Royal Road a ways, stopping at occasional overlook points while my mom took still photos and my dad overexposed hundreds more feet of movie film. Each reel lasted exactly three minutes. It wasn't until a couple weeks later, at home, that my father discovered the pitfalls of the "fast pan": If you move the movie camera too quickly past an object, you can't really see it very well.

At a vista turnout on the road to Cape Royal, I was about to try the diving gambit one last time (it was starting to get a little old by then). Standing at the edge of a sharp, perpendicular drop-off, and looking for a way to give my pretend swan dive a fresh twist, I noticed a trail running parallel to and just below the rocky rim, about ten feet down. My mother and father, arriving from the car, hadn't looked over the edge yet, so they weren't aware of the hidden trail.

Perfect.

"Hey, Mom," I yelled. "Watch this."

"Enough with the diving already," she said, starting to sound a little angry.

"Seriously, watch this."

With that, I actually did jump—not in an elegant, arms-first pirouette like you would into a swimming pool but in a foot-first dive, like I still do into a pool. I was actually airborne for five or six feet (I was five-foot-three at the time), then I hit a small scree slope and slid easily the rest of the way down to the trail, which ran along a fifteen-foot-wide ledge.

My mother immediately assumed that I had leaped to my death. Her bloodcurdling shriek was long, loud, and agonizing. I felt instantly terrible. Suddenly it no longer seemed funny.

"Don't worry," I quickly shouted when I hit bottom. "I'm OK."

For some reason, my mother couldn't hear me. I could hear her crying and wailing, only a few feet overhead, and my father consoling her.

"Why would he do something like that?" my mother kept asking. "Why? Why?"

"Mom, I'm OK!"

I could see my parents peering over the rim above me. Except that they kept looking out toward the distant horizon rather than directly down. My father had his arm around my mother, and she kept covering her face and crying.

"Can you see his body?" my mother asked.

"It's an awfully long way to the bottom," my father replied. "We'd never be able to see the body."

"So what should we do? Find a park ranger?" asked my mother.

"I suppose," said my father. "I guess that means we'll have to drive all the way back to the lodge, because I sure don't see any park rangers around here. I hate to just leave him though."

"Where's he going to go?" asked my mother. "He's dead." My mother started sobbing once again.

"You don't need a park ranger," I yelled up at them. "I'm OK. It was a joke. I'm right here. I'll be back up in a minute. Don't leave! Please!"

And then they were gone.

When I attempted to scramble back up to the rim and follow them, the slope was just a little too steep and sheer. After two or three failed attempts, I stopped to look around. It quickly occurred to me that I had no idea where the trail originated, where it went, or how or where it tied back into the road.

That was when I heard the sound of a car pulling away.

With no other obvious course of action, I sat down and tried not to cry.

PART 7

After a minute or two of sitting and feeling sorry for myself, unable to climb back up to the observation point and not knowing in which direction to follow the trail, I started walking, slowly and sadly, in what looked like the uphill direction, which I figured would probably lead back up to the rim and then to the parking lot. After about two hundred feet of walking, however, I discovered that the apparent uphill trend was only a small rise and that the direction I'd chosen, in fact, led rather steeply downhill.

I was about to turn around and go the other way when I noticed, perhaps 150 feet away and off the trail, a grove of small, stunted pine trees on a little ledge with a beautiful red-rock wall behind it. A small, clear creek ran through the middle of the little ledge and then tumbled down a seemingly endless staircase gorge into the canyon depths. The creek was lined with emerald-green grass that set off the brilliant red-rock walls and contrasted with the dull yellow-brown of the rest of the level ground.

There appeared to be a small natural grotto between the trees and the brilliant red wall. Next to the trees I could see some people. I walked over to investigate—to get a closer look at the grotto and ask the people there if they knew the quickest way back to the overlook and parking lot.

As it turned out, there were only two people. The man looked to be in his mid-fifties. He was short, kind of pudgy, and had a short salt-and-pepper beard, a crooked nose, and a disarming smile. The woman appeared to be ten or fifteen years older, in her late sixties. She was slim and elegant, with long gray hair piled on top of her head. They both wore old-fashioned artist smocks, like you see in the movies.

The woman sat on a chair in front of an easel, where she daubed gently with a long-handled brush at an oil painting. At one side of her, a small folding cross-legged canvas table, like a tiny army cot, supported an artist's palate much like my father's. At her other side, an opened wooden box full of paint tubes and brushes lay on the ground. My father had an artist's box almost exactly like it.

The man was standing behind the woman, watching her paint and commenting occasionally. There was a large blanket on the ground nearby, of Navajo design. (I knew that because we'd passed several roadside stands where Navajos sold blankets and turquoise jewelry.) On the blanket were a large wicker picnic basket, china plates, a bottle of wine and wine glasses, a baguette of French bread, and a selection of expensive-looking cheeses cut up into large cubical chunks in a bowl. Nearby, tethered to a tree and nibbling the green grass, stood a bored-looking mule.

Rounding out the little scene was a large wooden camera mounted on an immense tripod. I'd never seen a camera or tripod that big. It would definitely have taken a mule to carry them. I assumed that the camera belonged to the man, since the artist's supplies obviously belonged to the woman.

The pair smiled and waved as I approached.

"Beautiful day, isn't it?" said the man.

"Sure is," I replied. I was pretty shy around most adults back then, but I could usually be drawn into conversation.

"What are you doing all by yourself way out here?" he inquired.

"I jumped down to the trail from the vista point over there, and I can't find a way back up," I said, pointing. I saw no reason to go into detail about my stupid prank or its unintended consequences.

"Well," said the man, "if you walk back up the trail the way you came, you'll reach the main trailhead at the lodge in about six miles. However, if you look carefully as you pass beneath the turnout where you jumped down, you'll see a little side trail at the far end, heading back up to the parking lot. That's how we got here."

"Thank you," I said. I was pretty curious about the couple but also felt an urgent need to return to the overlook as quickly as possible, even though I knew my parents weren't there.

"Do you have time for a drink of water?" the woman asked. "And maybe some bread and cheese?"

"No thanks," I said. "I'd better get going."

"OK," said the man. "I hope everything works out."

Despite my desire to get back, my curiosity about the couple got the better of me and I lingered for two or three minutes.

"Nice painting," I said, peering over the woman's shoulder.

"Thank you," said the lady. "Are you interested in art?"

"A little," I said, "my name is Art and my father is an artist."

"What kind of artist?" asked the woman.

"I've heard him describe himself as a 'New Deal Social Realist.' He did a bunch of post office murals for the government."

"Very impressive," said the man. "You should be proud."

"I guess," I said to the man. "That's an awfully big camera. Have you taken lots of pictures today?"

"A few," said the man. "A camera this size doesn't lend itself to taking tons of pictures. Also, I'm not happy with the light and shadows right now. They should get better later in the day. The biggest trick in photographing nature is being willing to wait for the exact right moment. The camera is big because it uses large film. Glass plates, actually. It captures absolutely everything, down to the smallest insect crawling on a blade of grass, and it makes my photos extremely sharp."

"Well, you sure picked a great spot."

"Didn't we though?" said the woman. "And what kind of an artist are you, young man?

"I'm no artist."

I hesitated for another minute, rationalizing once again that my parents probably weren't there anyhow.

"Well, you seem like an artist," said the woman. "And you obviously have a strong artistic heritage. Here's a little test to tell if you're really an artist at heart. Does the Grand Canyon's scenery cause a quivering in the pit of your stomach and make you feel slightly out of breath?"

"I hadn't really noticed. Maybe."

"It certainly does for me," said the woman. "If you don't mind a word of advice, the next time you look at some really exquisite scenery, pay attention to how it makes you feel in the pit of your stomach. If you can put that into words, you might just end up the next great nature writer. Like Henry David Thoreau, John Muir, or Aldo Leopold."

"I'll try," I said, wondering who all those people were. "But I really have to go now. Thanks for everything."

"You're very welcome," said the man, nodding and smiling. "Good luck to you." The woman also turned and smiled at me, then went back to her painting.

Grand Canyon vista point, 1968

PART 8

Back on the trail, a minute or two later my father appeared over the rise, walking toward me. I'd never seen my father on a trail before and it looked kind of odd. I was extremely relieved to see him but afraid that he'd be really mad. He didn't look mad, however. For one thing, he was smiling.

"Sorry to scare you," I said. "Did you really think I was dead?"

"Nah. Your mother and I could see you the whole time. We were just having a little fun and trying to teach you a lesson. But don't ever try anything like that again."

In the distance, the man and woman waved at my dad and me; we both waved back and smiled.

"If you can tear yourself away from your buddies over there, we need to get back to the car and hit the road," said my dad.

In the car, as we resumed our journey, my father related the story of my rescue to my mother.

"He was having quite a conversation," he said.

"Did you think to ask their names or introduce yourself?" asked my mother.

"No. I was in too much of a hurry. But the woman was a real good artist. She was painting the Grand Canyon with what looked like the ghost of an Indian floating over it. He was a photographer and had a giant wooden camera."

"You don't suppose they were Georgia O'Keeffe and Ansel Adams?" said my dad.

"I thought Georgia O'Keeffe and Ansel Adams died a long time ago," I said.

"As far as I know, they're both very much alive," said my dad. "I've read in art magazines that she lives in New Mexico and he lives in San Francisco, that they're very close friends, and that he likes to visit her in New Mexico."

"It probably wasn't them," said my mother.

"No," I replied, "it was them all right."

I did not tell them the details of my conversation, about nature and creativity and all. I figured it would only get their hopes up about my being an artist some day, and I didn't want to disappoint them. What I really wanted was to get home and go back to spending my summer evenings playing street ball with Bernie Goldstein, Wayne, Steve, Ronnie, and sometimes Jill.

But still, a seed was planted that day that ultimately resulted in this kid from Detroit writing more than a dozen books on hiking, nature, and the outdoors. And I owe it all, or at least some of it, to Ansel Adams, Georgia O'Keeffe, and George Caleb Bingham.

TO VISIT

The hike: I was hiking on the Ken Patrick Trail, not far from where the path crosses the Cape Royal Road and heads out to Point Imperial, just before the Cape Royal Road's junction with the Point Imperial Road.

Distance: I hiked less than one-quarter mile each way. The main trailhead is six miles west, in the same parking lot as the North Kaibab Trail.

Directions: To reach the Ken Patrick trailhead from St. George, Utah, and I-15, head east on UT 9 a few miles north of St. George and follow UT 9 and UT 89 to Kanab, Utah. In Kanab, pick up UT 89A and follow it to Jacob Lake, Arizona, where AZ 67, the North Rim Road, begins. The trailhead parking lot is two miles north of Grand Canyon Lodge.

3.

The Lady in the Woods

PART 1

The first person in the entire universe that I told about that awful party when I was seventeen was my daughter, Sara. The party took place in October 1960, during my second weekend as a freshman at Antioch College in Yellow Springs, Ohio. It was my very first experience with out-of-control alcoholic behavior. I told Sara about the party in the summer of 2000, forty years later. That's how embarrassed I was about it.

There was a second party, two weeks after the first, that I still can't bring myself to tell Sara, or anyone else, about. My behavior at that party was even more embarrassing, depressing, and puzzling than at the first.

If it hadn't been for the Lady in the Woods, whom I met as a direct result of the two parties, I don't know what I'd have done.

The weekend of the first party—a mixer thrown by the sophomore class for incoming freshmen—started out extremely well. I don't know how I pulled it off, but I actually landed a date. A sweet, kind, and gentle date, who was also extremely pretty in a wholesome sort of way. I had an affinity in those days for sweet, kind, and wholesome prettiness. I still do.

The young lady's name was Lisa Dougherty.

Even my roommate was impressed. "Nice going, Good Time," he said.

My roommate, Jon Rubinstein from Scarsdale, New York, called me "Good Time" because I happened to have the same last name as a character in a Damon Runyon story he'd read. The character was named Good Time Charlie Bernstein. Jon thought that fit me well. At the time, it did.

Jon's approval of Lisa was important to me. I liked and admired Jon, who had finished first in his high school class, obtained a perfect score on the SATs, and planned to become a lawyer. There were a lot of people like that in the Antioch College freshman class of 1960. In contrast, my high school grades and SATs were fairly mediocre and I had no idea why Antioch accepted me.

What I envied most about Jon was that he knew exactly what he wanted to do with his life. At the time, I had no idea whatsoever what I wanted to do with my own life. I kept feeling like Noah probably felt when cast adrift in the ark—that I was wandering aimlessly and probably headed in an entirely wrong direction.

PART 2

I first met Lisa Dougherty in the college cafeteria. After one minute, I was smitten from the fuzz of my crew cut to the bottoms of my canvas-top sneakers.

Lisa was diminutive and blond, with penetrating blue eyes that knew instantly if something was bothering me or if I was not being 100 percent honest with her or myself. She was also self-effacing and shy, which mystified me because girls as pretty as Lisa were usually pretty stuck up. But most of all, Lisa was kind, caring, and generous. She did not have it in her to be any other way.

To my astonishment, Lisa didn't just mumble, "Sure why not?" when I asked her out. "I'd be delighted to be your date," she said without hesitation. And she seemed genuinely pleased.

Lisa had a part-time job at the college library and got off at 9:00 p.m. on Saturday night. We agreed that I would pick her up at 9:30. The party started at 8:00 and would probably go until midnight or later.

By 8:15 I was neatly attired in my best narrow tie and corduroy sports jacket and was pacing back and forth in the dorm room, driving Jon crazy. Jon was also going to the party. Every freshman and sophomore on campus was going to the party. There just wasn't much else to do on a Saturday night in Yellow Springs, Ohio. They could have thrown a frog dissecting demonstration and half the campus would have shown up.

"Why don't you come with me, Good Time?" said Jon. "It'll keep you occupied."

"But my date isn't until 9:30."

"So you'll go to the party, stay for an hour, then pick up Lisa and come back."

I'd never thought of that. Jon Rubinstein, apparently, had not been first in his class at Scarsdale High School for nothing.

The annual freshman-sophomore mixer was held in one of the new dormitories, which housed sophomores, juniors, and seniors. Freshmen lived in the old clapboard dormitories. With Antioch's unique nation-wide work-study program, that fall nearly the entire campus consisted of freshmen and sophomores. There would be many more upper-class people on campus during the winter and spring quarters.

Jon and I arrived to find the dormitory's dayroom bustling with neatly dressed students. There were crepe paper streamers on the walls and ceiling, an overflowing snack table, and loud music from the 1950s. The room also reeked of cigarettes but I didn't notice because I happened to be a prime contributor to the stench.

As was usually the case when I attended parties, I immediately plopped down on a couch and waited for somebody to talk to me. The truth was that, for me, the concept of a "mixer" was ludicrous. I could no more mix at a party than mice could mix with coyotes.

I hated parties and hoped things would improve later on, when Lisa was with me. I didn't plan to stay long, either then or later with Lisa—except that there was nowhere else to go.

Jon made an effort to sit with me for a few minutes. But he was a gregarious type, and pretty soon I was alone, depressed, and uncomfortable, just as I always was at parties.

And then I saw it. It was large and red and shining. It beckoned to me like a tarted-up prostitute in San Francisco's North Beach. It was the answer to my problems. How could I resist? I stood up, walked over to the punch bowl, and filled one of the little waxed-paper cups with the sweet red nectar. Then I took a small, tentative sip. The mixture, as nearly as I could determine, consisted of cherry Kool-Aid, 7UP, and vodka. It was the vodka that interested me most, although I liked cherry Kool-Aid and 7Up well enough. Who doesn't?

That sip was not the first time I'd consumed alcohol, but it was the first time I'd had vodka. And that big, beautiful, seductive red punch bowl was the first time I'd ever had a large quantity of alcohol placed directly in front of me, to have my way with as I pleased.

Drink casually in hand, I sidled back to my spot on the couch, plopped down, and took another sip. And another. Then, when I thought nobody was looking, I downed the rest of the drink in one gulp.

Then I did something that, to this day, I cannot explain. I walked back to the punch bowl and drank nine more glasses of punch, one after the other. Maybe it was because I was very tense and hoped the drinks would settle me down. Maybe it was because I was a latent alcoholic and that first swallow triggered something in my body chemistry. I'll never know.

According to my daughter, college freshman have been known to do that sort of thing. And they pretty much never have a logical explanation.

All I knew at the time was that when I finished the ten drinks, I was as sober as a Latin school headmaster. But I also knew, with absolute certainty, that within a few minutes I'd be slobbering drunk—or possibly dead. I'd never been falling-down drunk before and did not look forward to it. Especially since I had to meet Lisa in less than half an hour—poor, sweet, kind, beautiful Lisa.

While still reasonably sober, I decided that it was probably best to leave the party before I made a fool of myself, if I hadn't already done that. I entertained a faint hope that I might be able to sober up by 9:30. A very faint hope.

Without saying good-bye to Jon or anybody else, I wandered outside into the warm Ohio night, intending to walk around for a few minutes, or maybe try to score a cup of coffee somewhere, then head over to Lisa's dorm.

PART 3

I remember only fragments of the next hour. I think I spent most of it in an alcoholic blackout, although at the time I'd never heard of such a thing. I recall walking across the main lawn of the campus, past Antioch Hall. Then I remember finding myself in what appeared to be a wooded area. I had no idea how I got there, but I was running along a trail in the dark, panting, gasping, and terrified. I kept tripping and falling. I was dizzy, and my legs didn't seem to want to cooperate. But whenever I fell, I scrambled to my feet and started running again.

The only woods near campus were in Glen Helen, the thousand-acre nature preserve owned by the college. I couldn't imagine how I had ended up in the glen while walking from one dormitory to another since the entrance was two blocks out of the way.

Besides, I was not a nature person in those days. Glen Helen, the shining jewel of the Antioch campus, was not a place I would go voluntarily. I was a big-city kid from the teeming streets of Detroit.

I did not spend much time pondering the situation, however. The one thing I knew for certain was that somebody or something was chasing me. Or at least I believed that somebody or something was chasing me. Why else would I be running? Since I couldn't recall who or what was chasing me, I just kept going, even though I was running very slowly and kept falling down.

It occurred to me afterward that whoever or whatever was or was not chasing me had to have been pretty slow not to catch me.

I did have the presence of mind to realize that the trail was heading downhill, which meant I was going *into* the glen, not out. Once I reached bottom, a maze of pathways supposedly led to the park's interior. The only way back to campus, as far as I knew, was the route I was on—the very same trail on which somebody or something was chasing me into the dark unknown, into the trees, shadows, and unfamiliar terrain of the night woods.

After a while the path came to the bottom of the hill, leveled off, and began following a little creek. I couldn't actually see it in the dark, but I knew that a creek ran along the bottom of the tree-covered gorge. I'd seen it from the deck at the trailhead in front of the nature center. I'd been on the deck exactly once, during a guided tour of campus with my parents the first day.

In addition to a terror of getting beaten up, mauled, killed, and/or eaten by my pursuer, I worried that if I continued much farther, I'd never find my way out. At least not in the dark. Among other things, that would mean standing up poor Lisa.

That was when I bumped into somebody. At first I thought it was a tree. Then I concluded that my mysterious pursuer had caught me and the jig was up. Except whoever or whatever I'd bumped into was in front of me, not behind me. The impact was pretty violent, knocking the wind out of me and sending me sprawling into the dirt for the hundredth time. I did catch a brief glimpse of the person I had bumped into. It was a tall, dark-haired, pleasant-looking woman in jeans and a flannel shirt.

I later found out that she was the Lady in the Woods.

Then my alcoholic blackout kicked in again. When I next returned to consciousness, I was back on the main lawn of the campus, walking past Antioch Hall on my way to Lisa's dorm. I didn't feel nearly as woozy as I had in the woods, but I had a horrible headache, was out of breath, and still had a pretty unsteady gait.

In the light on the front porch of Lisa's dorm, I checked my watch. It was 9:50. I could see by the same light that I was covered with dirt and dripping with perspiration, there was a hole in the knee of my pants, and my shirt was untucked. I rushed to straighten myself up, tuck in my shirt, and brush myself off. When I touched the top of my head, my hand came back with blood on it. I debated going home, calling Lisa, and telling her I had suddenly taken ill. That would not only have been the absolute truth but also would have been the intelligent and compassionate thing to do. But I still wasn't thinking very clearly.

Instead I took a deep breath and knocked on the door.

"My goodness," said Lisa, looking horrified. "What happened?"

"Sorry I'm late," I said, trying to smile and act casually. "I went to the mixer a little early with my roommate and had a couple drinks. It was a silly thing to do, and I apologize for being late. I was trying to walk it off before I got here. I tripped on the way."

"Well, come on in," said Lisa, with a sigh. "I'll see what I can do to help."

That was when I noticed Lisa's party dress. It was green and beautiful, a one-piece minidress. She'd obviously gone to great lengths to look her best for me, just as I had for her. I wanted to cry.

Lisa's dorm radiated warmth and comfort. It was an older dorm, similar to mine, but it somehow felt nicer. Women's dorms do that. Lisa sat me down at a table in the little community kitchen and deftly made a pot of coffee.

"Don't worry about it," she kept telling me. "We don't have to go to the party. Everything will be fine. I'm not mad."

I'd have bought Lisa's reassurances except for something she said during my fourth cup of coffee. I hinted that perhaps she might consider a second date if I swore on a stack of Bibles that I wouldn't show up intoxicated. It seemed reasonable. At that moment, I fully intended never to ingest alcohol again as long as I lived.

"You're very nice, Art. Really. But my father was an alcoholic, and I promised my mother I would never date an alcoholic. I just hope you're eventually able to face whatever it is you're running from."

I wanted to reassure Lisa that I was not and never would be an alcoholic. That she was making way too much of this. That it was a fluke, an aberration. But the evidence, at least from her point of view, spoke for itself. So I kept my mouth shut and nodded in sad agreement. As it turned out, I kept my mouth shut for forty years.

PART 4

I spent the next two weeks trying to remember how I'd ended up in Glen Helen and what had been chasing me. But the memory was apparently lost forever in the drunken mists.

I also spent considerable time pondering exactly what Lisa had meant by "facing whatever I was running from." I was fairly certain it was just a figure of speech. But part of me kept wondering if she somehow knew about my mysterious pursuer in Glen Helen.

For the second embarrassing party, which took place in my own dormitory, I had no date. It was not the kind of thing to which you would invite an innocent female. We had all chipped in and purchased a keg of beer. The drinking age in Ohio was eighteen, and purchasing kegs and getting drunk was what freshmen did in those days.

I had never tasted beer before, just as I had never tasted vodka before the first party.

In our dormitory, the dayroom was in the attic, on the third floor. It was a run-down old room filled with frayed, overstuffed couches and chairs that looked as though they'd been there since the building's construction in the 1880s. The room smelled of lumber and soiled carpet.

I drank one glass of beer, my first ever, and remember being very analytical.

"Not bad," I commented to Jon. "A little bitter though."

"Beer is an acquired taste," he reassured me.

During the first two hours of the dorm party, I consumed a dozen glasses of beer. I recall being extremely pleased with myself, elated even, because unlike two weeks earlier, I'd spread my drinks out. At least I was making progress.

Needless to say, I ended up drunker than I'd been at the mixer. I didn't have a blackout, but I remember giggling like an idiot, falling down the stairs, and throwing up in the hallway. The only thing any of my dorm mates knew to do with somebody who'd overindulged was throw him in the shower, fully clothed, and let cold water run on him.

That was precisely where I ended up. I was later told that I put up a surprisingly spirited fight. As I recall, I didn't particularly object to being thrown in the shower. I just didn't want to make it easy for them.

It was my roommate, Jon, who subsequently related the story of the great Bernstein shower-throwing incident. He described it, of course, from his own point of view. My point of view, after I sobered up, was that I'd acted like an idiot and deserved whatever happened. In fact, the cold water actually helped. I didn't admit it to Jon, but in a perverse way, I sort of enjoyed the experience.

According to Jon, my dorm mates almost abandoned the idea of throwing me in the shower because they were afraid I'd hurt myself in the ruckus. Once I was in the shower, however, according to Jon, I went completely limp and kept flopping out. A couple people had to stand there with a foot on my rear end, holding me in. Some of them ended up almost as wet as I did.

While I was in the shower, five of the people who carried me there availed themselves of the toilet, immediately next to the shower stall.

"While they were all standing there peeing," said Jon, "your arm suddenly flopped into their line of fire. It was funny as hell."

I did not think it was funny.

The night they threw me into the shower was also the night I discovered that Jon was a pretty decent person for a strikingly good-looking, self-assured rich kid. He helped me to our room and stayed up with me all night. Every time I moaned, he grabbed me by the hair and swung my head out over the wastebasket, in case I was about to throw up, which I did several times.

According to Jon, I was not the drunkest person at the party that evening. Three other people had also been thrown into the shower.

It was scant solace.

PART 5

It happens like that sometimes. You stay up late partying like mad, get roaring drunk, fall into bed, then wake up bright-eyed and raring to go at some ungodly early hour. It happened to me the morning after I was thrown into the shower.

I woke up at 5:00 a.m., which for me was unheard of. I tried to go back to sleep. I even took some aspirin to assuage my throbbing head. I did manage to doze off for another twenty minutes, then I woke up for good. The aspirin had softened the headache considerably, but I felt an overwhelming need for fresh air.

At 5:45, a few minutes before sunrise, I stepped out into the fresh, sweet-smelling, early-morning midwestern autumn.

I didn't recall ever having gotten up that early before. I was pretty much a night person. My main activities, hanging out with friends and trying to meet girls, were predominantly nocturnal. Or they were as I practiced them. I'd been up at 6:30 before, to go to school or to the lake with my parents. But 5:45 was ridiculous.

I had no idea where I was going when I stepped out of the dormitory. The cafeteria and library were closed. All the stores and restaurants in town were closed. All my friends were asleep. I didn't want to talk to anybody anyhow. I wanted to run away, to never show my face in public again. I was convinced that something was terribly wrong with me. And yet some unknown element in the crisp, early-morning air made me feel good. Made me feel more at peace with the world and myself than I'd ever felt before. I never realized that simply getting up early could do that to you.

This oddly inappropriate sense of peace and happiness confused me even more than my drinking and depression.

Then I did the unthinkable. With absolutely nothing else to do, I headed for Glen Helen. I wanted to get away from the campus—and the town. I had to think things through, and it seemed important to be by myself. The glen seemed to me as good a place as any for a long walk by myself.

I paused at the deck in front of the nature center and looked down into the little gorge. When I say "little," it is from the perspective of forty years later, having been to the Grand Canyon and rafted several great white-water rivers of the West. To a seventeen-year-old Detroiter, Glen Helen was immense.

Basically, the glen consisted of a fairly steep hillside covered with hardwood trees. The hillside sloped down to a little willow-lined creek, with an elevation drop of maybe 150 feet. At the bottom, trails went off in both directions along the creek and up the other side of the gorge. The far slope was more densely wooded (because it faced north instead of south, I later learned), but it wasn't as steep as the slope adjacent to campus. The far side of the glen contained a number of side creeks and hidden draws. There was also supposed to be a fairly impressive waterfall somewhere, but I never found it.

On that sunny weekend in mid-October, southern Ohio was approaching the height of its color season. The glen was stupendous in its mantle of vibrant shades of red, yellow, and orange. It also smelled wonderful. I discovered that long, deep breaths of morning air filled with the aromas of autumn, though intoxicating in their own way, can get rid of a hangover faster than any medicine.

I hiked in the glen for about thirty minutes. I made it to the bottom of the hill, walked up the creek a ways, and then turned off onto a side trail for a considerable distance. Eventually I turned onto another side trail, then another. I kept changing directions because it always seemed as though the scenery would be just a little prettier on the new trail than the one I was on.

I was pretty sure I'd be able to find my way back. All I had to do was head downhill and downstream.

This time I wasn't worried about anything chasing me. I figured the pursuing demons of night from two weeks earlier were long gone, if they ever really existed. The glen seemed so peaceful and beautiful that I couldn't imagine anything bad happening.

I believed that—until something started chasing me.

A little over a mile from campus, I found myself in a dense stand of woods beside a little side creek near some tan rock outcrops. I was hiking up the trail when something rushed out of the bushes immediately behind me and started barking. I jumped two feet off the ground and nearly had a heart attack.

Then whatever it was started nipping at my heels. It sounded like a giant, angry Doberman or German shepherd. I instinctively began running, without looking back. I had no chance of outrunning a large angry dog, but I didn't know what else to do.

After less than twenty feet, a woman appeared on the trail in front of me. It was the same woman I'd bumped into during my night run two weeks prior. It was the Lady in the Woods.

"Now you hush, Precious," she said, wagging a finger. "Leave the nice man alone."

I looked behind me and discovered a tiny, nervous, fluffy red Pomeranian, jumping up and down and yipping. The animal had an unusually deep voice for a miniature lapdog. Or at least that's what I told myself.

I hoped that the silly little dog was not what I had been running from two weeks earlier. That would have been really embarrassing.

"Hi," I said to the lady. "Nice day."

"It's a beautiful day."

"Do you come here often?" I asked, nervously trying to make conversation.

The woman laughed. It wasn't a belittling laugh but a gentle, sweet laugh that gave me the opportunity to see her wonderful smile. She appeared to be in her mid-thirties. Slender and attractive, she had long, dark, free-flowing curly hair, intense brown eyes, and an unusually soft demeanor. She wore an Antioch College jacket, Levi's, hiking boots, and a knitted hat.

Women did not normally wear hiking boots in 1960, and I remember thinking it was a little strange.

"I live here. My name is Helen Burch. Everyone calls me the Lady in the Woods."

"Why do they call you that?"

"Because I live right here in the glen."

"Really? I didn't know you could do that."

"I'm sort of the caretaker. I have a cabin not far from here. It was built in 1763. Very historic. Would you like to see it? I'm about to cook breakfast."

"Sure."

In a little hollow not five hundred feet from where Helen's dog jumped out at me, there was indeed a tiny log cabin beneath some dogwood trees.

A few minutes later, I was inside the cabin and sitting at a large pedestal table, which appeared handmade and very old. I was devouring a plate of bacon, scrambled eggs, and toasted homemade bread with jam. Cholesterol notwithstanding, it was wonderful. The aroma of bacon cooked on a woodstove was glorious. After Helen served the meal, she sat down beside me at the table.

"So tell me," I asked, between coffee sips and bites of egg, "how does one go about landing the job of Glen Helen caretaker?"

"I don't know; I just applied for it. It sort of helped that my great-grandfather was the person who gave the property to the college. And that my great-great-great-grandparents built the cabin."

That was when I made the connection between the names Helen Burch, Glen Helen, and Hugh Taylor Burch. The latter was a revered Antioch icon who had donated the Glen Helen land to the college in the 1920s. As I understood it, he named the land for his daughter, who was born in the 1890s.

"How long have you been caretaker?"

"A couple years. It took me a long time to find myself. My father was an engineer, and my mother was a social worker. In college I used to tell everyone that I wanted to be an engineer or a social worker. But it was a lie. Finally I decided on a direction for my life that was completely mine and not my parents'. And here I am."

As it happened, my own father was an engineer (when he wasn't being an artist) and my mother was a social worker. However, Helen sounded so matter of fact that you'd have thought everyone's parents were engineers and social workers. The only difference was that Helen's father drove a train while my father designed machinery.

"So you ended up devoting your life to communing with nature?" I concluded.

"Something like that."

"I don't know much about nature. I'm from Detroit."

"And I'm from Cincinnati. But don't worry. You don't have to commune with nature if you don't want to. Personally, I enjoy it."

"I've enjoyed this morning."

"Glad to hear it. Come back anytime. I'm usually around. And the cabin is never locked."

Helen and I talked for nearly two hours. I left feeling much better about things. And no, I had no problem finding my way out of the glen and back to the campus.

"Guess what?" I said to Jon when I got back the dorm. Jon was still in bed. It was only 8:45 a.m. after all. I was finally starting to get tired myself by then.

"What is it, Good Time?" Jon mumbled. "What are you so happy about?

"I met the Lady in the Woods."

"Congratulations. Who the hell is the Lady in the Woods?"

"She's a caretaker who lives in a cabin in the glen. She made me breakfast."

"The Lady in the Woods? Never heard of her. And I never heard about a cabin, either. But I'll take your word for it."

PART 6

Although I'd had a few significant experiences with nature and the outdoors in my life prior to the visit with Helen Burch, the visit was a turning point because it substantially redirected my thinking. Much of the impact was gradual though.

I never did make it back to the cabin, even though I intended to do so just about every weekend. However, I did visit Glen Helen frequently after that because early mornings, woods, and nature had suddenly taken on new meaning. I left Antioch after a year because my parents couldn't afford it, and I have never been back.

In 1964 I obtained a B.A. from the University of Michigan, fully intending to become a social worker like my mother. Except that she actually enjoyed being a social worker and found it fulfilling. I worked as a social worker, on and off, for eight years.

Then, following memorable trips out West in 1966 and 1967, in 1968 I made the decision to enroll at the University of Michigan School of Natural Resources. In 1972 I received the degree of Master of Science in Natural Resource Management.

While I never again drank twelve beers or ten glasses of vodka punch at one sitting, I wrestled with alcoholism until my third child was born. I officially quit drinking in September 1982 and have not consumed alcohol since.

While researching this story in 2000, I decided to give the Antioch College Glen Helen Nature Center a call from my home in Oregon and see if I could find out anything more about Helen Burch and the old Burch Cabin.

"The cabin's not there anymore," said a pleasant female voice.

"That's too bad," I said. "I understand it was very historic. Built in 1763. I visited it in 1960, when I was a freshman at Antioch. When did they tear it down?"

There was a long pause on the other end of the telephone line.

"You're joking, right?" said the woman, finally. "The Burch Cabin burned to the ground in 1948. Helen Burch, the caretaker, who lived there with her little dog, died in the fire. According to the newspaper report, the dog died too."

The lady on the phone was wrong. There was a cabin in Glen Helen in 1960 and there was a woman named Helen Burch living in it. I can prove it too. Ghosts from 1948 would not wear hiking boots, Antioch jackets, and Levi's. Of that I am certain.

TO VISIT

The hike: Trails of the Glen Helen Ecological Preserve, Antioch College, Yellow Springs, Ohio

Distance: One and a half miles (one-way)

Directions: In Ohio, take I-70 between Columbus and Dayton to US 68 South, which heads toward Yellow Springs and Xenia. In Yellow Springs, turn left at the second stoplight onto East Livermore Avenue. Proceed through the Antioch College campus (which closed in 2006) to the east end, where the Glen Helen Ecological Preserve begins. Park at the nature center and trailhead.

Additional information: Day-use only

4

The Barrens

PART 1

When I was twenty-one years old, in November 1964, I ran away from home in search of greener pastures and the correct pathway to take me through life. I ran all the way to New York City.

The previous spring, in 1964, my plan for the fall had been to attend the University of Michigan School of Social Work. But my father passed away during the summer, and when autumn rolled around, I discovered that I was no longer interested in social work, or in school for that matter.

My father was a talented artist who had worked for the Works Progress Administration (WPA) during the Franklin Roosevelt years, painting a number of post office murals in Michigan and Illinois. In order to make sure he could support his family, when he got married in 1939, he found a regular job that he hated, as a mechanical engineer, and became a weekend hobby painter. His plan was to go back to painting as a profession after his three children were grown. Unfortunately, he didn't quite make it. When I was twenty-one, he died of a sudden heart attack at age fifty-two.

I had been lukewarm about social work to begin with, and when my father passed away, unfulfilled in life and entirely too early, I resolved that whatever I did with my life, it would be meaningful and rewarding. I did not want to end up like my father.

Nevertheless, having no other plans and at my mother's urging, I enrolled in the School of Social Work in October, as originally scheduled. I then spent a month staring out the windows of my classrooms, not studying and not sleeping at night.

PART 2

I formally withdrew from school on a Wednesday afternoon in November, loaded my few belongings into my car, and left for New York immediately after dinner. I drove through the darkness on the Ohio and

Pennsylvania Turnpikes for hour after hour, listening to strange radio stations from far-away places like Waterloo, Iowa, and Fargo, North Dakota.

Two weeks later I managed to land a pretty good job. Needless to say, it was as a social worker. But it was only a six-month temporary job to keep me alive while I explored other options. I was an intake worker at the world's second-largest mental hospital, which had nine thousand patients in 1964. That was before they let all the mental patients out on the street and closed most of the big mental hospitals because the courts had ruled that detaining someone against their will for "psychiatric evaluation" was, in most cases, a violation of their civil rights.

The hospital, in a quiet village on Long Island Sound forty miles from New York City, was serene and beautiful. While working at the hospital, I dated a young woman named Mikki, who was a nursing student at Brooklyn Jewish Hospital. She was doing a practicum at my hospital in psychiatric nursing. We spent many happy weekends and evenings discovering the wonders of Greenwich Village, Canarsie Pier, and Nathan's at Coney Island, the original hot dog stand.

More than anything else, I liked the patients. One patient with whom I became especially close was an Italian fellow in his late twenties. His name was Sal, which was short for Salvatore, which means "savior." Sal had spent his entire life in the Little Italy section of Lower Manhattan, and his family was strongly mob connected. He was in the hospital because of an attempted suicide while in jail at Rikers Island on a minor offense.

The hospital psychiatrists believed that the suicide attempt was not sincere and, mostly because of his mob connections and criminal history, diagnosed him as a "sociopathic personality." That meant he was technically "without mental disorder," which meant he would quickly be either released or sent back to Rikers.

The diagnosis identified Sal as having an inborn and incurable "inability to internalize the morals and values of society." It was the exact same diagnosis the doctors automatically applied to alcoholics and homosexuals. The category also included cold-blooded, unfeeling murderers.

Sal regarded his diagnosis as an irreversible life sentence that meant he would continue to get into frequent trouble, always be in and out of jail, never truly feel love for another person, and constantly manipulate others to satisfy his immediate needs.

One trait, however, set Sal apart from every other petty New York gangster. Sal wrote beautiful, sensitive poetry. He wrote about his girl-friend, about what it's like to be in jail, and about how it feels to be unable to control your violent impulses. He also wrote about nature. His poems did not sound as though they had been written by a mobster and criminal sociopath.

For three weeks Sal was a patient in the minimum-security intake ward to which I'd been assigned. Then he was released. A month later I received a message that Sal was back in the hospital, this time in the maximum-security ward. He'd been arrested for attempted murder and then tried to hang himself at Rikers Island.

My visit with Sal was the one and only time I was ever in the maximum-security ward. An oversize skeleton key, carried by all employees including myself, allowed me unescorted access into the building and into the dayroom of Sal's ward. This dayroom was one of the most frightening places I've ever been. The huge, barred room was furnished with wooden benches, which accommodated maybe a third of the patients, and a TV behind a protective Plexiglas shield. The walls and the shield were caked with dried "stuff," whatever it was, and the room reeked of fecal matter, sweat, and vomit. It was jam-packed with shouting, cursing, psychotic-looking men acting out various stages of rage. Thrown objects kept flying past my head. Skir-mishes broke out every few seconds. Hieronymus Bosch could not have imagined a more terrifying place.

I quickly made my way through the melee to the attendant's station. Along the back wall, I passed a row of patients in "double restraints," who had been straitjacketed and then shackled to a mattress-less bed frame. One of the men in double restraints was Sal, looking sad and tired. After announcing my presence to the head attendant, I talked to Sal.

It turned out that Sal was in double restraints not because he was a suicide risk but because he'd beaten another patient nearly to death. The other patient had attacked him first. The attempted murder back in the city, which landed him on Rikers Island, was perpetrated against a guy who had threatened his girlfriend.

Sal asked if I would talk to the head attendant about letting him out of the restraints. I said I would.

"Hey, man," Sal said, as I was about to leave. "I thought about you one day while I was out. Me and my girlfriend drove out to the Pine Barrens, over in New Jersey. You'd like the Pine Barrens. I know you get a kick out of nature and stuff."

"Thanks," I said. "Maybe I'll check it out."

"The Forked River Mountains," said Sal.

"I beg your pardon?"

"I said the Forked River Mountains. That's where we went. Great place. Full of surprises."

That was the only time during the conversation that Sal smiled.

The truth was that I had no intention of driving halfway across New Jersey, which had never impressed me as very scenic, just to see some barren place that was covered with pines. I did not tell him that though. I just smiled and acted interested.

The next morning, shortly after I arrived in my office, I received a phone call from my supervisor. She informed me that Sal had died the previous night.

"The staff at maximum security thought you'd like to know," she said.

According to my supervisor, as a result of my intervention, Sal had been released from the bed frame and straitjacket. While being interviewed in the attendants' station (maximum-security attendants rarely ventured into the dayroom if they could avoid it), he'd apparently fished the pull-tab off a soda can out of the wastebasket. He had hidden it his pocket until night and used it to slice open his wrists.

PART 3

Were it not for Sal's passing, I never would have tried to find the Forked River Mountains. But I figured I owed it to him. Conning me into driving all the way to central New Jersey was Sal's last act of sociopathic manipulation, unless you count stealing the pull-tab. Still, Mikki and I liked to take drives out of the city every now and then. The urge grew particularly compelling as spring gathered into full blossom after a long and dreary winter.

Mikki proved to be an excellent traveling companion. She was game for just about anything, appreciative of good scenery, and easy to get along with. In addition, she was well organized and good at following maps. What more could I want in a traveling companion?

Locating the Forked River Mountains was not easy. They didn't appear on any map that I could find. On the New Jersey map, I did manage to find a little town on the Atlantic shore, forty-five miles north of Atlantic City, called Forked River. That sounded promising. Actually, Mikki found it by looking through the index of towns on the back of the map. For a tiny state, New Jersey has an awful lot of towns. And for a densely populated state, it contains an awful lot of blank holes. Most of those holes, it turned out, were the Pine Barrens.

On a warm morning in late April, as apple and cherry blossoms filled the East Coast with visual and aromatic magic, Mikki and I jumped into my big old Plymouth and headed out of town on the New Jersey Turnpike and Garden State Parkway to Forked River. Our sole objective was to drive around, visit some pretty places, hopefully have a look at the mountains (although I could not imagine there being anything in New Jersey that resembled real mountains), and honor Sal's memory.

Technically, the town of Forked River, New Jersey, was not exactly located on the Atlantic shore, although it was a classic coastal fishing village. It was located on Barnegat Bay, part of the Intracoastal Waterway. A long, narrow barrier island on the other side of the bay faced the actual ocean. Nor was the town exactly on Barnegat Bay either. It was situated on an inlet just off the bay, on the wide estuary at the mouth of the Forked River.

Except for the estuary, the Forked River wasn't much of a river. True to its name, the stagnant, slow-moving waterway forked five miles upstream into the North, Middle, and South Branches.

If the Forked River wasn't much of a river, the town of Forked River wasn't much of a town. In 1965 it consisted of a gas station, a smoky little cafe, a few stores, and a cluster of houses. The population was perhaps one or two thousand. The stores catered mostly to commercial and recreational fishermen.

Mikki and I invaded fairly early in the day. We stopped by the little convenience store, called a "general store" back then, to purchase a bag of pretzels and inquire about the Forked River Mountains. The store had an ancient, musty smell. The owner, or somebody, collected antique kitchen utensils. Old eggbeaters, whisks, and unidentifiable gizmos covered with gears and cranks dangled by the hundreds from the ceiling, suspended by wires.

We approached the proprietor, who was standing near the cash register, about the Forked River Mountains. The white-haired guy in his late sixties must have weighed four hundred pounds. His apron was the size of a bedsheet.

"You wanna see the mountains, do you, kiddos?" he replied with an effusive grin. "Well I think I can help."

"Great," I said. "How do we get there?"

"It's not quite that easy, kiddos. The mountains are on private property. I need to call the owner and let him know you're coming so he'll have the gate unlocked. It's no problem though." The man picked up the telephone receiver and started to dial.

"Hold on a second," I said. "Can't you see the mountains from the road?"

"You can see them from County Road 614, but they're way off in the distance and don't look like much. I can get you right up close. To the top even, if you want, although that requires a little hiking. You kiddos like hiking?"

Then the man started dialing again.

Going hiking had never entered my mind. Or Mikki's, I presumed. Hiking just wasn't in our repertoire of things to do, even though we both enjoyed nature and the outdoors.

"How long are the trails?" I quickly interjected, which to my relief caused the man to pause in his dialing. "And are they very hard?"

"Not hard at all. Pretty soft in fact. Very sandy. They're also pretty easy. Not too steep and only a couple miles long. You might want to buy a compass though. Not that you're likely to get lost. But there are surprises."

"Let me guess. You just happen to sell compasses."

"Sure do, kiddo."

"What do we need a compass for?" asked Mikki.

"In case we get lost," I repeated. The store clerk nodded in support. I certainly did not want to get lost.

"I don't see how a compass will help us if we get lost," said Mikki. "But if you want a toy to play with . . ."

"We'll take the compass," I said. "What else do we need?"

"Well, let's see. A map. Sandwiches. Couple cans of soda. That should do her."

"We'll take all of that," I announced, glancing toward Mikki to make sure she agreed with the decision. She smiled and nodded.

As the shopkeeper made the phone call to the landowner, then prepared the sandwiches, I continued asking him questions.

"Do you send a lot of people hiking there?"

"Two or three a month. Tourists are more interested in the coast than the Barrens. Everybody loves water."

When the man was done making the sandwiches—salami and lettuce on rye with mustard—he gave us instructions on how to use the compass and how to find the property entrance. The gated turnoff onto a dirt road was located eight miles from town, on the left. The mailbox read BARNEGAT JONES.

Just as we were leaving, the man also mentioned that the property owner expected us to fork over $1 for the privilege of driving and walking on his land. I felt a twinge of annoyance that he hadn't mentioned this earlier. But I was now kind of interested in the prospect of scaling the mighty Forked River Mountains. Mikki agreed that the hike definitely sounded fun.

It was certainly worth a $1 investment, plus another $4 investment in sandwiches, soda, and a compass. Everybody made money off us that day.

PART 4

The short drive up the North Branch of the Forked River, then over a low rise past the "mountains," was lovely. Just the sort of outing Mikki and I were looking for. Much of the North Branch was a stagnant, smelly channel with lush, brilliant-green vegetation choking the shore. Once out of the river valley, we found ourselves driving on a narrow, paved county road through an unbroken but light-filled forest of pines and oaks, with occasional openings of grass, small farm tracts, and swamp.

Five miles from town the mountains came into view, off to the left. The four-mile road segment between the North Branch of the Forked River and the Factory Branch of Cedar Creek crested gently, almost imperceptibly, at about fifty feet above sea level. To the northwest a series of broad hills, maybe three miles away, nudged skyward to perhaps two hundred feet in elevation.

Those, we guessed, were the Forked River Mountains. As nearly as I could tell, there were three of them, in a small cluster.

"Some mountains," I said to Mikki.

"I like them," she replied. "I think they're cute."

A two-hundred-foot-high mountain is minuscule, even by New Jersey standards. By contrast, the highest point in New Jersey (brilliantly called "High Point"), a ski area in the state's extreme northwest corner, soars to a whopping 1,800 feet above sea level.

Although I found the Forked River Mountains kind of silly looking, I liked the Pine Barrens. I especially liked that they were in New Jersey. When you think of "remote," the last place that comes to mind is New Jersey, with its small area, heavy industry, and teeming population, not to mention New York City pressing against one border and Philadelphia crowding the other.

The Pine Barrens, Mikki read as we drove, from a brochure she'd picked up in the general store, cover a million acres and are "a land of lakes, swamps, floating bogs, many rivers, and one hundred miles of coast protected by offshore bars." The soil in the Pine Barrens is acidic and very sandy, with a hardpan layer in some places that stunts the trees. In most places, the Barrens are densely forested with small pines and even smaller oaks. They are anything but barren.

More than anything else, I liked the smells, especially after we got off the paved road and onto the private property. The sweet scent of pitch pine was the most obvious, as well as the dank smell of decaying organic matter in the creeks, stagnant ponds, and swamps. Then there were the blossoms. And the wildflowers. And the warm spring breezes. Each lent its own special perfume to the mix.

We located the Barnegat Jones gate easily enough, on the left just as the county road drew even with the mountains. The dirt driveway was straight as a yardstick for two miles until it crossed a railroad track. Immediately over the tracks, we turned left onto another dirt road, following instructions from the guy in the general store. Half a mile later, we arrived at a little clapboard farmhouse with a lawn, fenced pasture, newly plowed field, big red barn, and friendly collie.

From the look of things, I guessed that the farmer mostly cut down trees for a living and then milled them into lumber in his barn. There were stacks of rough-cut lumber all around the property. The land did not look badly abused, however. I saw no clear-cuts, skid trails, or even many tree stumps.

A slender young man in overalls, with short, platinum-blond hair and an almost albino complexion, came out of the house to greet us and collect our dollar. I could see his wife inside and a cute little toddler girl in a diaper playing on the front porch. The man looked maybe twenty-eight years old. Thirty at the oldest.

"Howdy," he said, extending a hand for me to shake. "I'm Barney Jones. Hope you have a good time today. If there's anything I can do for you, let me know."

Wow, I thought, farmers really do say "howdy" when they greet people. And they really do wear overalls. I doubt if I'd talked to more than three or four farmers in my life up to then.

Barney Jones had set up a couple of picnic tables under a large oak tree at the edge of the woods, two hundred feet from the house. He'd also built an outhouse nearby. Two trails took off near the picnic tables, one to the right and one to the left. Immediately beyond the twin trailheads, Mikki and I could see the gentle, tree-covered rise of the "mountains." The peaks did not look very far away, and the hike did not appear very difficult.

"You folks got a map?" asked Barney. "If not, I can sell you one for a dime." Mr. Jones pulled a map out of the pocket of his overalls. It was identical to the map for which I'd just paid a quarter at the general store.

"Sure do," I said.

"Good," said the young man, looking slightly disappointed. "Best way to get to the mountain is to go in on the left-hand trail and come out on the right-hand trail. Or you can go in on the right-hand trail and come out on the left-hand trail. Either way. If you follow the map, you shouldn't have any problems. And if you get lost, or run into any surprises, just head south to reach the mountain and north to come back." Barney could see that I was holding a compass.

"What kind of surprises?" I asked.

"Never can tell," said Barney. "Nothing serious."

"There aren't any bears or anything, are there?"

"I never seen one."

After lunching on the salami sandwiches at the picnic table, Mikki and I set off on our little trek, taking the left-hand trail as Barney had suggested. Mikki insisted that we take a compass reading at every intersection (there were several side trails). I'm not sure if she had any real reason for this, except to get our money's worth out of the compass. After all, how lost could we get on a self-contained trail system on only about four square miles of ground? According to the compass and map, the path from the left-hand trailhead headed south-south-east.

It was not a particularly pleasant trail. Too much dense brush encroached from the sides and clawed at our legs as we passed. Also, there were too many bugs, the soft sand created extra strain as we walked, and there wasn't much scenery. At least not near the bottom. The pine smell was kind of pleasant though, and I liked the gnarled little pine trees for which the Barrens were named.

A half mile along the gently upward-sloping path, we arrived at a junction near a picturesque old barn in a field of wildflowers. By "picturesque," I mean the barn was falling apart. Neither Mikki nor I felt inclined to linger, although we enjoyed the wildflowers.

The junction near the barn was shaped like a pitchfork, presenting us with three options. According to the map, the right-hand prong headed south and led, after a mile, to the vista point atop the main peak. The other two prongs just sort of drifted off into the woods. A check of the compass confirmed that the right-hand prong indeed headed due south. Beyond the vista point, the right-hand fork supposedly doubled back 180 degrees and emerged back at the farmhouse as the trail on the right (remember, we'd started our hike on the trail on the left).

"Are you satisfied?" I asked Mikki after taking the compass reading and then shoving the instrument back into my pocket.

"Exceedingly," she grinned.

Five minutes up the new path, which was steeper than the initial trail segment leading to the old barn (although still not very steep), I began feeling slightly dizzy. The dizziness was accompanied by a cold sweat and a wave of mild nausea. It felt like what I would later recognize as hypoglycemia, except not as severe.

"I don't feel so good," I whined, pausing to let my stomach settle and regain my equilibrium.

"Neither do I," said Mikki, also pausing.

"Must be the sandwiches," I conjectured. "Although they tasted OK to me."

We both stood and rested for a couple of minutes. Then whatever had been afflicting us went away.

"I wonder what that was," I said. I didn't really believe that our sudden malady had been caused by the sandwiches. The discomfort had descended too quickly and then went away just as quickly.

"Could have been anything," said Mikki, the nursing student, after we felt better. "Maybe the sandwiches, maybe fatigue. Or there might be power lines nearby. That could do it. Or perhaps a magnetic anomaly. Or gamma rays from a flying saucer."

"I don't see any power lines or flying saucers."

"Well, then, I guess we'll never know," said Mikki with a shrug.

We continued hiking.

Half a mile later the path emerged at a little clearing at the hilltop vista point that was our destination. It was indeed very scenic. We could see all the way back to the farmhouse.

"Nice view," I said, "for New Jersey."

"Very nice indeed," Mikki agreed, "except that the Empire State Building is five times as high and Mount Everest is 145 times as high."

We lingered a few minutes but quickly ran out of ways to occupy our time. So we prepared to head back.

"Don't forget the compass reading," said Mikki, wagging a finger.

"Yezzum," I dutifully replied.

According to the compass, the path we intended to follow, the continuation of the path we came in on, headed north and not south. According to the map, the path was supposed to head south and not north. The compass reading made no sense, because we'd just come from the north and had been heading south. We had not passed, nor did the map indicate, any major curves in our route up to that point.

"Let me see," said Mikki.

I showed her my reading. She agreed that the compass showed the continuing path as heading north instead of south. According to the map, if we continued straight ahead on the trail, we should go south for another quarter mile and then and only then would we loop back north.

As an experiment, I made a 180-degree about-face. The compass still showed me facing north. And no, the needle was not stuck. When I rotated the casing, the needle held fast to its direction. In case the needle had somehow become attracted to my magnetic personality, I handed the compass to Mikki. Both trail directions registered as north for her too.

"So what should we do?" Mikki asked. "Assume the compass is wrong and hike forward, or go back the way we came to make sure we don't get lost?"

"Beats me," I said. "I wonder what Sal would have done. He's the reason we're here after all." Mikki had never met Sal but had heard a lot about him from me.

"He'd probably smash the compass to smithereens, pick a direction to go at random, and then write a poem about it," said Mikki.

We decided to stick to the tried and true for the return trek, going back the way we came instead of completing the loop. Half a mile later, we arrived back at the old barn. Except we emerged on the middle prong, the one that according to the map trailed off into the woods and dead-ended. We should have emerged on the right-hand prong, the one we went in on.

The compass still showed us heading north, and it still also showed the opposite direction as north. That was when we decided to quit taking compass readings.

From the barn we retraced the trail back to the farmhouse, again following the same trail we came in on and passing the same now-familiar landmarks. However, to our astonishment, we emerged at the right-hand trailhead, the one we did not go in on, rather than the left-hand trailhead.

Having entered on the left-hand trail and come out on the right-hand trail, there was only one possible conclusion: We had completed our intended loop. We had no idea how, but we had. And we couldn't begin to imagine where we'd have ended up had we continued straight ahead at the summit.

PART 5

Mikki and I were exceedingly relieved to be back at the farmhouse. Barney Jones was sitting at the picnic table when we arrived, drinking a beer and playing with his little girl.

"Everything go OK?" he inquired.

"Just fine," I lied.

"That's good. A lot of people have trouble finding the far end of the loop and end up coming back the same way they went in."

"Not us," I said. "We just followed the map. We did run into some surprises though."

The man smiled knowingly. "That happens a lot," he said. "Especially to people who insist on bringing a compass along because they don't trust their own instincts."

On the way home, we couldn't help thinking that Sal would have had a huge laugh over our little predicament. And Sal could have used a few more laughs during his life. And maybe that, after all, is what's really important.

Here's to you, Sal.

TO VISIT

The hike: Unknown trail in the Forked River Mountains, in what is now Pinelands National Preserve, near Forked River, New Jersey

Distance: Three-mile loop

Directions: Take I-95, the New Jersey Turnpike, south from New York City. Where the turnpike crosses the Garden State Parkway, near Perth Amboy, go left (south) on the parkway toward Atlantic City. Proceed to exit 74 and follow CR 614 north, away from the town of Forked River, for about five miles.

Additional information: In 1965 I was told to look for a gated road on private land, with a three-mile hiking loop. These days, if you wish to hike in the Forked River Mountains, you must arrange an escorted tour with the Ocean County Parks Department or the Forked River Mountains Coalition.

5

Stop the World, I Want to Get On

PROLOGUE

Looking up at the trail in front of me, I was reminded of a story I once heard a TV evangelist tell. It was about a guy who died and at the gate to Heaven was told that he would only be allowed in after spending a year in Hell. A year goes by and he's still in Hell and can't find anybody to ask about it. Then ten years go by. Then a hundred. One day, while he's slaving away in endless misery amid the fire and brimstone, the Devil wanders past; the guy sees his chance and corners him.

"I thought I was only supposed to be here a year," the man says to the Devil. "Shouldn't I have been sent upstairs a long time ago?"

"Hell, son," says the Devil, looking at his watch with a gleeful leer, "you haven't even been here five minutes."

That's exactly how I felt that day in 1967 when I hiked California's Whitney Summit Trail to the top of the highest peak in the United States outside Alaska. For five and a half hours I'd been dragging my out-of-shape body straight uphill in the thin high-mountain air, gasping for breath and wanting desperately to turn back. Then, at the trail's halfway point, just when I was starting to feel as though I'd finally made a little progress and might actually succeed, I arrived at the base of the notorious trail section described in the brochures as "The Ladder."

The Ladder consisted of a series of ninety-nine short, sharp, extremely steep switchbacks, with no shade whatsoever, up an almost vertical white granite cliff that brought the trail from the bottom of the glacial cirque at Mount Whitney's base to the crest of the ridge that led to the 14,505-foot summit. In 2.2 miles, the Ladder ascended from twelve thousand feet elevation to 13,700 feet.

I'd already hiked five and a half of the trail's eleven miles and succeeded in ascending from 8,100 feet elevation at the trailhead to twelve thousand feet at Consultation Lake, which lay at the base of the Ladder. Looking up at the cliffs and trail ahead of me, it became painfully clear that everything I'd already accomplished, as difficult as it had been, was merely prelude and that, like the guy in Hell, I'd barely gotten started.

With a deep sigh of exhausted resignation, I did what I'd been doing since the trailhead—I took just one more step.

And I said to myself for the thousandth time, "This is for you, Nancy."

And with each step, although the pain and exhaustion might have increased tenfold, the guilt receded by a millionth of a micron. And that's why I kept going.

PART 1

I'd first met Nancy Whitney four years earlier, in 1963, when we were both juniors at the University of Michigan. The day we met was absolutely beautiful. As I walked to my sociology class, the university, after months of hibernation under gloom and snow, was yawning and stretching to life. On the campus's central lawn, cut by a maze of walkways called the "Diagonal," or "Diag," once-barren oaks and elms sported a brand-new watercolor splash of yellow-green. A few days earlier, the temperature had struggled to reach 40 degrees, and now it flirted with 70.

In addition to trees, the lawn that day was adorned with dozens of sorority princesses, sitting on blankets, jackets, or bare grass, basking in the awakening. The women, nearly every one of them among the fairest flowers of middle- and upper-class Detroit suburbia, reveled in their good fortune in being alive, young, affluent, and attractive on such a day.

As a nonaffluent, nonfraternity, fairly shy twenty-year-old, I had little in common with sorority girls, hadn't a clue how to relate to them, and therefore avoided them. I rationalized this avoidance by telling myself that I didn't like them. Still, they were rather pleasant to look at on a beautiful spring day.

I would shortly discover that Nancy Whitney was a hundred times better looking than any sorority girl. She was also smarter, more interesting, and, best of all, absolutely attainable. Even by me.

The classroom was a large, impersonal lecture hall within the neoclassic bastion of Angell Hall, the university's main classroom building. I seated myself at the most rearward of its long Formica tables. The drone of a verbose professor, like a refrigerator motor on its last legs, echoed off the walls. He expounded, as I recall, on primary group socialization in the Solomon Islands. Or something equally mind numbing. The man had written a book on the subject, but that didn't make his presentation any more interesting.

I sat behind a blond in a powder-blue cashmere sweater. Fifteen minutes later, as I stifled my thousandth yawn and scribbled notes into a large spiral notebook, I was attacked by a floating pollen speck carrying a hostile allergen. My nose began to itch and my eyes filled with water. I felt like a clogged up mustard squirter being stepped on by an elephant.

My sneeze was loud, violent, and juicy. I tried to cover it but, to my horror, I soon became aware of a small yellowish glob clinging like a garden slug to the back of the cashmere expanse in front of me. Like a cockroach in a spotlight, I searched frantically for a loose bit of molding to scurry under. I skulked down in my seat, praying that nobody else would notice.

Then I observed a feminine-looking hand, writing in the corner of my notebook paper in super-neat draftsman printing that looked as though it could have been done by a typewriter.

"Nice shot, loogey boy," it said. Simultaneously, a low but distinctly female voice with a thick New York accent whispered in my ear. "Are you going to tell her?"

She pronounced "her" as "huh."

I grunted imperceptibly and kept my eyes on my notebook. I did not want to know who was speaking to me. In fact, I wanted to run as far and fast I could.

"Telling her would be the honorable thing to do," I scribbled beneath her message, still too embarrassed to turn my head. "I probably won't though."

I went back to my note-taking but could hear my co-conspirator suppressing a slight giggle.

"It's not funny," I wrote.

"No, but it is a-mucin," she wrote back.

Whoever was sitting next to me apparently possessed a sense of humor sophisticated enough to get off a decent pun. That meant she was definitely not a typical sorority type. It also meant she probably wasn't very good looking.

I turned, finally, to have a look at her and actually felt my eyeballs bulge slightly. I couldn't imagine sitting beside such a magnificent-looking human being without noticing. I prided myself on noticing absolutely everything.

She was ten times better looking than the cashmere girl. They were not flouncy, artificially augmented, sorority-cute looks, either, but a beauty that radiated from the soul, with tragic, penetrating eyes that seemed to follow you wherever you went. It didn't matter that her long auburn hair seemed slightly untended or that she wore no makeup. Her chestnut complexion, full lips, and fiery eyes evoked a kaleidoscope of exotic imagery. Had I not heard her speak, I'd have guessed her origin as Middle Eastern.

The steamy intensity of her eyes and mouth seemed at discord with her clothing. She wore a prim white blouse buttoned to the neck, and she smelled faintly antiseptic, like rubbing alcohol. Her writing implement was not the usual ballpoint but a fine-point "00" drawing pen. An art major, no doubt.

"What's wrong?" she whispered. "You OK?"

"I'm fine," I whispered back.

When the professor dismissed the class a few minutes later, the phlegm-buoyant blond in front of me pulled on a white blazer, stuck her chin in the air, and marched out the door. I prepared to beat it out the door myself. As I hoisted my book bag over my shoulder, my erstwhile pen pal, whom I could now see was wearing blue jeans—another indicator of an "artsy" type—accosted me once again, in the now almost empty classroom.

"Hi," she said in a clipped, slightly tough sounding voice (actually, with her New York accent, it came out more like "hoy"). She extended her arm to signify a desire to give me a man's handshake. "I'm Nancy Whitney." The handshake was strong and confident, yet unexpectedly gentle.

I felt awkward to say the least. The best reply that I could come up with was, "Hi. I'm Art Bernstein."

"I hope my teasing didn't embarrass you. That was the funniest thing I ever saw. And you picked the perfect person."

"That's OK," I said, wondering what the hell she was up to. Then she sprang it on me. She wanted something.

"Hey, listen, Art, I wonder if I could borrow your notes from the last lecture (which she pronounced "lek-sha"). I promise not to sneeze any loogies on them."

"OK," I said, handing her the notes. "But if you lose them, we're both screwed. I'll flunk the course, and you'll be dead."

"Keep your pants on, Hot Shot. I'll see you in two days."

"OK," I said, desperately wracking my brain to come up with something a little more witty than just saying "OK" over and over.

As I bounded out of Angell Hall's rear entrance and back toward the library, I noticed that springtime's incubating warmth and burgeoning sensations suddenly felt far more intense than they had a scant forty minutes earlier.

PART 2

Two days later, I excitedly rushed off to class, arriving five minutes early to allow time to locate my new acquaintance. It may be the most excited I have ever been about a class. Nancy arrived with my wayfaring notebook, a few minutes late and full of apologies. She then invited me to join her for coffee at the Michigan Union Grill after class.

The "MUG" was an immense cafeteria and student hangout in the basement of the Michigan Union, directly across from Angell Hall. The place, which seated about five hundred people and teemed constantly with students and faculty, served awful food and reeked of stale gravy. It was one of the places where students such as myself, who didn't belong to a fraternity or sorority, hung out.

Nancy and I chatted and laughed for more than an hour. I learned that she was indeed from New York—Brooklyn in fact. She was not an art major but an architecture major—one of very few female architecture students in 1963.

Nancy proved her worthiness as a friend the day she returned the notes. They came with a small gift—a little cellophane bag of mello-crème pumpkins neatly tied in an orange ribbon. I had no idea how she knew that mello-crème pumpkins were my favorite candy. I couldn't recall ever telling anyone, and I had no idea how she managed to acquire that traditional Halloween treat in April. I asked, but she would never tell me.

By the end our coffee-in-the-MUG date, Nancy Whitney had firmly established herself as my best friend, possibly the best friend I would ever have. She finished up that first date by taking me on an architectural tour of the university campus, pointing out all sorts of oddities that I passed by every day but never noticed, including a concrete bas-relief of baboons playing bongo drums, located next to the loading dock behind the administration building.

I slept with Nancy twice. We could easily have become much more romantically involved but it would have lasted maybe a few weeks and I'd have ended up in the trash heap like all her other lovers. Although I loved Nancy from the day I met her, I quickly figured out that she went through men like Jimmy Durante with a cold went through tissues. Instead I assumed the role of the one constant in her life, the friend who was always there to pick up the pieces. Even when she was seeing somebody else, she usually spent more time with me.

Of all the friends, lovers, and romantic hopefuls that constantly swarmed around Nancy, she was absolutely devoted only to two and would drop everything if she thought we needed her. The other friend was a tall, chubby redhead, also from New York, named Linda Lowe.

Most of the world might have described Nancy as a manipulative sociopath—and that's if they were being kind. But with Linda and myself, she was the exact opposite. She asked only one thing—never spoken but always implied—that we never, under any circumstances, judge her lifestyle.

PART 3

In 1967, as I prepared for the "hike to end all hikes" in honor of Nancy's memory, I had no way of knowing that it would lead to my own lifelong addiction to long, difficult, high-mountain trails. I selected Mount Whitney to climb mostly because Nancy and the mountain had the same last name.

Although Mount Whitney is the highest mountain in the contiguous United States, you could get to the top without technical climbing gear. The Whitney Summit Trail gains 6,100 feet in eleven miles, rising to 14,505 feet while zigzagging up and around what was described in the brochures as some of the most spectacular and dramatic high-mountain scenery anywhere.

When the time came for my two-week summer vacation from my job in Detroit, I jumped into my little convertible and followed old Route 66, which was then and is still I-40.

I turned off at Barstow, in the middle of California's Mojave Desert, and in the dark of night headed north 150 miles on US 395 to the little desert town of Lone Pine.

After eating dinner in Lone Pine's only cafe, I turned off US 395 and onto Whitney Portal Road. There were no directional signs, only a regular street sign. The pavement ended after a couple of blocks, and the road began climbing the mountain ten miles later.

Where the road began climbing, it veered off to the right, angling steeply up an almost sheer cliff face. It made a 180-degree switchback after a mile or so, then continued angling up the same cliff face in the opposite direction, eventually entering a narrow canyon. Although it was dark out, I had seen photos of Mount Whitney from Lone Pine. The peak was a triangular, almost vertical white granite rock face with three slightly shorter granite spires jutting up in a row beside it. All four peaks were framed by the canyon into which I'd just turned.

The road ended at a Forest Service campground at 8,300 feet elevation, with a little creek running down the middle. I enjoyed the mingling of warm, rising desert air, cool breezes dropping down from the mountains, and sweet pine scent. I parked the car, gobbled a couple of Oreo cookies, and went to sleep in the driver's seat. It was about midnight.

I slept for four hours, which is pretty decent for me in the front seat of a car. It wasn't nearly adequate, but I figured it was far more sleep than I'd have gotten in a tent. That's why I intended to hike up and back all in one day instead of hiking for a couple of miles and camping out as the brochures suggested.

And, yes, I was nervous. For one thing, it never occurred to me to spend some of my time in Detroit getting in shape. I just didn't think in those terms back then. I was soon to learn exactly how sore and out of breath it was possible for a supposedly healthy twenty-four-year-old to become.

It was still dark when I woke up. Soon after, the first glimmers of sun coming from the east revealed dazzling white monolithic cliffs on either side of the canyon, rising up thousands of feet. I was especially intrigued by the little pine trees with corkscrew trunks that I later learned were foxtail pines.

My equipment was minimal because, since I did not plan to camp out, I had no need for a backpack, tent, clothes, or cooking equipment. I carried a two-quart blanket canteen, a secondhand Nikkormat 35mm camera, five rolls of film, two chicken salad sandwiches my mother had made three days earlier, a dozen Oreo cookies (they didn't have trail mix or energy bars in 1967), and a tube of sunscreen. I wore a light jacket and a baseball cap and kept film, cookies, and sandwiches in the jacket pockets.

With a deep sigh of trepidation and resignation, at the first light of dawn I started up the steep and twisty pathway through a series of large white boulders. I was on my way.

The first thing I thought about as I hiked up the steep initial pitch was Nancy. She was the reason, the only reason, I was here, and I knew that she loved nature and hiking trails. The trails we'd gone on together during pleasanter times, at Muir Woods and Big Sur, were nothing like this, but she had thoroughly enjoyed them. And I had enjoyed seeing her so delighted.

I paused for a second and bowed my head in my friend's memory. Then I took a deep breath in the intoxicating morning air and continued on.

PART 4

In addition to being a straight-A student, Nancy was a serious narcotics addict. She had very little money to support her drug habit, and only rarely did she manage to acquire hard drugs such as heroin. The rest of the time she used whatever she could scrape together or mooch, which usually wasn't much. She did, however, manage to get the FBI after her once, which she rode out by hiding in my room rather than going home. We spent a very cozy couple days.

The most readily available true narcotic in 1963 was paregoric (camphorated tincture of opium), an over-the-counter cough and diarrhea remedy from which morphine could be extracted. The extract wasn't anything close to pure morphine, and as a street narcotic it was considered the bottom of the barrel. Nancy used a lot of morphine extracted from paregoric.

Normally Nancy kept her drug crowd separate from her other friends. However, she did invite me to watch her shoot up one time when she and a friend scored some genuine Mafia heroin. She said she wanted me to understand what drugs represented for her, even though she claimed that the last thing she wanted was for me to actually try it and risk becoming addicted.

Her final word on the subject was, "Sorry, kid, but I just can't see you as a junkie."

I did watch and I did learn a lot though. The next night, back in the MUG, we talked about it.

"Don't you ever worry about going to jail or overdosing or wrecking your brain?" I asked.

"I know I should, but for some reason I don't. I've always been a risk taker. In fact, the danger, the thrill may be more exciting than the actual drug. As for wrecking my brain, there's a big debate as to whether I even have one."

"If you want thrills, why don't you just take up skydiving or something?"

"Not risky enough," Nancy laughed. "Why don't *you* take up skydiving?"

"No way," I said. "Too risky."

"I guess that's the difference between you and me," she said. "I'm too much of a risk taker, and you're not enough of a risk taker. Go figure."

"I'm a risk taker," I protested. "I hang out with you, don't I?"

Nancy laughed, then she got serious and looked me in the eye, as though something was on her mind.

"You're not a risk taker. Not at all. And if you must know, I think you'd be a lot happier if you spent more time participating in life and less time as an onlooker. Narcotics aside, of course."

"How can you say that? I participate in life. What more should I do?"

"I don't know. Anything as long at it feels risky and you grow from the experience."

"Give me an example."

"Ask out a sorority girl."

"I have nothing in common with them."

"I think you're just intimidated by them, which is stupid because you have some amazing things going for you. More than you could possibly realize. The only way around that is to ask one out, no matter how afraid you are, and then keep trying until you get it right."

"That's easy for you to say. Just about anybody would go out with you."

"Don't be so sure," said Nancy.

"What else could I do to get more involved?"

"Well . . . you could go to Las Vegas and bet all your money at the roulette table, on red or black. You'd have a 50 percent chance of doubling your money and a 50 percent chance of losing it all."

"Too risky. I could never do that. Besides, I'm under twenty-one and I don't have any money to bet."

"Sign up to be a volunteer fireman."

"I'm not coordinated enough. Besides, can you see me as a fireman?"

"I absolutely can. How about joining the army?"

"I couldn't sleep in a barracks with everybody snoring."

"Take part in a civil rights demonstration."

"I support the cause, but I don't personally like any of the local leaders. I find them too pushy."

"Go skydiving."

"I might get killed. Besides, would you go skydiving?"

"Definitely. And I'd be scared to death."

"I've never seen you scared."

"Hah! I'm scared most of the time. But I don't let fear control me."

"I don't let fear control me, either."

"If you say so. OK, then, go climb a really high mountain."

"Are you going to shoot up again tonight?" I asked, changing the subject.

"No," she replied. "And I wouldn't tell you if I was."

"Too risky, huh?" I said.

Nancy smiled and gave me a hug.

I felt very disappointed. Apparently I didn't even need to use heroin to become addicted, just be in the same room with the stuff. It was weeks before I stopped thinking about it.

It was also weeks before I stopped wondering if Nancy was right or wrong about my being too much of an observer in life and not enough of a participant.

PART 5

After fewer than fifty steps along the Whitney Summit Trail, I was positive I was going to die if I kept going. Sweat poured off me, even though it was only about 45 degrees out. I breathed in deep, gasping wheezes. My heart pounded, my legs ached, my stomach quivered with anxiety, my eyes felt like I hadn't slept in a year, and I desperately wanted to go home. In fact, I came within a step or two of turning around and giving up.

If this was what Nancy meant by "risk taking," I didn't like it and the heck with her. But I had made a promise to Nancy and myself. And step by step, I plodded on. And slowly I began feeling a little better.

After fifteen or twenty minutes of steep ascent through a tree-shaded boulder field, the path came out in a lovely little green meadow full of wildflowers and dome tents and surrounded by vertical cliffs. For the first time, I felt a bit of elation, even a twinge of hope that I just might make it. But I knew I hadn't even gone a mile.

The trail leveled off briefly at the meadow. The sun rose fully, and I could see down the canyon eastward to Lone Pine and across the desert to the Panamint and White Mountains. Eventually I would also be able to see Telescope Peak on the west side of Death Valley; Humphreys Peak, which is the highest point in Arizona; and the faintest outline of the Grand Canyon, three hundred miles away on the distant horizon.

As the trail continued up and around the rock, boulders, and ledges, I passed mile markers one and two. It gradually warmed up, and people began to appear. Most were headed in the same direction as I, overtaking me from behind. Later on, I would begin to see people coming in the opposite direction.

As long as I eventually achieved my goal, I told myself, I didn't care who passed me up. One disgustingly fit looking fellow, decked out in a mule-pack of expensive-looking gear, saw fit to comment as he passed by at twice my speed.

"Slow and steady wins the race," he said with a nod. I think he meant to sound encouraging, but to me it just sounded patronizing.

Approaching mile marker three, the trail passed Lone Pine Lake, a beautiful little pool surrounded by green grass, wildflowers, and a few foxtail and limber pines. There were dozens of tents there, with many of their occupants cooking breakfast over a Coleman stove or otherwise preparing for the day's ascent.

The path soon exited the little basin containing the lake and started seriously uphill again, traversing more meadows, rock formations, ledges, large gravel piles, and occasional small ponds. Each successive meadow was drier than the last, with less grass and fewer and smaller trees.

Eventually the summit came into view, looming three or four thousand feet overhead. I couldn't make out the three spirelike subpeaks, but the main summit was obvious—a sheer, massive, barren, immense, completely vertical cliff soaring up from a treeless, rocky basin. From about the third mile on, the summit was always there, solid, immovable, and discouragingly far away and high up—simultaneously beckoning and taunting.

At five and a half miles—the halfway point in distance, elevation, and time—I arrived at Consultation Lake, elevation twelve thousand feet, the largest and most spectacular lake on the route. The lake completely lacked shoreline vegetation, or any other vegetation. Nestled on barren ground against the base of an immense cliff, surrounded by melting snowbanks amid car- and house-size boulders, Consultation Lake at first appeared like nothing more than a large, temporary snowmelt puddle. It wasn't until I looked down from farther up the path that its large size—about twelve acres—became apparent.

Just beyond Consultation Lake, the trail's most difficult section began, the section that nearly did me in. This was the notorious Ladder, with its ninety-nine switchbacks. The path here climbed quickly out of the moraines and gravel fields at the base of Whitney's main summit and charged up a nearly vertical paralleling cliff to the ridge crest at 13,700 feet. The trail gained 1,700 feet in 2.2 miles, forcing its way up barren rock in rapidly thinning air, with virtually no shelter from the oppressive solar radiation.

Consultation Lake in 1967

If you somehow reached the ridge crest, another 2.8 much more level miles of trail took you to the final summit.

PART 6

At a keg party at a friend's house attended by Nancy, Linda Lowe, and myself, my relationship with Nancy started to shift from merely a wonderful friendship to an intense and difficult adventure that frequently made me think about turning back. Normally flirtatious and talkative, Nancy seemed sullen that night. Finally, Linda and I pulled her into the kitchen and asked if anything was wrong.

"I did something really dumb," Nancy informed us.

"You, do something dumb?" said Linda. "I'm shocked. What happened this time?"

"I'm pregnant."

"Oh!?" Linda and I replied in unison.

"I can't have a baby. Can you see me as a mother? Give me a break."

Then she launched into a little sarcastic improvisational scene: "This, my darling son, is a hypodermic needle. It can be your best friend or your worst enemy."

"Maybe having a baby will settle you down," I offered, drawing a Dixie cup of warm beer from the keg.

"I don't want to settle down. I haven't slept with every humanoid on the planet yet. Only about half of them."

"So have an abortion," Linda suggested. That was before *Roe v. Wade*, when abortions were still frighteningly illegal. "I'm sure you could get the money from the baby's father, if you know who it is, or maybe from one of your rich boyfriend wannabes."

"I am having an abortion. Tomorrow."

"And you're scared. Is that the problem?" I inquired.

"Don't be ridiculous. It would take a lot more than that to frighten me. I'm just not in the mood for partying right now."

The following night, I visited Nancy in her tiny room in a run-down rooming house. The walls were brightly covered with art prints, especially Salvador Dali. Nancy wore a nightgown and a bulky bathrobe and looked haggard and pale. She kept going to the bathroom to change sanitary pads.

"Are you OK?" I asked several times.

"I think so. You know me, I bounce back. Except for this damned bleeding."

It didn't seem wise to leave her alone. After a couple hours, when she continued to disappear into the bathroom every few minutes, I began worrying.

"I think we should go to the emergency room," I said after each trip. At around 10:00 p.m. she finally relented. I phoned for a cab, and we rode to the University Hospital together. Nancy seemed extremely weak and drowsy and didn't say much during the ride. On arrival, she was given an immediate blood transfusion and wheeled off to surgery, where she had an emergency dilation and curettage, or "D and C," which is a scraping of the uterus.

A doctor later told me that had we waited another twenty minutes, Nancy would have died. He also said that they had a terrible time finding a healthy vein for the transfusion because of all the narcotics injections.

Following the operation, I sat beside a sleeping Nancy in the recovery room, which reeked of ether and rubbing alcohol. After a while she opened her eyes with a far-off and dreamy look. When she saw me, she smiled weakly.

"Artie the hero!" she whispered. "Thank you for saving my life."

"No big deal," I smiled.

"You wouldn't be so smiley if you knew the truth."

"The truth?"

"The abortion wasn't done by a doctor. It was done by a guy named Mike on a kitchen table. You won't tell anyone, will you?"

"Trust me," I sighed as Nancy went back to sleep.

PART 7

By the summer of 1964, President Kennedy had been assassinated, my father had died of a heart attack at age fifty-two, and I had graduated college and was living in Detroit and working downtown as a welfare worker. Nancy also had graduated and, according to Linda Lowe, was back in New York using more drugs than ever and living on the streets in Greenwich Village.

In 1966, two years after graduation (and a year after a stint in New York during which I tried and failed several times to track Nancy down), I was sick of Detroit and sick of social work. The problem was that I had no other marketable skills. It was time, as Nancy would say, to take a risk.

My best friend in Ann Arbor, aside from Nancy and Linda, had been a law student named Basil Acidophilus. After getting his law degree, and mostly to avoid the Vietnam draft, Basil moved to Berkeley, California, to pursue a master's degree in economics. Between 1964 and 1966, every few months I'd get a call from Basil extolling the wonders and delights of San Francisco, Berkeley, and the hippie revolution. Neither of us, of course, had any interest in hippie social or spiritual philosophy. We were, however, extremely interested in the hordes of promiscuous and vulnerable young women that the movement was attracting to San Francisco and Berkeley.

In June 1966, driving a brand new Plymouth convertible and with virtually no plans, I quit my job and headed westward to investigate the "Summer of Love." I arrived in Berkeley on a sunny California day and parked in front of Basil's run-down hotel on Shattuck Avenue. The building was eight stories high, had seen much better days, and was home mostly to ex-students, dropouts, and others who hadn't quite gotten it together.

I went inside and asked for Basil at the desk. While I was at it, I rented a room of my own. The dark, creaky, musty, and extremely basic room—a seventh floor walk-up—cost $3.50 a week.

The first thing Basil said to me when I met him in the lobby was, "Nancy's here."

Basil knew Nancy from Ann Arbor, although not nearly as well as I did.

The second thing he said was, "*Please* take her off my hands. I'm begging you. She's jolly well driving me crazy. I've been supporting her and that's OK, but please, let her drive *you* insane for a while."

"Is she on drugs?" I asked.

"No doubt. I avoid giving her cash, but she spends a lot of time on the street; there's no telling what she's been up to."

As I was unpacking, Nancy came in and we hugged long and hard. I was genuinely glad to see her, and she seemed excited to see me. Except that she looked terrible. She'd lost weight, her skin seemed pale and pasty, and her hair had lost its beautiful sheen and didn't smell very good. Her jeans and shirt were still clean and tasteful, though, and she wore just a touch of makeup.

"I can't believe it's you," she said, after three or four more hugs. "And in California. How exciting is that?"

Over the next couple weeks, Nancy, Basil, and I took in the sights of the Bay Area. We drove down to Santa Cruz and the Monterey Peninsula. We drove north, over the Golden Gate Bridge, to Sausalito, Muir Woods, and Stinson Beach. We went to Chinatown, Fisherman's Wharf, Golden Gate Park, Haight-Ashbury, the Palace of Fine Arts, North Beach, and the Coit Tower. We went east to Lake Tahoe, Reno, and

Yosemite. And we spent hours cruising up and down Telegraph Avenue, Berkeley's teeming miniversion of San Francisco's Haight Street.

Things started to sour between Nancy and me after I took a two-week trip to visit my father's relatives in Los Angeles. The night of my return, Basil and I sat in the Steppenwolf Bar on Telegraph Avenue, downing beer after beer. A blaring rock band on the smoky stage made it difficult to hear each other.

"How's Nancy doing?" I shouted.

"Not well. I've offered a million times to take her to the state employment office. I've also been watching the want ads for her, but she bloody well won't follow up on anything. There were a couple ads for architectural draftsmen that she could do in her sleep."

"Are you still giving her money?"

"Not as much. She always has a guy in tow. But it's not like the old days. Now she picks up stupid kids from Iowa, here to 'check out the scene.' And even they catch on pretty quickly that she's just after their money to buy drugs. Do you think I should stop giving her money?"

"I'm not sure. We don't want her to starve, but we don't want to be enablers, either."

"What's an enabler?"

"Someone who makes it easier for an addict to be an addict. I learned about it in a psychology class."

"If you think we should back off, I'll trust your judgment, although if she was starving, I could never refuse her. And if she sincerely wanted to change her life, we should definitely be there for her."

At the time, it seemed like an excellent plan.

PART 8

It was on the section between Consultation Lake and the ridge crest that my resolve to climb Mount Whitney in Nancy's honor began to seriously deteriorate. I discovered, among other things, that there are other symptoms of exhaustion (and dehydration and altitude sickness) besides sleepiness.

With my slow, deliberate plodding pace and frequent short rests, I somehow managed the first fifty or sixty switchbacks up the trail's notorious Ladder section. Gradually, the sun became even more intense and the air much thinner. My field of vision began to narrow due to dehydration, and every time I got up from a rest, I found myself gasping for air after only two or three steps. That was around noon, when shade was at an absolute minimum.

It eventually got to where I would rest for five to ten minutes, then slowly try to walk for two or three minutes, then rest again, then walk for one minute, then rest again—all the while blinking constantly to clear my vision. I found myself looking for occasional overhanging rocks that cast maybe a square foot of shade on the trail. Upon spotting such a shade patch, I'd immediately drop onto my back and stick my head under it for a few minutes of relief from the relentless solar glare.

"One more step," I kept telling myself. "Then you can turn back. Just one more step." And so I kept going.

Finally I could go no farther. Lying on my back with my head stuck in a small shadow, I stared up at the summit, still impossibly high up and far away.

If only I could fly, I thought, I'd be there just in a few minutes and all this torture would be over.

The thought seemed to metamorphose into a kind of dreamy unreality, fed by exhaustion, dehydration, and thin air. I became convinced that I actually could levitate my body and soar on updrafts to the summit. All I had to do, I reasoned, was stand up, step over the edge, and think light thoughts.

Slowly, out of breath and aching, I forced myself to stand. To my delight, I discovered that I already seemed to be levitating. I was positive that my feet were not touching the ground and that I was floating in air. All I had to do was gently propel myself toward the summit and I'd sail on the wind like a feather.

I walked, or glided, to the edge of the trail and a sheer, five-hundred-foot drop-off, and stuck a foot over the edge.

PART 9

Nancy's life, and my own, came crashing down the night after I returned to my room after a night of bar hopping on Telegraph Avenue and found a note in my box, folded in half and stapled. When I opened the note, it said, in typed words with a plain, utilitarian signature at the bottom:

Dear Art (or should I say "Dear Gorgeous"):

You have the most beautiful body I've ever seen. If interested, I'll be eagerly waiting in Room 522, any time. Don't get paranoid if I'm with another guy. I'll get around to you. And, yes, it's free.

Anxiously,
Roxy

A little while later, as I lay in bed in my underwear reading a book, Basil knocked and then entered.

"Have you ever heard of a girl named Roxy?" I inquired.

"Indeed. I had sex with her in response to a mysterious note. Why? Did you get a note also?"

"Yeah. What's she like?"

"Rather nice, actually. A bit overweight but not bad looking. It seems that she and her cousin bet each other $100 to see who could sleep with a hundred different men first. When I met Roxy, the cousin was at sixty-one and Roxy was at fourteen. Hence, the mass mailing."

The next night, following yet another alcoholic foray on Telegraph Avenue, I again came home early and this time ended up watching TV in the hotel lobby. Behind the TV, a large plate-glass window made up the front end of the lobby. Through the glass you could see Shattuck Avenue and people walking past under the yellow streetlights.

I sat down next to a chubby black girl with a crew cut, who was watching the *Dean Martin Show* in black and white.

"I don't believe we've met," said the girl, turning toward me. "I'm Roxy."

I did a slight double take and tensed up.

"I'm Art." I forced a smile at her, then returned my attention to Dean Martin. "Get my note?" asked Roxy, inching her chair toward me.

"Oh yeah," I mumbled.

"Interested?"

"Maybe."

She reached over and rubbed the back of my hand, which I reflexively moved away.

"Not in the lobby," I explained.

"Then let's go upstairs."

"Right now?"

"If not now, when. And if not you, who?"

Nancy's sudden breathless burst through the doorway instantly cut short the negotiations.

"Am I glad to see you," said Nancy, dropping to her knees in front of me. Tears and dirt smudged her face. Her eyes were red and swollen as though she'd been crying, and an angry purple bruise puffed up one side of her jaw. Sobbing and out of breath, she looked up into my eyes.

"What happened?" I asked.

"I guess I really did it this time. You know that guy I told you about?"

"The rich kid from Iowa?"

"Yeah, that's him. He wanted me to buy him some acid because all the dealers thought he was a narc. He gave me $200 and said I could keep $50. Well, he found out the acid only cost me $40 and went crazy. He stuck his hand in my jacket pocket and yanked out the money. He ripped the pocket right off. Then he called me a thief and a whore and slugged me in the face. When I started to cry, he only got madder. He carried me outside by the belt and threw me into the street, then he kicked me in the ribs."

The side pocket of her purple nylon windbreaker had indeed been torn out.

"So he's not as big a patsy as you thought," I said.

"I guess not."

I leaned forward with a sigh and took her hand.

"For what it's worth," I announced, "I think you've finally hit bottom, and that may turn into a good thing. If you're ready to try to pull yourself back up, Basil and I will do whatever we can to help."

In retrospect, my statement was naïve and dismissive. In 1966, however, it was common wisdom. For one thing, there was no such thing in those days as a drug rehabilitation center.

She stood up slowly, withdrawing her hand, and wiped her cheeks without expression.

"Stay with me tonight," she whispered. "You've done it before. And you're wrong. Very wrong. I haven't hit bottom. For once, I'm genuinely scared."

"I'll absolutely stay with you. Just give me a couple minutes."

"Please come now."

"Just a couple minutes."

I felt that refusing Roxy's offer should be handled with tact. I couldn't just walk away.

"Good-bye, Art," said Nancy. She walked slowly and achingly up the stairs, in short, exhausted steps, favoring her injured ribs.

"Two seconds," I shouted after her. "I promise."

Nancy didn't look back.

"That girl loves you," said Roxy when Nancy had gone.

"And I love her," I said. "I hope I wasn't too harsh, but she does tend to use people."

"What's wrong with letting someone use you? Especially a friend in trouble."

I paused over her statement and slouched in my chair.

"You might have a point," I said. "I'd better go see her."

I started to get up.

"When will you and I get together?" Roxy asked.

"Tomorrow. The night after. I don't know."

"Can I leave you with a little something so you don't forget?" she said with a wink and a leer.

"I guess."

Roxy leaned over and gave me a long, deeply probing kiss. We ended up making out for several minutes, even though I knew I ought to leave and take care of Nancy.

Our embrace was interrupted by a falling blur outside the window behind the TV and a muffled thud. Roxy and I rushed to the doorway to investigate.

As I looked out onto the night street, a spasm of nauseated horror knocked the wind out of me. I tried repeatedly to will away what I saw. I clamped one hand across my gut and welded the other over my mouth.

Nancy, frail and oddly dwarfed, lay peacefully on the sidewalk. Her pallid head bobbed slightly from side to side. My still-recoiling body forced itself to her side.

"Nancy?" I whispered.

Her eyes half opened and looked at me.

"Now," she said in a faint gurgle, "I've hit bottom."

Then her beautiful eyes closed forever.

PART 10

I stood midstride at the brink of the Whitney Summit Trail with my foot dangling into space, preparing to levitate to the summit. I was a split second from falling five hundred feet straight down and crashing into the solid granite.

At that very instant, a hand—or something—grabbed the back of my collar and yanked me back onto the trail. I stumbled for a second and then quickly regained my balance and most of my senses. I turned around to thank whoever or whatever had saved my life, but there was nobody there.

The hand that pulled me back was absolutely real. It was not my imagination. Of that, I am certain. What happened next, however, is not so clear. I heard a voice. It was not an audible voice, like you would hear if someone was standing next to you. But I definitely heard something.

A rather deep female voice with a thick New York accent said, or seemed to say, "No shortcuts, Bernstein. Get back on the trail. All we need is for us both to end up dead."

For a few seconds I felt a strong sense of Nancy's presence. And then she was gone. Immediately after, my head cleared completely and I felt a surge of genuine energy for the first time in hours.

I knew then that Nancy really did forgive me for what I had done, and I climbed to the top of the ridge with renewed determination, despite the tears trickling down my cheeks.

PART 11

Hours after Nancy's leap from the hotel roof, after the Berkeley police had left and the crowd had disbursed, I stood by myself, not moving from the spot, in the terrible silence of the night street. In the light from the hotel window, I cast a long shadow onto Shattuck Avenue. Still clutching my mouth and stomach, standing inside the yellow outline the police had drawn around Nancy's body, I tried in vain to persuade myself that it was not my fault.

The next day, Nancy's parents arrived. They were distraught, of course, but not entirely surprised. They cleaned out Nancy's room and arranged to have her body flown back to Long Island for burial.

While going through Nancy's belongings, they found a sealed envelope with my name on it. They also found similar envelopes addressed to them and to Nancy's younger sister. The mother knocked on my door and handed me the envelope with my name on it. We chatted for a minute before she left.

I sat down on the bed and felt myself choking up again, as I had been doing for most of the night and morning. I opened the envelope and unfolded the paper inside.

Here's what it said:

To my dearest and best friend, Art–

If you are reading this, it means I finally got up the nerve to do what needed to be done. I'd been thinking about it for months and neither you nor anybody else could have prevented it. My life had become completely out of control, and I saw no way to reverse it. If nothing else, I'm off drugs now.

As for you, I advise what I've always advised: Participate more in life rather than observing from the sidelines, and take greater risks even if they leave you vulnerable and uncomfortable. Because if you never take a risk, you will never grow. I see wonderful potential in you but only if you learn to charge into the oncoming headlights rather than just stare at them.

My suggestion—find a high and difficult mountain—higher than you could ever climb safely and comfortably—and go climb it, even though you are frightened, exhausted, and can't take another step. It will change your life.

Do this one last thing for me.

And give my regards to Basil.

All my love forever,
Nancy

PART 12

I have no idea how I managed it, but forty minutes after my aborted "shortcut," I actually reached the ridgecrest. The next 2.8 miles rose yet another eight hundred feet, but that was easy compared with what I'd already completed.

At 3:00 p.m., I reached the boulder-and-snow-patch-strewn plateau with the little stone cabin. About half the size of a football field, it was the highest point in the United States outside Alaska. It was then that I took out the piece of paper I had brought with me, Nancy's letter.

In planning the trip, once I settled on Mount Whitney, I'd spent months trying to figure out the most deeply moving, symbolic, and meaningful gesture I could make in Nancy's honor. I wrote rough drafts of long and poetic speeches, thought about bringing flowers, and considered poking a stick in the ground and writing her name on it.

In the end, I decided to keep my mouth shut for once and just let myself experience the moment. I walked as close to the edge as I dared. And then, in a moment of inspiration, I got down on my knees and folded the letter into a paper airplane. Then I stood up and sailed the letter over the edge.

"This is for you, Nancy," I whispered. "I couldn't have done it without you."

It wasn't much of a speech, but I liked it.

I watched the small white triangular object sail in a gentle, looping glide high above the basin, over Consultation Lake and out over the desert. I'm not sure when I lost sight of it, because the barely perceptible white dot seemed to linger a lot longer in my memory than in reality.

Satisfied, and feeling a little better, I shouldered my canteen and camera, adjusted my hat, and started back down. I felt pleased that I had succeeded in my quest. But I felt even more pleased that Nancy, for the first time since I'd met her on that beautiful day in Ann Arbor, was finally at peace.

TO VISIT

The hike: Whitney Summit Trail
Distance: Eleven miles (one-way)

Directions: Between Bridgeport and Lone Pine, California, US 395 follows the base of the spectacular eastern face of the Sierra Nevada. In Lone Pine, turn west onto Whitney Portal Road and drive fourteen miles through the highly scenic Alabama Hills and up to Whitney Portal. As of 2005, the road is paved, the campground has been greatly enlarged, and the trail is extremely crowded. You can write in advance for a permit to hike the trail or take your chances at the little store at Whitney Portal.

6

The Trail That Didn't Want Me

PROLOGUE
In life there are many trails. A few open new and wondrous horizons and change you forever. Most are good, bad, or indifferent but in the long run don't matter all that much. However, when a chosen path sends out incontrovertible signals that it is not right for you in your life, no matter how determined you might be to pursue it to the end, you probably would be well advised to seek an alternate route.

PART 1
In winter 1999–2000 I received an invitation to speak at the "Lunch-time Health Forum" lecture series for the staff at Providence Hospital in Medford, Oregon. They presented speakers on health issues, and as a local hiking guru, I guess I qualified. I've been known to lecture on hiking from time to time.

We met in a rather stark conference room with gray tables arranged in a circle. About forty people showed up—doctors, nurses, technicians, and other staff—all with lunches. They proved an unusually pleasant, intelligent, and responsive group.

Instead of showing slides and boring them with a shotgun blast of local hiking opportunities, which around Medford are far too numerous to detail, I spent ten minutes talking about noncompetitive physical conditioning and endorphins and stuff like that. Then I simply threw it open for questions.

The first inquiry came from a gray-haired doctor in his late sixties, who timidly raised his hand.

"This may sound dumb," he said, "but what precisely is a trail?"

I'd never been asked that before, and the answer proved far more complicated than I'd have guessed, because every definition I could think of seemed to have several exceptions. After that, the questions flowed like Kool-Aid in a day camp.

"Have you ever been seriously injured while hiking?" a chubby nurse asked.

"Yes. I've had two sprained ankles."

"Have you ever gotten lost?"

"Four times. But I obviously found my way back each time."

"Have you ever turned back halfway into a hike?"

"Frequently, usually because I was exhausted or the trail took much longer than anticipated."

"Have you ever been really frightened on a hike?"

"Many times, but I usually try not to let it bother me and to keep going anyhow."

"What kinds of things have frightened you?"

"High up on the list was the time lightning struck a cliff fifty feet above where I was standing. It knocked me over, made my hair stand on end, and made electricity arc between my fingers. But I didn't turn back because I was already on the way back. Bears and rattlesnakes will also get my adrenaline going, but not enough to cause me to turn back."

"So you've never turned back because something scared you and for no other reason?"

"Just once, in 1965, when I was twenty-two years old. The strangest thing about that hike was that I really couldn't pinpoint exactly what frightened me. All I knew was that for some reason, I got the distinct feeling that the trail didn't want me there."

PART 2

It was a few days before Christmas and, finding myself for once with a surplus of time and money, I decided to drive down to Florida for a couple days. I'd always wanted to see Florida. In elementary school, many of my classmates went to Florida over winter or spring break, returning with deep, off-season tans. Everybody but me.

With five days to kill and a blizzard about to move into southern Michigan, the timing seemed perfect. It seems counterintuitive, but when you drive the 1,200 miles from Detroit to Miami, one-third of the trip is inside Florida. I left at 5:00 p.m. on December 20. It got light somewhere in Tennessee and dark again as I entered Florida. (There's not much daylight that time of year.) I spent several hours sleeping in my car in a freeway rest area near Lake Worth, Florida.

Most of day two was spent motoring down Florida's Atlantic coast past Daytona Beach, St. Augustine, Cape Canaveral–Cape Kennedy, Palm Beach, and Fort Lauderdale.

Late in the day, after a wide loop around Miami, I headed out the spectacular Key West Highway. I loved the concept of driving one hundred miles straight into the warm ocean at Christmas. I loved the sunny, 80-degree weather. I loved the water that looked like a giant, sparkling swimming pool. I loved the lack of surf. I loved the mangrove trees with their stiltlike roots. I loved the strange pink birds and the hardwood trees that had not lost their leaves merely because it happened to be winter.

Key West was unbelievable. Despite the tropical sunshine, the moss-draped live oaks, the gnarled old banyan trees, and the majestic palms, the town's graceful elegance brought to mind a New England fishing village, or maybe the Hamptons on outer Long Island. I envied the charter-boat operators in the town harbor, lazing around in their Hawaiian shirts, their only mission being to haul rich people out to fish for marlin and sailfish.

After taking in the sights of Key West, including the southernmost point in the southernmost city in the continental United States, I slept for a few hours on a white sand beach in a little state park on one of the keys. These days you wouldn't do such a thing unless you were insane. The world, with a few notable exceptions, was much safer back then. Or at least I thought it was.

The next morning, day three, I reluctantly dragged myself out of the soft sand, took a washcloth bath, and changed into clean clothes in the restroom. Then I drove into the town of Marathon Key for breakfast. The little restaurant appeared clean enough except for thirty or forty strips of flypaper dangling from the ceiling, which badly needed to be replaced. Also, the place reeked of rancid grease. But I was starving so I chose to overlook those shortcomings of ambience.

After I'd spent a few minutes examining the menu, a waitress in her forties, with stiff, bouffant hair, way too much makeup, and a food-stained, candy-striped apron, approached to take my order. I could barely understand her thick Southern accent.

"Y'all wanna poo incognito?" she asked, readying her pen over the order pad. At least that's what it seemed like she said.

I placed my order without responding to her inquiry about pooing incognito. I ordered eggs over medium, toast, hash browns, and pork sausage. When my food arrived, a few minutes later, it was exactly as I had envisioned, except for a small deposit of white slop near the edge, with butter melting on it.

"What's that stuff?" I inquired.

"Grits."

That was the only thing she said that I understood. And even that wasn't easy because she actually said, "gree-yuts."

"I didn't order grits."

"Comes wi'the foo fanny."

"Oh, OK."

Then she said something that completely baffled me. In fact, it was at that very instant that the trip began to turn strange.

"Y'all watch out for Martians, now."

Having no idea what she actually said, and little hope of comprehending any possible clarification, I ate my breakfast and did not press for details. I did not eat the grits, although I did take a small taste. Then I got in my car and headed for the Everglades, still puzzling over the waitress's remark.

I eventually decided, as I drove back to the mainland and through the town of Homestead, that what I'd heard as "Martians" was possibly "Marathonians," which I conjectured were residents of Marathon Key, where the restaurant was located. Even with that brilliant bit of insight, however, the statement still made no sense. It did not explain why I should watch out for people from Marathon Key, if indeed that was what she'd said, which it probably wasn't.

PART 3

Things seemed normal enough when I arrived at the massive Everglades Visitor Center and Entrance Station, just inside the park near Homestead. There were hundreds of cars, and people were milling everywhere. As I pulled into a parking place, I must have inadvertently cut off a young man in a beat-up old Volkswagen Beetle whose car had been spray-painted black. The guy beeped his horn at me then flipped me off. Not knowing what I'd done and with no desire to find out, I smiled politely and continued parking my car while avoiding eye contact.

As I got out of my car and walked toward the building, I heard somebody behind me shouting obscenities. It might have been the fellow in the Volkswagen or it might have been some road-weary parent chastising his kids. I didn't look around to find out. I figured if it was the guy in the Volkswagen, it was best to simply get lost in the crowd rather than confront him.

I'd caught a brief glimpse of the Volkswagen driver when he flipped me off. He was about my age and wore a black T-shirt. He looked very unkempt and unpleasant. Of course after three days on the road, sleeping in my car and in the sand, I myself was hardly the epitome of kempt pleasantry.

I spent maybe ten minutes in the visitor center and then started down the road to Flamingo Village. As I departed the center, I noted that the Volkswagen was parked four or five spaces away from me.

It took me a while to realize that there were no other cars on the Flamingo Road. The first inkling came several miles down the highway when I pulled into a parking turnout with a short nature walk. I found it a little odd that I was the only visitor on a weekend in December at 10:00 in the morning. I didn't see any cars or people in the parking area or on the wooden boardwalk through the swamp, just lots of pink, white, and red birds and an alligator. The same was true at Mahogany Hammock and a couple other turnouts.

At first I attributed the lack of cars and people to a momentary aberration. I compared the phenomenon to something I'd learned in elementary school science class years earlier: There are trillions of oxygen molecules in the air in constant random movement around the room. It is theoretically possible that, for a brief instant, they could all end up on the same side of the room, leaving the other side devoid of oxygen. Highly unlikely, but possible.

When I arrived back from the ten-minute hike at Mahogany Hammock, the lack of vehicles and humans evolved in my mind from curiosity to a slight, gnawing threat. There, parked right beside my car, was the black Volkswagen. There were no other cars, nobody in the Volkswagen, and I hadn't encountered anybody on the trail (which made some sense, since it was a loop). It also made sense, I tried to assure myself, that somebody who entered the park the same time I had and was driving the same main road would also stop at a major turnout.

But why the Volkswagen and no other cars? The guy in the Volkswagen was the only person I didn't care to see again.

The lack of other cars, the mysterious, slightly threatening Volkswagen, and the waitress's Martian remark all seemed to roll together in my mind as the notorious Bernstein imagination began running wild. It sounded ridiculous, but Martians were the most reasonable explanation I could come up with for the lack of other cars. Had the road been closed due to a chemical spill or an escaped convict, which might also account for the sudden dearth of traffic, there would have been cars in the opposite direction, or police, or something.

Only Martians have been known to stop all traffic dead in its tracks in all directions. Every time you hear about somebody seeing a flying saucer close up, the person's car always mysteriously dies. And it invariably starts up again the instant the flying saucer leaves.

Of course my Martian theory had its holes. Presuming that every car but mine had mysteriously stalled because of magnetic rays emitted by a hovering flying saucer, there should have been stalled cars everywhere, with people running up and down the highway screaming in terror. And there should have been a flying saucer overhead.

As I started my car at Mahogany Hammock and prepared to continue the journey, it occurred to me that the Martian theory did not account for the continued flawless functioning of my little powder-blue Plymouth. Why was my vehicle alone impervious to the alien rays while all the other cars were dropping like mosquitoes zapped with insecticide? And above all, why was the black Volkswagen also impervious to Martian electronic interference?

Unless . . . unless the Volkswagen was actually a disguised "away" vehicle from the Martian mother ship. And the driver, the guy in the black T-shirt, was a Martian. And I alone had been singled out for abduction.

The story made perfect sense. I tried to dismiss it as silly and tell myself that there were no Martians and that very soon I'd begin seeing traffic again. But my imagination, and my obsessive brain, would not

Everglades viewing area

be assuaged. Especially when I drove the final 18 miles to my intended destination, the Bear Lake Trail, and still didn't see another car.

PART 4

Before heading out Bear Lake Road, I stopped by Flamingo Village, which turned out to be one of the most beautiful places I'd ever seen, before or since. It consisted of a vast palm-dotted lawn facing the ocean, with mangrove swamps on both sides and the intoxicating aroma of warm ocean air permeating everything. The only problem was that there wasn't much to do in Flamingo Village unless you happened to own a sailboat, which I did not. Aside from that, the only activities I could find were walking around and browsing in the little store. I ended up the proud owner of a brand-new Popsicle and a bunch of postcards.

And, yes, there were people in Flamingo Village. Lots of people: pasty-faced, Hawaiian-shirted tourists with Brownie cameras, and children frantically dashing every which way, basking in the momentary release from their automotive oubliettes. And of course there were lots of parked cars. But I never saw any cars or any people until I was in the actual parking lot. I never saw a car or a person on the highway. Not one. Except for the Volkswagen at Mahogany Hammock.

On arriving at Flamingo Village, I was immensely relieved that the "no cars, no people" state of affairs had finally ended. I laughed to myself over the silliness of my Martian theory. There had obviously been other cars on the road after all. I just hadn't noticed them.

I stayed in Flamingo perhaps twenty minutes, after which I drove back to the Bear Lake Road turnoff and followed the two-mile, arrow-straight route to the trailhead at the road's end. To my dismay, once I left the village, all the cars and people vanished again. Again I tried to persuade myself that it was my imagination. I passed no cars on the highway and no cars on Bear Lake Road, but I didn't expect there to be many cars on Bear Lake Road.

Arriving at the trailhead, I reassured myself that at least there were no black Volkswagens parked there. Or Martian spaceships.

I got out, locked my vehicle, and started hiking up the 1.6-mile trail, which began at a small, stagnant, brackish-smelling pond. The route traversed a dense tropical hardwood forest of mahogany and buttonwood, full of strange little air plants, near the edge of mangroves. It paralleled a canal teeming with squawking waterfowl, egrets, herons, flamingos, and bald eagles. Lengths of wooden boardwalk kept my feet dry through the swampy areas and minimized the chances of being attacked by alligators or poisonous water snakes.

I actually enjoyed the first few minutes of the walk. However, my anxiety level rose slightly when I started hearing footsteps behind me. Or what sounded like footsteps. The noise was faint at first. So faint that I didn't notice it for a while, so I can't say precisely when it started. When I became aware of the noise, a quarter mile into the hike, I again attributed it to my overly active imagination and snickered at myself for my silliness. Besides, what with the birds, alligators, raccoons, squirrels, deer, pumas, bears, insects, copperheads, and water moccasins, I was walking through a pretty busy and noisy place. Were something tailing me, or skulking alongside me in the woods, it should not have been a total surprise.

I stopped two or three times to look behind me. The trail was nearly straight, so if somebody or something was following me, I'd surely have seen it. Unless, each time, they ducked into the impenetrable under-brush at the last second.

Most disturbing about the noises was that instead of merely pumas or crazed stalkers, my thoughts kept returning to Martians. That obvi-ously was not logical at all. Why would a Martian follow me? It seemed to me that if Martians wanted to abduct or kill me, they would just do it, straight out. They wouldn't need to track me for miles and go to such lengths to keep out of sight.

Still, whatever was or wasn't going on, my intuition absolutely, pos-itively insisted that Martians were somehow involved. The idea would not go away.

After a while the footsteps behind me began to grow louder. So loud that there was no mistaking that something—Martians, rac-coons, another hiker, or whatever—was making a noise to my rear. The noise sped up when I sped up, slowed down when I slowed down, and stopped when I stopped. I repeatedly checked myself to make sure there was nothing dangling from my shoes, jiggling in my pocket, or slapping against my back or legs.

It didn't help that the forest was exceptionally spooky, like some-thing out of *The Wizard of Oz.* I could almost picture the trees with faces on them cursing and throwing apples at me. I reminded myself that I'd hiked through spooky forests before. There was Washington's Olympic rain forest, for example, with its giant conifers, musty smells, light-starved understory, and moss-draped branches. The Olympic rain forest, however, despite the Hansel and Gretel imagery, hadn't evoked any spooky intuition.

The Bear Lake Trail was feeling less safe by the minute. But I was determined to tough it out. If I turned back, I could never admit to anyone that I hadn't completed my only hike in the Everglades out of fear of Martians.

I pressed onward until the noise behind me started growing louder yet again. Then I began hearing rustling in the bushes around me. Not occasional rustling but constant rustling, as though every animal in the neighborhood was tracking me, watching my every move, ready to pounce. Finally, when I heard a distinct growling noise in front of me, I stopped dead in my tracks.

The instant I stopped, the universe fell silent. I took two or three hesitant steps forward and the noise started up again. Including the growling.

As an experiment, I turned around and walked a few steps back toward the car—and was greeted with nothing but profound and blessed silence. When I started back toward Bear Lake, the noises commenced once again. I figured the lake was half a mile away at that point.

At the rate the noises were escalating, there was no telling what would happen by the time I arrived at my destination. Reluctantly I opted for the direction of quietude and peace of mind. I opted to get the hell out of there.

I rationalized that I was tired, that it was getting late in the day, that the trail was way too long, and that it was not very interesting. None of those things were true.

The farther from Bear Lake I got, the more relaxed and relieved I felt. By the time I arrived back at the trailhead, I felt downright elated, if a little embarrassed.

As I was getting into my car, the black Volkswagen pulled into the parking lot. It frightened me for a second, especially when the driver got out and started walking toward me. Until I saw that he was smiling.

"Hey, man," he said, "how was Bear Lake?"

"Fantastic," I lied. "Lots of wildlife."

With a polite nod, the Volkswagen guy walked past me and started up the trail.

The fellow did not look like a Martian. In fact he didn't look threatening in any way. Still, I don't know why—call it intuition—I was glad I was not sharing the path with him, which would have been the case had I continued to Bear Lake instead of turning back.

When I pulled back onto the Flamingo Highway and headed back toward Homestead, there was traffic all over the place, in both directions.

And the world was whole once again.

PART 5

I spent the next night sleeping in my car in another freeway rest area, this one near Jacksonville. My plan was to swing up through Georgia and South Carolina, make the drive through Great Smoky Mountain National Park, then head home. I did not plan to hike in the Smokies.

As I drove toward Jacksonville, I spent most of the time trying to figure out what had happened on the Bear Lake hike and what all those strange noises and premonitions were about. I came to no conclusions except that the whole business made no sense. When I awoke in the morning, the events of the previous day seemed much less threatening.

Actually, when I woke up my thoughts had to do solely with filling my gut. Breakfast is my favorite meal, especially a nice, greasy, fried-egg breakfast in a roadside cafe. One of my first acts of the day, at around 7:00 a.m., was to stop and eat.

Unlike the previous day, I selected a nice, new, clean, mostly plastic restaurant at a freeway interchange. The establishment was spotless and smelled of butter and syrup rather than dead flies, rancid grease, and mildew. It boasted a charming little gift section that sold plaster figurines of kittens, puppies, and elves. They also sold Florida souvenirs, including the now highly illegal stuffed baby alligators.

I ordered the same meal as I had in Marathon Key—eggs over medium, toast, hash browns, and sausage. This time I understood every word the waitress said. And there were no grits with the meal, although there were grits on the menu.

While eating, I decided to purchase that day's issue of the *Miami Herald*. I get bored pretty easily when I'm by myself and I enjoy the local newspapers. I planned to save the paper and read it at lunch too.

Out of habit, the first place I turned to was the sports page. For some reason, basketball and football scores fascinate me. After extracting every iota of relevant information from the sports page, which took about thirty seconds, I moved to the front page, which also had a marked paucity of attention-grabbing material. The lead story, as I recall, was about Senator Strom Thurmond of South Carolina, the same person who ran for president in 1948, marrying a twenty-three-year-old beauty pageant winner.

Page two proved just as uninteresting as page one. Page three would have been even more boring, except for a small article near the bottom.

The headline said, "Suspected Killer Eludes Capture in Everglades." I read it only because I happened to have been in the Everglades the previous day. The tragic, frightening story had to do with a family—mother, father, and four-year-old daughter—who were robbed and shot to death while camping in a state park near Homestead. The alleged perpetrator fled into the Everglades and apparently was still on the loose. They had a description of his car from an eyewitness.

It was an old Volkswagen Beetle that had been spray-painted black. The police had identified the alleged perpetrator from fingerprints at the crime scene. He was a notorious twenty-three-year-old drug dealer and habitual miscreant from Miami.

His name was Oscar Henry Mars.

I was later told by friends that Bear Lake is a very nice place. I plan to go back one of these days. The next time, I hope to make it all the way to the lake.

TO VISIT

The hike: Bear Lake Trail, Everglades National Park, Florida
Distance: 1.6 miles (one-way)
Directions: Take the main road (FL 9053) from US 1 in Homestead, Florida, into Everglades National Park, toward Flamingo Village. One mile before Flamingo (thirty-eight miles from the park entrance), turn right onto Bear Lake Road. It's two miles to the Bear Lake trailhead.

7

The Power Source

PART 1

This story, which ends with the possible impending destruction of Mount Shasta, California's most impressive summit, began on a warm September evening in 1970 when J. Herbert Gumble answered the door naked. J. Herbert, whom most people called "JH," was my coworker at the Siskiyou County Welfare Department in Yreka, California, where I'd just been hired after moving out from Michigan. He and his wife, Barbara, had invited my wife, Patricia, and me to dinner.

In addition to being my coworker, JH was a New Age guru and self-anointed priest, although he downplayed that particular sideline around my wife and me because he knew we weren't interested.

A major reason for our move to Yreka was that it was near Mount Shasta. I'd seen Mount Shasta for the first time when passing by in my car a couple of years earlier and had become mesmerized. That happens to a lot of people and is why the Mount Shasta area was in 1970, and still is, a mecca for oddball religious types like JH.

Mount Shasta is a solitary, 14,161-foot volcano that stands guard over the California Far North. For those living in Shasta's shadow, I quickly discovered, the influence of the massive, glacier-covered peak is pervasive. Shasta greets you every morning, puts you to bed at night, and enters your awareness frequently throughout the day. You rarely go more than an hour or two without thinking about the mountain.

In addition to being a welfare caseworker and a high priest, JH was an exhibitionist. Having heard that about him, I was not surprised when he answered the door naked. I was not pleased either. He reputedly showed off his body to anyone who would look, especially young women. Barbara Gumble, a tall, serious, short-haired brunette, was not an exhibitionist.

Thirty-eight years old in 1970, JH had curly blond hair; a lean, well-proportioned body; and a big, long, hooked nose. As for the rest of his anatomy, I didn't look so I can't say. The fact that my wife was twenty-three, quite pretty, and very shy was probably all the incentive

JH needed to drop his drawers. My wife did not look either. At least she claims she didn't.

Barbara and JH lived in a tidy little house on the edge of town, with pasture on one side, a stand of piney woods on another, and the newly constructed I-5 passing by. It looked sort of like the house in the Andrew Wyeth painting *Christina's World*, a white clapboard structure rising starkly out of a field. Like the painting, it radiated great rustic charm. Also like the painting, when you looked more closely, there was something not quite right about it.

The official excuse that JH offered for being naked was that he was in the middle of ironing his pants.

"Come on in," he said. "I'm ironing my pants."

He was, too. There was an ironing board set up in the living room.

What mostly drew JH and me together as friends were the problems we'd both been experiencing at work. To be accepted in Siskiyou County, California, in 1970, it helped to be a narrow-minded bigot, which we were not, although we were fairly bigoted against narrow-minded bigots. Welfare recipients and hippies were particular targets of community scorn. The town boasted a disproportionate share of welfare recipients and hippies in 1970. Anything bad that happened—from lost kittens to lightning striking a tree—was blamed on welfare recipients and hippies. Signs in the windows of some of the stores and restaurants in town proclaimed, WE DO NOT SOLICIT HIPPIE PATRONAGE.

JH, myself, and our supervisor, a secret cocaine addict named Bob Piggins, were all suspected (correctly) of being hippie sympathizers and were considered just a little too liberal and "big city." JH and his wife hailed from the bustling and cosmopolitan metropolis of Chico, California. But they had lived in San Francisco. So had our supervisor, a Yreka native.

I'd met Patricia in Detroit two years earlier. The main thing we had in common was a burning desire to move out West. In May 1970 Patricia and her two-year-old daughter, Jennifer, accompanied me to San Francisco. I was hired at the Siskiyou County Welfare Department in Yreka two weeks later.

In 1970 Yreka was the Wild West, gold rush, logging, and cattle-ranching seat of California's northernmost county. Pat immediately found work as a legal secretary, and the very first cases she handled had to do with claim jumping on gold mines. Talk about culture shock.

The very best thing about Yreka, of course, was that Mount Shasta lay only thirty miles away. There were much closer towns to the mountain, such as Mount Shasta City, but thirty miles was near enough for the town of five thousand to fall well within the mountain's spell and aura. Since 1970 I have seen Mount Shasta probably five thousand times. I've seen it in summer, fall, winter, and spring; morning, noon, and night. I've hiked trails on every side of the mountain and have watched from the summit, huddling in front of my wind-whipped tent, as the mountain's pointed shadow slowly crept across the much lower mountains to the east.

I have come to two conclusions: Mount Shasta never looks the same twice, and it invariably evokes an overwhelming sense of awe.

After a huge turkey dinner, JH (now wearing pants) and I sat in the living room sipping Rainier beers.

"Damned nice country around here," I commented, lazing back on the couch as the aroma of turkey gravy wafted in from the kitchen. The only things preventing me from falling immediately asleep were JH's presence and an intensifying pressure in my bladder from all the beer.

"I'll say," said JH with a knowing grin. JH was the master of the knowing grin. "You got Mount Shasta. You got the Marble Mountain Wilderness. You got the Trinity Alps Wilderness. You got Crater Lake and the redwoods. If I were one of those hiking fanatics, I suspect I could hike a different trail every day of my life, all within a hundred-mile radius of Yreka, and never run out of trails."

"I thought you liked hiking," I said.

"I love hiking. But not every day of my life."

"So tell me," I said, "what's the prettiest natural place in the area? Not counting Mount Shasta."

"That's easy," said JH, with a knowing, sleepy grin. "Ney Springs."

"What's so special about Ney Springs?" I asked, stifling my own yawn.

"A lot of things," said JH, uncapping another brew. "But mostly it's incredibly beautiful."

"I guess I'll have to check it out. How do I get there?"

"As it happens, you're in luck. I'm going there next weekend. My church is having its semiannual Equinox Festival and Ruckus. You and Pat want to come? It'll be lots of fun."

"I'm not sure," I replied with a suspicious squint. "I'm not big on religion."

"You said you wanted to see Ney Springs," said JH, pretending to look hurt. "You don't have to be a church member, and you don't have to participate. A lot of people just come to watch."

"I'll think about it."

"I'll pick you and Pat up at 6:00 p.m. I hope you won't be offended by a couple dozen naked girls dancing around in a drunken frenzy."

On reflection, I decided that I wouldn't mind going.

PART 2

A few days after my dinner at JH's house, and before the big ceremony at Ney Springs, he and I met for lunch at the McDonald's in Mount Shasta City. We were both in the field that day, visiting clients.

"Ever heard of Lemurians?" JH inquired through a mouthful of Big Mac. Had he asked the question twenty-four hours earlier, I wouldn't have had the faintest idea what he was talking about. As it was, he created a prime opportunity for me to strut out a bit of newly acquired knowledge.

"I have indeed," I replied, pleased with myself for having passed his little pop quiz. "Some guy in the Buckhorn Tavern was telling me about them last night. As I understand it, Lemurians are the descendants of the escapees from the lost continent of Mu and they supposedly live underneath Mount Shasta. What I can't figure out is how someone can live underneath a mountain. You don't believe in Lemurians, do you?"

I would have been very surprised to learn that JH believed in Lemurians. J. Herbert Gumble believed in J. Herbert Gumble. Everything else was a scam. I knew that, and he knew that I knew.

"Of course I don't believe in Lemurians," said JH. "But to fully appreciate Ney Springs, and the spiritual power of Mount Shasta, you have to understand the local legends. Especially the Lemurian legend. It's fascinating but a rather long story, so I may not be able to finish it today."

"I'm all ears," I announced.

"Although everybody around here has heard of Lemurians," JH explained, "not many know how the legend got started. Or what it means. Even fewer people know about the connection between the Lemurians, the spiritual power of Mount Shasta, and Ney Springs. Have you ever heard of the Continental Drift theory?"

"Umm, sure," I said, somewhat startled by the sudden non sequitur. "In geology class back at the University of Michigan."

"The Continental Drift theory was first expounded in the 1860s. Its originator, some German guy whose name I forget, gave the name, 'Gondwanaland' to the giant, protocontinent from which all others are derived."

"I know about Gondwanaland," I said, pleased with myself. "Nobody today believes there was ever such a place."

"What matters is that part of the hypothetical Gondwanaland, a subplate composed of present-day East Africa, Madagascar, and part of India, was named 'Lemuria' after an animal called a lemur, which lives in all three places. It's the lowest form of primate."

"Are you serious?" I said, laughing. "I made a joke about lemurs and Lemurians last night. The guy I told it to never heard of lemurs."

"That doesn't surprise me. But my source happens to be the California State Library in Sacramento. Anyhow, about ten years after the subcontinent of Lemuria was first described, a Russian mystic in New York named Helena Blavatsky published a book in which she described 'Seven Races of Man.' Race Number Two were the Lemurians, an apelike people who laid eggs, were hermaphroditic, stood fifteen feet tall, and had eyes in the back of their heads and four arms. We're Race Number Five, in case you're interested."

"And this theory, no doubt, was subsequently borne out in archaeological research?"

"Don't be silly. As it happens, though, Madame Blavatsky's big contribution to the Lemurian legend was to mistakenly move Lemuria from the Indian Ocean to the Pacific."

"Interesting," I said, for want of a better comment.

"It gets crazier," said JH. "You're probably wondering about the connection between Lemuria and the lost continent of Mu."

"Not exactly. Is there a connection?"

114

"Most people assume they are one and the same because of the name similarity. But they're not. Not at all. The protocontinent of Lemuria and the lost continent of Mu are connected only by their identical middle syllable. That and the fact that both were supposed to have been in the Pacific. Except for Lemuria, which was actually in the Indian Ocean."

"The guy in the bar last night told me that Lemurians are from Mu. I guess he was wrong."

"People from Mu are called Muvians and people from Lemuria are called Lemurians. It's very confusing. But then it's all nonsense anyhow. The Mu theory traces to the 1500s when a missionary named Diego de Landa, working in Mexico, published an alleged Mayan alphabet, which he claimed proved that the region's native tribes were descended from the Lost Tribes of Israel. Since Mayan writing was pictographic and not phonetic, his alphabet was completely bogus."

"It certainly would not have been the first recorded incidence of bad archaeology," I commented.

"Nor the last," said JH. "Anyhow, in 1864 a French mystic named Brasseur used the de Landa alphabet to translate a Mayan inscription into a story about a 'land called Mu, which sank beneath the Pacific in a great catastrophe.' Mu is the middle letter of the Greek alphabet. Brasseur thought the Mayans were escapees from this lost continent. Actually they were clearly related to, if a little more advanced than, the tribes around them."

"How does all this relate to Mount Shasta and Ney Springs?"

"I'm getting to that. In 1894 one Frederick Oliver, under the name Phylos the Tibetan, wrote a book called *A Dweller on Two Planets* about a traveler who meets a Chinese holy man while climbing on Mount Shasta. The holy man runs a temple dedicated to preserving the ancient writings of Mu. The traveler visits the temple, is introduced to the wisdom of Mu, and, incidentally, psychically visits the planet Venus. It was intended as fiction but many people took it seriously. Some still do. You can purchase the book at most bookstores hereabouts."

"I guess some people will believe just about anything."

"Tell me about it. In fact, there are still followers of Madame Blavatsky around. Anyhow, the story then jumps to 1924 and a man named Edgar Larkin. Larkin was a small-time entrepreneur who operated a little telescopic observatory for tourists, mainly to augment the income from an adjacent inn he managed for the Southern Pacific Railroad. It was called Mount Lowe and it wasn't far from Mount Wilson, a real observatory near Sacramento. Mount Shasta was a favorite target of his telescopic observations. So Larkin, probably to attract business, and having read the Oliver book, began spreading stories about seeing Lemurians dancing on Mount Shasta in white robes. He described them as 'taciturn' and said they held secret nightly rituals by the light of green campfires."

"How did he know they were Lemurians? Did they have four arms and eyes in the back of their head?"

"Larkin never mentioned anything like that. I guess he just assumed they were Lemurians because they were on Mount Shasta dancing around green campfires. In any case, not long after, a San Francisco journalist named Lanseur created a sensation with a story about observing Lemurians on Mount Shasta as he rode past in a train. Which is pretty observant considering you'd have to be 150 feet tall to even start to be visible on Shasta from a passing train. He described them in great detail, even though nobody else on the train saw them."

JH had finished his meal and was gathering his briefcase preparatory to leaving. I looked at my watch and saw that it was indeed time to go back to work.

"You never got to the connection between Mount Shasta, Lemurians, and Ney Springs," I said.

"I guess that will have to wait," said JH, suddenly looking very businesslike as he dashed out the door.

PART 3

JH filled me in on the rest of the story a couple of days later, on the way to the Full Moon Festival and Ruckus. I expected him to be dressed in garish ceremonial garb, but his clothes were pretty subdued for 1970: widely flared bell-bottomed jeans and a tie-dyed T-shirt. My own apparel wasn't much different.

It was late in the day, around 7:00 p.m., when we departed. Soon after, we were in JH's car on I-5 between Yreka and Mount Shasta City. Ahead and slightly to the southeast, Mount Shasta glowed red in the setting sun.

Patricia didn't want to go, and neither apparently did Barbara Gumble.

"Have you ever heard Mount Shasta spoken of as a spiritual 'power source'?" JH asked.

"Of course," I said. "Everybody has."

"And do you know what that means?"

"Certainly," I replied. Then I paused. I knew that JH's next question would be to ask me to explain the meaning, which I suddenly realized I could not do. "What does it mean?" I said.

"A spiritual power source is a place where the presence of God can be felt more readily than other places. If you're looking for spiritual highs, it helps to find a power source. Mount Shasta is supposed to be one. Oak Creek Canyon, near Flagstaff, Arizona, is another. And Taos, New Mexico. And Mount Desert Island in Maine. There are a bunch of them."

"I presume that's why there are so many religious nuts wandering around Yreka and Mount Shasta City. No offense."

"None taken. It's exactly the reason. Except there's one thing the religious nuts, as you so aptly put it, don't know."

"And what might that be?"

"Glad you asked," said JH, grinning knowingly and looking pleased with himself. "According to a Karuk Indian shaman I know, a fellow named Augie Atteberry, Mount Shasta is only a secondary power source. The mountain draws its power from another, much stronger, primary power source. Without the primary power source, Shasta would be nothing but a big, pretty volcano, like Mount Lassen or Mount Rainier. Its mystical aura would go out like a snuffed candle."

"And where might this primary power source be?" I asked, although I had pretty much guessed the answer.

"The primary power source from which Mount Shasta draws its spiritual power," JH announced, "is Ney Springs. According to the legend, it is the job of the Lemurians to protect Mount Shasta's power, both on the mountain and at Ney Springs. And it is the job of believers in the legend to protect the Lemurians."

"You show me a Lemurian and I promise to protect him," I joked.

"I just might do that," said JH with a knowing grin.

At Mount Shasta City, JH turned off the freeway and then drove up a series of paved side roads that headed away from town. Then he drove up a bunch of gravel roads that headed into the mountains. Then he drove up what seemed like an impossible maze of dirt roads, ending at a nondescript spot by a creek where a dozen or so other cars were parked. Then he got out and we started walking up a very steep road that was too badly rutted to drive on. The road followed high above the creek, which JH identified as Ney Creek.

It was just about dark when we started walking. JH brought a flashlight, but we didn't really need it what with the road and full moon. From what I could see, this was not the prettiest spot in the Mount Shasta region. It was pretty but not extraordinary.

The most striking thing about the walk to the ceremonial site along Ney Creek was the smell, which grew stronger as we drew closer. It was a distinctly sulfurous smell, like rotten eggs or the boiling mud springs I'd seen and smelled while touring Yellowstone Park with my parents sixteen years earlier. It smelled like the bowels of hell.

The ceremonial site was a level wide spot at the end of a closed-off road that branched off the first road we walked up. Large, roaring campfires burned on either end of the level spot. In between, three stone circles had been laid out, marked by river cobbles six to eight inches in diameter. The center circle looked to be about ten feet across, while the side circles were about six feet. Outside the circles, dozens of stone cairns, or rock piles, dotted the little flat. They ranged from one to three feet high. Some looked very precarious, as though the stones had been painstakingly balanced.

Everyone seemed glad to see JH. Especially the members of his "church," who swarmed around him, besieged him with questions, and sought his guidance in what seemed to me very trivial matters, such as where they should stand or how they should wear their hair.

It wasn't difficult to distinguish the members of JH's church from the onlookers. The church members were 80 percent female and nearly all young and pretty. The few male members weren't bad looking either. Except for JH.

"Just hang out and have a good time," JH instructed, leaving me to my own devices. "After the ceremony, I'll take you up to the hot spring and waterfall. It's only a few minutes' walk from here."

I positioned myself near one of the fires, which a massive logger type fed frequently from a nearby pile of cordwood and small logs. JH had identified this individual and a few others as "security people." As nearly as I could tell, the job of the security people was to (1) tend the campfires; (2) keep an eye on the half dozen picnic coolers filled with crushed ice and cans of Rainier beer, from which everyone in attendance, including myself, freely helped themselves; and (3) keep unauthorized and overzealous spectators, again including myself, out of the ritual dance.

According to JH, another of their tasks was to "watch out for trouble." The thought that there might be trouble made me uneasy. I pictured hordes of townsfolk suddenly descending on us, brandishing clubs. I looked around for an escape path, just in case.

The ritual began twenty minutes after our arrival. By then thirty or forty spectators, mostly harmless hippie types, had also arrived. The ceremonial participants, JH and his church members, numbered around twenty.

The proceedings started with JH standing alone in the middle of the center circle, with the other participants standing in the side circles. He raised his arms to the night heavens and chanted, "Oo-ram-na, ram-na, te-osh, te-osh, te-osh, praya makooya lemuriati."

Years later I visited a Christian church where some of the members spoke in tongues. They reminded me of JH's ritual chanting. Except for the "lemuriati" part at the end.

When the chant was done, a fellow sitting at the edge of the ceremonial flat with a set of bongo drums began playing. His rhythm was soon joined by hand clapping from spectators and participants. By then the participants had all downed two or three beers, so their inhibitions were, shall we say, diminished. Not that they had many inhibitions to begin with.

If other inhibition-diminishing drugs besides alcohol were being ingested, I wasn't aware of it, although it wouldn't have surprised me. JH had been known to drop a little LSD now and then. He had also been known to smoke a little marijuana. And hashish. And occasional opium. He considered cocaine and heroin dangerously addictive, however. I did not use any drugs besides alcohol in 1970, but most people I knew in Yreka used alcohol, marijuana, hashish, and LSD.

The dancing began innocently enough. The church members performed a chaotic, free-form fandango that looked pretty much like the frug, a popular dance from the late 1950s. They danced both inside and outside the circles. Since the dancers paid no attention to the circles, I wondered what the circles were for. I figured I'd find out soon enough.

It wasn't long before JH, predictably, had dropped his drawers. And his shirt. And his underwear. He did keep his shoes on, though, probably because of all the rocks lying around. Needless to say, the parishioners quickly followed suit.

The nude dancing and chaotic shouting continued for nearly an hour amid the happy aroma of the fires, pine trees, and sulfur. The rhythm of the bongos grew gradually faster and the dancing became more and more frenzied, with ever-increasing physical contact between dancers. Some enthusiastic spectators tried to get into the swing of things too, but anyone attempting to crash into the ritual circles was gently but quickly nudged back by the security people.

I would never admit it to JH, but I would have loved to join the dance. They looked like they were having a fantastic time. Instead I stood on the sidelines, ogling the naked girls and thinking snide thoughts about how dumb the ritual was.

Still, I couldn't help but admire the stamina of JH and his friends. I'd have keeled over in exhaustion after ten minutes. It occurred to me to look for the hot spring and waterfall by myself, which according to JH were only a few hundred feet up the first road. But I wasn't about to wander off by myself in the dark.

The only person I talked to was a young hippie girl with curly red hair, a wool poncho, and an exceptionally vapid smile.

"Nice ceremony," I said.

"Yeah, man," she said. "Cool, huh?"

"Ever been to the hot spring and waterfall?"

"Yeah, man. They're really cool."

"The hot spring is cool?"

"Yeah man. It's really cool."

The conversation ended when the two campfires suddenly went green. I'd never seen a green campfire before. With the change in color, the blazes greatly increased in size and intensity. I had to take several steps back away from them and shield my eyes with my hand. I didn't notice anybody tossing chemicals into the fire, but I figured that's what had happened. I wondered if the fires could be seen through a telescope from near Sacramento.

With a brilliant, eerie green glow illuminating the proceedings, the pace of the dancing, shouting, drumming, and hand clapping intensified even more. After a while somebody, probably JH, shouted, "Here they come!"

The dancing abruptly stopped and the celebrants stepped out of the circles. Crowding around, they continued their rhythmic clapping and the bongoist kept bongoing.

"They're coming! Fantastic!" JH yelled. "Here they are! We're doing it. Yes! Yes! Yes! Wow!"

Then the drumming ceased and everybody began cheering. I tried to get a look at the circles to see what was going on, but everyone kept crowding and shoving and I couldn't see very well. I was also a bit tipsy from having downed three or four beers. From what I could make out, the circles were completely empty. I did get a sense of something moving in them, though, just out of my field of vision.

Then the ritual was over. The fires stopped being green and diminished to barely glowing, definitely red embers. And the darkness of the woods, held precariously in check by the festivities, descended on the flat.

"Now can we see the hot spring and waterfall?" I asked JH as soon as I was able to get his attention.

"Oops. I forgot about that. Listen, can I take a rain check? Besides, they're better when it's light out. Why don't I just give you directions?"

"Whatever," I said, a little disappointed.

"What did you think of the ceremony?" asked JH during the drive home.

"It looked like a lot of work," I replied. "But I really couldn't see very well, especially at the end."

"Did you see the stone cairns come alive, turn into Lemurians, and start to dance inside the stone circles?" JH inquired.

"No," I said. "Did you?"

"Nope. But a lot of people believe they did. In any event, Mount Shasta's spiritual power is assured for another month."

JH grinned knowingly.

PART 4

I didn't look for Ney Springs again until the following spring. I hadn't forgotten about it though. Not at all. As I visited more and more of the vast and magnificent natural areas and wilderness around Yreka, I found myself increasingly intrigued by the idea of "the most beautiful place of all."

I'd have gone back to Ney Springs much sooner, but it snowed early and to a low elevation in the winter of 1970–71, and most of the mountain roads quickly became impassable. The first snowfall came in late September. It wasn't just a few flurries either; it was a major blizzard. I remember that particular storm because I rescued some stranded southern Californians in a Volkswagen minivan with flowers painted all over it, on Etna Summit Road.

In May 1971, following JH's directions, I finally set out to find Ney Springs. I didn't anticipate that it would be a very difficult task, because Ney Creek and all the roads touching it are shown on the local national forest map, although Ney Springs and the waterfall are not. Having been to the spot before, I figured I could probably find the place even without JH's instructions.

Boy, was I wrong. I started up the paved road to Castle Lake, as JH instructed, then turned off on the first gravel road to the left. Then I got totally lost and could have kicked myself for not paying more attention to JH's route the night of the ceremony. Absolutely nothing looked familiar, as though they'd moved the place—lock, stock, and cairn.

After driving up and down every gravel side road along the eight miles of Castle Lake Road, which frequently flirted with Ney Creek, without finding a trace of Ney Springs, the ceremonial site, the waterfall, or the sulfur smell, I went home feeling very frustrated.

"I don't know what you did wrong, man," said JH on the phone afterward. "Sounds like you were on the right track."

I spoke to JH only one more time after that, then lost contact with him for twenty-six years. I returned to Michigan to get my master's, then in 1972 I came back out West and got a job as a Children's Services case worker in Grants Pass, Oregon, eighty miles away.

JH visited Patricia and myself in Grants Pass only once. His wife was not with him, and he made amorous passes at Pat, her sister, and her best friend. When I called JH a low-life womanizer, he accused me of being narrow-minded, judgmental, and inhibited.

"You need to expand your awareness and not be so uptight," he said with a knowing grin.

I freely acknowledged that he was absolutely correct. That did not, however, prevent me from booting him out of the house and telling him never to come back.

I think my final words to him were, "Take your knowing grin and shove it."

It was twenty-six years before my next attempt at sleuthing out Ney Springs. I'd thought about it a lot during the intervening years but never made it back to Castle Lake Road or the upper Sacramento. Then, in late fall of 1997, our oldest daughter, Jennifer, then twenty-nine, decided to rent some rooms for her family and ours for Thanksgiving at a charming bed-and-breakfast just outside Mount Shasta City. The place boasted a terrific view of Mount Shasta from the living room through a large picture window. A telescope in the living room was permanently pointed at the mountain. I looked for evidence of Lemurians through the telescope, but there was not a green fire to be seen anywhere.

Jennifer and her family lived in the San Francisco area. They had come up for the opening day of ski season and to celebrate Thanksgiving with us. My wife and I and our youngest daughter, Anna, then fifteen, also stayed at the bed-and-breakfast. Our middle daughter, Sara, then twenty-three, couldn't make it.

Now it so happens that the B&B was located not far from Castle Lake Road, where the mysterious and elusive turnoff to Ney Springs was also supposedly located. With a couple of hours to kill after breakfast on a cold but sunny Sunday morning, I decided to go for a ride. And while I was at it, to have another go at locating Ney Springs.

This time I actually made it to a place that looked very promising. I ended up on a dead-end dirt road on the banks of the Sacramento River, one hundred yards from the mouth of Ney Creek. I enjoyed a beautiful cross-country walk to the creek mouth through willows, cottonwoods, and bigleaf maples in fall color.

The creek mouth, in fact, contained a very nice waterfall. But it wasn't the right waterfall, and it definitely wasn't the site of the 1970 ceremony. For one thing, the sulfur smell was missing.

On the same excursion I tried another side road. This one dead-ended at Ney Creek, a mile upstream from the mouth. I was certain I'd been there before, with JH, and began getting excited. But again, there were just too many side roads, and I didn't have the time or inclination to check them all out.

Before returning to Oregon, I did one thing that proved immensely helpful. I stopped by Fifth Season Outfitters, a large and bustling outdoors store in Mount Shasta City. The owner, a blond, Nordic-looking type appropriately named Leif, happened to be a friend of mine—his store sold many of the hiking guidebooks that I'd written since 1989. Leif was a knowledgeable informant on local hiking opportunities.

"So how do I get to Ney Springs?" I inquired.

"Interesting question," Leif replied, with a knowing grin, as he leaned on the glass counter beside the cash register. The store was crammed to the rafters with noisy skiers bearing credit cards. In summer it would be crammed to the rafters *with actual rafters* who had their sights on the Klamath, McCloud, Scott, and Salmon Rivers. "Where did you hear about Ney Springs? Not many people know about it, and those who do prefer to keep it a secret."

"A fellow told me about it years ago. He said there's a fantastic waterfall there."

"There is indeed. And an old bathhouse too. At the hot spring."

"So how do you get there?"

Leif proceeded to describe the exact route I'd just taken, the one where the road dead-ended at Ney Creek, a mile above the mouth. He said there were a bunch of old roads in the vicinity, most of them closed off, but that if I simply walked upstream for a quarter mile, I couldn't miss it.

My next visit to the Mount Shasta area came the following summer, on the Fourth of July 1998. Following Leif's directions, I parked where the gravel road dead-ended at Ney Creek, a mile upstream from the creek mouth. Then Pat and I started hiking upstream, along the creekbank.

It was fairly rough going for the initial two hundred feet or so. The bank was extremely rocky and choked with willow, alder, and other impediments to rapid movement. The creek was fast moving and very pretty. What impelled us to continue, five minutes into the excursion, was the faint smell of sulfur. All we had to do was follow the odor.

Not long after, we came out on a narrow, steep road that had obviously been closed off years earlier. Trees and shrubs slowly encroached at the edges. We continued upstream, following the road for perhaps an eighth of a mile. The road dead-ended at a little shaded flat beside the creek.

On the shaded flat, Pat and I encountered three stone circles and hundreds of rock cairns. It was obviously the site of the 1970 Ruckus. The place looked exactly as it had all those years earlier, as though the most recent ceremony had been held only a couple of days prior.

Most of the hippies and religious mystics from the 1970s were long gone from Mount Shasta City by 1998. Either that or they had blended in with the general populace (where they contributed significantly to the local economy). JH, I assumed, hadn't been around in years. Nevertheless, somebody, somewhere, somehow was obviously still watching out for the Lemurians and "protecting Mount Shasta's power source."

That pleased me very much.

I had told my wife and kids many times about the ceremony and the dancing Lemurians. It was a family legend. One of Patricia's great regrets was that she hadn't accompanied me on that balmy night, twenty-eight years earlier.

"Barbara Gumble told me I wouldn't enjoy it," she explained.

"Barbara Gumble was wrong," I replied.

Since the closed-off road did not continue upstream, where the hot spring was supposedly located, we explored the flat with the stone circles for a while before continuing our journey along the creekbank. As we progressed, the sulfur smell grew distinctly stronger.

A few hundred feet beyond the ceremonial site, I noticed another road, up the hill from where we were walking. I scrambled up the extremely steep slope. Within five minutes Pat and I were walking side by side up the high road, looking for the hot spring. We could tell from the aroma that it was very near.

The high road was extremely rough and rutted but obviously still in use. I had no idea how it connected with either the ceremonial road or the spot where we'd parked. I intended to find out on the way back.

After five minutes we arrived at Ney Springs, a beautiful little grotto overgrown with horsetails and skunk cabbage, with a little stone wall built into the hillside. A pipe emerged from the wall, and milky, sulfur-smelling water emerged from the pipe. The water dropped into a little concrete basin, which it overflowed. Below the basin, the water collected around the horsetails and skunk cabbage then ran across the road and down the forested hillside to the creek. I could tell from looking at the water that it was hot because of the steam. But I still felt compelled to feel it.

Poking a finger into the washbasin, I had to admit: The water was hot. Not scalding but hot enough. It also reeked of sulfur.

The grotto containing the pipe and skunk cabbage lay on the right side of the road. On the road's left side, a steep, one-hundred-foot-long path led sharply down to the creek. At the bottom of the path there was more concrete work, which Leif at Fifth Season Outfitters had said was the foundation of an old bathhouse, built in the 1920s. The top of the bathhouse was long gone. In the middle of the concrete foundation was a small cistern, perhaps four feet in diameter, with a plywood lid. The cistern was filled with warm water and had two submerged wooden benches inside.

Despite the water's noxious aroma and murky whitish color, it looked very inviting. Where the water overflowed the cistern and ran into the creek, the rocks were stained with a white patina. Immediately downstream, the creek had been dammed into a clear sapphire-blue, ice-cold pool. The pool had no doubt been built for the benefit of those desiring to shock their system with a sudden leap from the warmth of the cistern. Hot-spring fanatics love things like that.

After checking out the hot spring, we hiked back to the road and continued following it uphill, in search of the most elusive and purportedly beautiful prize of all, the legendary Ney Creek waterfall, JH's "most scenic place."

Beyond and above the hot spring, the road became much steeper and even more deeply rutted. It was almost a quarter mile from the spring to the spot where the narrow trail to the waterfall left the road. There was no sign at the junction, but the path was well marked and easy to find. Someone had erected a small rock cairn at the turnoff, not unlike the cairns back at the ceremonial flat. I wondered if the cairn might be a Lemurian standing guard over the treasure.

The trail was an eighth of a mile long and contoured across a nearly vertical slope. The route was mostly level, though, and followed a nar-

Ney Creek Falls

row ledge, except near the end, where it scrambled down the rocks to the base of the falls.

As you approached on the trail, you first heard the falls as a roar in the distance. Then you smelled the mist in the air (the sulfur essence was long gone). Then you caught a glimpse of the crashing water, then a wider glimpse. Finally, Ney Creek Falls were revealed in their full awesome majesty.

JH had been correct. In retrospect, though, perhaps it was probably better for me to wait twenty-eight years before witnessing the most exquisite of all waterfalls. Had I seen it in 1970, when my quest for the perfect waterfall was just starting, it would have diminished all the others.

One thing I've learned about waterfalls, though, is that each has its own mystique and unique beauty, and it's foolish to compare them.

I'd estimate the waterfall's height at 150 feet. Maybe a little less. It's not an immense height, but it's enough to be impressive. The water's ordeal begins far overhead, in a vertical-sided rock chasm. The churning white fluid enters, then instantly drops thirty feet into a little collecting pool to catch its breath for a split second. While in the collecting pool, the water somehow twists 90 degrees. It then charges out in full force and fury, fanning out over a magnificent white rock face before dropping into a much larger collecting pool at the base of the plunge.

There were places on the rock face where you could probably sit and enjoy a shower in late summer after the early-season flow slacked off. When Pat and I visited on the Fourth of July, however, the abundant, roaring water would have crushed anything that dared get in its way.

Pat and I climbed down to the edge of the lower collecting pool and let the mist wash over us.

PART 5

Finally finding Ney Springs and the waterfall in 1998 got me to thinking about old J. Herbert. Although we hadn't parted on the best of terms in 1972, I wanted him to know that I agreed with his glowing description of the area. Upon Googling him, I learned that he still lived in Yreka. So I called him up and arranged to drop by.

I found JH living in a retirement residence. His wife had divorced him years earlier and subsequently so had two other women. He'd spent the last twenty-two years of his working life selling automobile insurance.

At the time of my 1998 visit, JH told me he was seventy-two.

"That doesn't add up," I said. "You said in 1970 that you were thirty-eight."

"So I lied," said JH, with a knowing grin.

He certainly looked seventy-two. He was still tall and lean, but what little hair remained was white. He struck me as a little depressed.

"Are you still protecting the Lemurians at Ney Springs?" I asked.

"I try," he sighed. "We kept up the semiannual Ruckuses for seven or eight years, then for the next few years I went there whenever I could with a group of friends. But for the last dozen years, I've mostly gone alone. I bathe in the hot spring, make sure the stone circles and cairns are all in place, and then I sit naked in the middle circle with my guitar, sing old folk songs, and greet any Lemurians who happen to wander past."

"You still do that? After all these years? I thought you didn't believe in Lemurians?"

"I don't. But somebody has to protect the power source. There's nobody else so I just keep doing it. It's actually very pleasant."

PART 6

In August 1999 Pat and I returned to Ney Springs with Anna and her best friend, Phaedra. We'd spent a year talking the place up, and Anna was anxious not only to see the waterfall but also to bathe in the cistern and visit the ceremonial flat with the stone circles and cairns. Her real desire was to witness the monthly ceremony. Or better yet, to participate in it. At age seventeen, Anna's biggest regret in life was being a teenager thirty years too late for the hippie era.

"You didn't miss much," I liked to inform her when she inquired about what the world was like back then. In Anna's mind, Pat and I had squandered the greatest cultural era ever to reveal itself to humankind.

As we drove to Ney Springs in 1999, my wife warned the girls about the smell. "Be prepared to hold your nose," she said. She was exaggerating of course. But a year earlier we had been assaulted by sulfur from the moment we stepped out of the car.

This time, when we got out of the car, we smelled nothing. I sensed immediately that something was wrong. I began feeling uneasy and a little worried. I'm not sure why I was worried, but I was.

"It's a very pretty creek," said Anna. "But I don't smell a thing."

"You will," I tried to assure her. "Wait until we get to the ceremonial flat."

A year earlier the aroma at the flat had been pungent. This time we smelled only pine needles, wild lilacs, and a rushing mountain stream. While those were wonderful aromas, they were not what we had anticipated.

The whole aura at the ceremonial flat had changed. On our 1998 visit, Pat and I had sensed the spirits of lots of people having fun. This time the place felt dead, abandoned. We looked around for some indication that everything was OK but found none. The stone circles had been scattered, and the cairns were all knocked over. From the vegetation around the scattered river cobbles that once formed the circles and cairns, it appeared as though the destruction had occurred gradually, through weathering over several years. Had I not been to the site a year earlier, I'd have guessed that it hadn't been used in a decade or more.

The devastation made me slightly ill in the pit of my stomach. I found myself worrying about the fate of the Lemurians, the protectors. Then I hastily reminded myself that there was no such thing. At least according to JH.

Anna kept staring at Pat and I, as though we'd made up the story about the sulfur smell, the ceremonial flat, the hot spring, and the waterfall.

"For this you dragged us all the way to California?"

We insisted that the place had been very different a year earlier, but I don't think Anna or Phaedra believed us.

We walked up to the hot spring, and still there was no sulfur smell. Feeling a sense of dread that I could not explain, I extended a finger and stuck it in the water. My worst fears were instantly realized. The water coming out of the pipe in the stone wall was cold as a January night. So was the water in the cistern by the creek. The cistern water was green and slimy, and you'd have to have been insane to bathe in it. The row of boulders that created the beautiful pool in the creek had also vanished.

The Lemurians were not being protected. Something was definitely wrong.

"Oh, well," I said, trying to sound nonchalant. "Let's hike up to the waterfall. That can't possibly have gone anywhere."

"Unless the Lemurians took it," Anna joked.

The waterfall, much to my relief, remained unchanged. It was as gorgeous and awe inspiring as ever. Anna acknowledged that it was among the prettiest she'd ever seen.

Anna and Phaedra had a fine time wading in the collecting pool and enjoying the swirling mist. So the trip wasn't a total waste.

PART 7

On the way home with Pat, Anna, and Phaedra, I decided to stop by and see JH and ask him if he knew what had happened. I was informed by the guy at the front desk of the retirement residence that JH had passed away quietly in his bed the previous December during the biggest winter storm since 1964, a storm that had caused most of the rivers and creeks in the area to substantially overflow their banks.

The storm at least explained what had happened to the cairns and stone circles.

When I arrived back in Oregon, I called up Monty Elliott, a geology professor at Southern Oregon University in Ashland, who explained why a hot spring might suddenly go cold. The same storm, combined with a record snowfall, would have raised the water table and cooled off the underground heat source. The spring, he said, might or might not heat back up following the next dry winter. (As of 2008, it was still ice cold.) On further investigation, I learned that 1999 was the first time, dating back at least to the California gold rush of the 1850s, that Ney Springs had gone cold.

I also heard an alternate explanation from a New Age type in Grants Pass, where I live. She suggested that the hot spring had cooled because Mount Shasta was gathering heat into itself. According to her, the only reason the mountain would gather heat into itself was because an eruption was imminent. I did not like that explanation.

I don't know the answer. All I know is that even though my lack of spirituality remains as unshaken as ever, I can't help thinking that the cooling of the hot spring was linked to the unexplained destruction of the stone circles. And that the loss of that spiritual nexus will ultimately affect the stability of Mount Shasta. And that somehow, the Lemurians are involved.

Here's the strange part: Even though I don't believe in Lemurians, I keep finding myself worrying about them and hoping that somebody has or will take JH's place as their erstwhile "protector." The reason, as nearly as I can figure, is that I don't just admire Mount Shasta as a beautiful mountain. It is my own personal power source (or one of my power sources). If Mount Shasta ever ceased to be a power source, I would be diminished, northern California would be diminished, and the world would be diminished.

There is also a broader lesson that I learned from all this: Whatever your personal power source might be, you need to always protect the Lemurians who keep the power flowing. Even if you don't believe in them. Because, as JH showed me, you don't have to believe in them to protect them.

TO VISIT

The hike: Ney Creek Falls Trail, Shasta-Trinity National Forest, Mount Shasta City, California

Distance: One-quarter mile (one-way)

Directions: Take I-5 to the Central Mount Shasta City exit. Turn west, away from town, toward the fish hatchery and then turn left (south), toward Lake Siskiyou (bear right at the fork). Just beyond the dam, turn left onto Castle Lake Road, then immediately turn left onto the first gravel road. Bear right at the junction a mile or so down. Just before the road crosses Ney Creek and is blocked by a gate, a primitive dirt road takes off uphill on the right. Drive up it as far as you can, then park and walk. It's about one mile up the road to a fifty-foot side trail on the right that leads to the hot spring. A second trail, this one a couple hundred feet long, takes off directly opposite, on the left, and leads to the bathhouse foundation by the creek. The now unmarked, quarter-mile path to the waterfall is also on the left, one-quarter mile up the road beyond the hot spring.

The Spilled Canteen

PART 1

Things first started to go wrong on the Big Trip of 1971 in El Paso, when we rented a room in a little motel. From the outside, the white clapboard establishment, with about twenty rooms facing a courtyard, looked reasonably nice, if modest. Amazed at how inexpensive the rooms were, we grabbed one without first inspecting what would be our home for the next several hours. Since then, my wife and I make it a practice to always examine a room closely before shelling out any money.

In September 1971 we were in Texas as part of an automobile trip from California to Michigan. My wife, her three-year-old daughter, Jennifer, and I were headed for Ann Arbor, where I had a one-semester teaching fellowship. Having a little time on our hands, we took an extremely long, scenic route from California to Michigan, ending up in Texas and Louisiana.

Even though it appeared halfway decent from the outside, the El Paso lodging must have been some sort of local flophouse. Inside, the room was not halfway decent. It was not a quarter of the way decent. In a city where 110 degrees is commonplace in summer, with nighttime lows in the 70s and 80s, there was no functioning air-conditioning. The furnishings were run-down, broken and frayed, and the room, upon closer inspection, was filthy.

We could have lived with that, though. What we could not live with were the drunks shouting, laughing, and cursing in Spanish in the parking lot all night long. Not that their language made any difference. Loud noises are annoying in any language when you're trying to sleep.

We might even have been able to tolerate the noise. What really upset us was the three or four times during the night when the drunken revelers loudly tried our doorknob. That especially freaked out Jennifer, who spent most of the night crying.

After hours of cowering and sweltering, morning finally came. Exhausted and grumpy, we bade a quick good-bye and good riddance to the motel in El Paso and hit the road.

PART 2

To fully grasp the significance of the Big Bend incident in 1971, you have to understand about Category Four animals. At the time, I'd never seen a Category Four animal. Or for that matter, a Category Three or Category Two animal. At least none that I was 100 percent sure of. I'd seen plenty of Category One animals, though. Everybody has seen Category One animals.

Here are the categories of animals under my system:

Category One: Real, documented, and verified animals, such as squirrels, rabbits, horses, three-toed sloths, gnus, tigers, ringtail cats, and whales.

Category Two: Animals sighted from time to time but never officially confirmed or verified. Some supposedly extinct animals fall into this category. Bigfoot, the man-ape of rumor and legend, would be a Category Two animal because, although the species is certainly documented, it remains unverified.

Category Three: Animals that exist in reality but which nobody has ever seen, so there are no rumors, legends, or reports about them. There could be many animals in this category, but of course nobody would know about them.

Category Four: Animals with no tangible existence in reality. These are spirit, imaginary, or ghost animals that can, under certain circumstances, seem very real indeed.

I believe that the animal I saw in Big Bend belonged to Category Four. The fact that I actually saw it argues against Category Three, because seeing a Category Three animal automatically takes it out of that category. The fact that nobody else has ever seen one (and I have since researched this) probably argues against Category One or Two and in favor of Category Four.

But of course nobody knows for sure. Texas, I should add, can be a mighty strange place as far as animals go. For example, the entire United States ranges of the javelina and jaguarundi are limited to Texas, Arizona, and New Mexico. If you're going to have a first-class "odd animal" experience, Big Bend National Park, in the remote and barren west Texas desert, is the place to do it.

PART 3

Even without being kept up half the night at the motel, the drive to Big Bend would have been exhausting. It was three hundred desert miles, in temperatures over 100 degrees. At least, I consoled myself, I didn't have to worry about the engine overheating in my little green 1970 Volkswagen Squareback, with the homemade plywood box on the roof. Volkswagen engines in those days were air-cooled and located in the rear.

We all looked forward to the next day, when I would go hiking at Big Bend while everyone else relaxed, slept in, and enjoyed the cool mountain heights of the Chisos Basin Campground.

We finally entered the park at around 3:00 p.m. and quickly discovered that all the places we wanted to go were at least an hour away.

Our first stop was beautiful Santa Elena Canyon. As we approached across the low, fiery desert, a huge cliff appeared in the distance. After a while we noticed a notch in the cliff. The notch was Santa Elena Canyon, a vertical-walled chasm cut at right angles into the escarpment. The left side of the notch was Mexico and the right side was Texas. The Rio Grande flowed through Santa Elena Canyon, then made a 90-degree turn and followed the escarpment base.

After miles and miles of driving, we pulled up to the Santa Elena parking area and made the short hike into the canyon, which can be followed by trail for perhaps a quarter mile. The contrast between the hot, arid Chihuahuan Desert, which smelled mostly of creosote bush and death, and the canyon's lush, shady coolness, was unforgettable.

We arrived at the Chisos Basin Campground at around six. It was a sunny, pleasant evening, much cooler at 5,400 feet than in the low desert. The road from the low desert up into the stark, chocolate-brown Chisos Mountains was curvy and beautiful. The campground, surrounded by jagged peaks and ridges, had room for a couple hundred people but only ten or fifteen slots were occupied. We set up our tent, and then Pat cooked dinner on the Coleman stove. We had deli potato salad and steak, both of which we'd purchased at the supermarket in Terlingua. That long-ago meal in Big Bend, grilled outdoors in the Chisos Basin Campground, may have been the tastiest chunk of meat I ever consumed.

Road into Chisos Mountains

The starry night was neither too warm nor too cold. After the experience with the motel and the long, hot drive, we all fell asleep immediately, confident that everything bad that could happen had already happened and that there would be only smooth sailing from there to Detroit.

PART 4

I woke up at 6:30 a.m. to a spectacular sunrise and the cool, sweet aroma of morning dew. As my wife and stepdaughter slept, I showered in the campground bathhouse, filled my all-important two-quart blanket canteen, and got dressed. Then I crawled briefly back into the tent and kissed Pat and Jenny good-bye, instructing them not to worry and to enjoy their morning of leisure.

I expected to be gone maybe five hours on the nine-mile hike. My normal pace on moderate-to-steep grades is two miles per hour. Having made forays into California's Marble Mountains and Trinity Alps only weeks before, and having just completed an eight-month stint with the

California Fish and Game Department, I considered myself in decent physical condition.

It was a quarter mile from the campground to the trailhead, located near the store and ranger station. I debated driving there but figured Pat might need the car. So I walked, which added about six minutes to my hiking time.

Once at the trailhead, I started briskly down the path, filled with joy and elation at the beauty of the scenery, the respite from the long, boring days of driving, and the goodness of a world that allowed me to witness such wonders.

The first thing to go wrong was that I missed the turnoff to the Pinnacles Trail. The path from the Chisos Basin trailhead is called the Laguna Meadows Trail, with the Pinnacles Trail breaking off to the left soon after. Both trails will get you to the Mount Emory turnoff, my destination, but Laguna Meadows does it in eight and a half miles as opposed to three and a half miles for the Pinnacles Trail.

After hiking nearly a mile, crossing two dry washes, and starting up a series of steep, rocky switchbacks with no junction in sight, I backtracked to the trailhead. According to the map, the Pinnacles Trail turnoff was less than a quarter mile from the trailhead. I have no idea how I managed to miss the turnoff, but on the second pass it was right there, obvious to one and all.

Having wasted forty minutes, and now feeling slightly rushed and annoyed instead of joyous and relaxed, I started up the correct path. The scenery was splendid. The Pinnacles Trail made its way around to Mount Emory's east side, crossing Pinnacles Pass between Mount Emory and Toll Mountain. A one-mile side trail took hikers from the pass to the summit.

As I walked, I passed other hikers every few hundred feet. Most were pretty friendly. I was put off, however, by a loud, poorly supervised Boy Scout troop whose members kept running back and forth along the path without looking where they were going, screaming at the top of their lungs. Nor was I pleased by the hikers smoking cigarettes, something you don't see in Oregon or California.

The path was fairly easy for almost two and a half miles as it made its way up the combined flanks of Mount Emory, Casa Grande Peak, and Toll Mountain. After that two and a half miles, the route steepened considerably, swung sharply left then right, then began a series of rocky switchbacks to Pinnacles Pass. I passed a few scattered trees and rock overhangs, but most of the route was lined with grass and brush and was out in the open. Even though it was only 10:30 a.m., I approached Pinnacles Pass sweating profusely. I'd estimate the temperature at perhaps 80 or 85 degrees, which is pretty warm for that high up. I also knew that the temperature would grow much hotter as the day wore on.

The narrow Pinnacles Pass, with Toll Mountain on one side and Emory Peak on the other, was lovely. The name "pinnacles" referred to the scattered, kind of pointy but stubby-looking rock outcrops in the area. I sat down on the edge of the trail, on the south side of the pass, beneath a large lone ponderosa pine, with my feet dangling over a drop-off. The trail started back down on the south side, toward the canyon of Boot Creek.

Despite the increasing heat, I'd been trying to avoid drinking from my canteen. My standard tactic on hikes, unless I'm dying of thirst, has always been to save the water until I arrive at my destination, then dole it out on the return trip. But with the steep switchbacks, the heat, and the lack of shade, I broke my rule and chugged down maybe a quarter of the contents. I immediately regretted drinking so much, because I still had the much steeper Mount Emory hike ahead of me.

When done drinking, I set the canteen down beside me. I did not put the cap back on because I planned to treat myself to one last sip before I started hiking again in a minute or two, after I'd rested a little and my initial huge drink had settled in.

In retrospect, the expenditure of energy required to screw the cap back on, then off, then on again would have been minuscule compared to the ultimate cost of my failure to replace the cap. I don't know how I managed it, but somehow as I gathered my old Nikkormat camera and prepared to get up, I knocked the opened canteen over the edge of the trail, down the rocky incline, and into the canyon. The container tumbled about fifty feet, then came to rest upside down in some bramble bushes.

"Crap," I said out loud, quickly assuaging my initial panic by reassuring myself that with all those hordes of fellow hikers, and "only" five and a half more miles to hike, I could manage without the canteen.

Possibly. The nearest potential water source, at Boot Spring, lay one and a quarter miles beyond Pinnacles Pass. Of course I'd also read in the park brochure that in September, the driest month of the year, Boot Spring was probably as dry as Mars (the brochure didn't use those exact words).

I was able to climb down and retrieve the canteen with little difficulty. But boy, oh boy, was it ever empty. On every hike since, I screw the cap back on immediately after each drink from my canteen, even if I plan to take another drink in a couple of minutes. I learned my lesson.

Forty minutes later, perspiring even more and anxious to start back down, I stood atop the flat, white rock summit of Mount Emory, surrounded by cliffs, Boy Scouts, and cigarette smokers. The view, spectacular wherever you looked, was better to the west than any other direction. To the east, Toll Mountain and Casa Grande Peak, although excellent to look at, continued to get in the way. To the south, the South Rim blocked the near view somewhat, but I could still see all the way to Mexico and eighty miles beyond.

I actually managed to scrounge a drink from a Boy Scout while on the summit. He was a fat, squeaky-voiced, nervous kid with an untucked shirt and an incipient, never-shaved mustache. The young fellow was very nice about it. I figured that since it was downhill all the way home, the offering from the Boy Scout should suffice for the remainder of the trip. I was wrong.

I started back down at 11:30. Remember that I'd hoped to be back at the trailhead by 1:00 p.m., and it was still two and a half hours away. While the return trip was all downhill, which made the going faster and easier, I now had the midday sun to contend with. And even though the 7,800-foot elevation cooled things considerably, there was still little shade and the solar radiation was intense.

By the time I got back to the pass, my mouth felt as though somebody had stuffed it with ultra-absorbent diapers. I had all the early symptoms of dehydration: fatigue, headache, slight dizziness, nausea, spots in my peripheral vision, extremely dry mouth, and bright yellow urine. I hasten to add that I'd experienced all those symptoms before, some many times. But never when totally without water in a place this hot and arid.

I'm not sure why I didn't just ask a passerby for a drink at Pinnacles Pass, as I'd done with the Boy Scout. It seemed like an imposition. They undoubtedly needed their water as much as I did.

The fact that I continued to perspire on the way down from Mount Emory was both a good sign and a bad sign. According to the *Red Cross First Aid Handbook*, it meant I still had the raw materials in my body with which to manufacture perspiration. It also meant I was depleting those raw materials. If and when my body ran out of water and electrolytes, I would be in big trouble. They call that "heatstroke," and it can be fatal.

Back at Pinnacles Pass, a passing hiker informed me that contrary to the park brochure, there was still a little water at Boot Spring. The news touched off a lengthy internal debate. Should I head back toward the trailhead without water or hike an extra one and a quarter miles—two and a half miles round-trip—to Boot Spring to obtain the precious fluid? The side trip would delay my arrival back at the trailhead by more than an hour, and I was already an hour behind.

I pretty much decided to forget Boot Spring and take my chances. Nevertheless, I inexplicably found myself walking a short ways down the trail in the Boot Spring direction, ostensibly looking for a good photogenic view into the canyon.

That was when I noticed a faint, unmarked side trail taking off to the left. It appeared to drop down to Boot Creek, meeting the stream in a quarter mile, at a point, I estimated after examining the map, one mile below Boot Spring. The map showed the creek but not the side trail. While kind of steep, the shortcut could possibly get me to water in far less distance than the Boot Spring hike on the main trail. I couldn't tell from my vantage point if there was water in that part of Boot Creek or not.

If I followed this path and did not find water, my situation would be worse than ever. On the other hand, if I did find water, my problem would be solved and I'd have lost only twenty minutes or so.

"Hmmm," I said out loud, unscrewing the cap from my canteen and peering with one eye into its dank, echoing emptiness. I took a dozen or so steps down the side trail, which turned out to be not as steep or faint as it appeared from the junction. I ended up following it all the way to the creek.

The creek was completely dry. My heart sank as I pondered the prospect of hiking empty-handed back up to the pass. Then I noticed that there seemed to be a fair amount of dampness in the creekbed under the top layer of pebbles and cobbles. And a lot of green streamside vegetation. If I hiked upstream a short ways, I wondered, would I find water in the creek, especially if I dug it out a little?

I was not anxious to return to the main trail without achieving my objective. Besides, my spot by the creek felt good, a little cooler than the main trail and much more secluded. The short side trip had transformed my journey from an irritating battle with crowds to pleasant seclusion, the way a hike should be. I walked a little farther upstream, looking for signs of water.

My judgment was not 100 percent just then.

After hiking one hundred feet or so, I scolded myself for taking such a huge risk. What I should have done was ignore my fatigue and thirst, tough it out, and get on home while I still had a little energy left. Were something to happen to me, if I passed out from heat exhaustion, nobody would ever find me here. I absolutely had to get back on the main trail. And soon. But I was too tired. And my head hurt. And I kept hearing an annoying buzzing noise in my ears. And man, was I ever thirsty.

I debated lying down, but I knew that would not quench my thirst. My most prudent course of action was still to get back to the main trail. And I still kept hearing that buzzing noise. In fact, it was growing louder.

I stood pondering for a minute or two, then started walking back toward the side trail with as much resolve as I could muster, which wasn't very much. I'd taken maybe three steps when I felt a stabbing, pinprick pain in my calf.

That's when I saw the rattlesnake. And when I figured out what the buzzing noise had been.

PART 5

According to the *Red Cross First Aid Handbook*, the recommended treatment for snakebite is to get to a doctor within two hours. It was, however, 12:15 p.m. Even if I had plenty of water, felt 100 percent, and had not been bitten by a rattlesnake, I was at least two hours from the trailhead. Probably more. The other recommended snakebite treatment is to do everything possible to slow your body's metabolism so that your kidneys can detoxify the venom before it does all the damage of which it's capable.

Slowing my metabolism was the best excuse I could think of to sit down, which was what I'd wanted to do all along.

I should add that I was terrified. Thoughts of dying whirled around my brain even though I kept reassuring myself that snakebites, according to the *Red Cross First Aid Handbook,* usually aren't fatal to adults. I'd read somewhere else that the rattlers don't always get their venom out when they bite. This guy, however, had gotten off a pretty good chomp. I would have been surprised if he'd failed to deliver his package. He apparently crawled up under my pant leg, so that I couldn't even rationalize that he'd bitten me through denim. The fact that he'd crawled up my pant leg is a testimony to my inattentiveness at the time.

At least the buzzing noise was gone.

I sat down on the ground in the scant shade provided by the creekside willow bush, pulled up my pant leg, and examined the wound. It was a flaming nasty red and hurt terribly. I squeezed the spot and two small drops of venom oozed out. I squeezed some more, with all my might, but those first drops were all I was going to get.

The circles of redness kept growing. And my lower leg was becoming numb, which could make it difficult to walk should I try to hike out. I was becoming more nauseated and dizzy by the minute. And feverish. The fever was a new, ominous development. I lay down in the shadiest spot I could find and prayed that my body would have the strength to fight off whatever was about to happen.

That's when I vomited. If I was dehydrated before, I was really dehydrated now. Without water, I could not wash the taste of vomit out of my mouth. I was able to scoot away from the little vomit puddle just before I blacked out.

I didn't completely black out. I guess you could describe my condition as semidelirious. Or that's how I remember it. I kept dozing, then half waking up, then dozing again. I dreamed I'd been bitten by a garter snake not a rattler and that I was running desperately up and down the trail, showing everyone the terrible, dripping, festering wound on my leg and begging for help. But they all kept laughing at me because, as everyone knows, garter snakes are completely harmless.

Eventually I returned to full consciousness. Or almost full consciousness. I knew I wasn't dreaming anymore because I was aware of minute details, such as the pebbles in the creek, the dust on my pant legs, the awful taste in my mouth, and the smell of puke a few feet away. Images in dreams are usually painted with much broader brush strokes and much less detail.

In that moment of clarity, it occurred it me that there was a good chance that I was about to die, in which case they probably wouldn't find me for weeks, if ever. I didn't much like the idea of becoming buzzard fodder, and I didn't want my wife to worry. I tried once again to get up, but I still didn't have the strength and my wound hurt too badly. My lower leg throbbed like a jungle tom-tom. And the nausea, dizziness, thirst, and fever had not abated. Not in the slightest.

All in all, I preferred the delirium.

That's when I heard a rustling noise in the bushes. I looked in that direction and saw nothing at first. Then I noticed an animal hiding in the foliage.

"Come on out, fellow," I said, holding out a bit of sandwich. "I won't hurt you."

Slowly, warily, a strange-looking creature crawled out of the bushes. It was about three feet long with a doglike face, very short legs, and long, smooth white fur that dragged on the ground. It had a musky smell that I found kind of pleasant.

The animal reminded me of a cross between Flub-a-Dub, from the old *Howdy Doody* show, and Falcor, the friendly Luck Dragon from the movie *Never-Ending Story*. Flub-a-Dub was a marionette with floppy dog ears, feet like a seal, a duck's bill, a cat's whiskers, a bunny's tail, and a body that was mostly a plaid dog coat. Falcor was twenty feet long and had a sweet, doglike face and a long, furry, snakelike body with silvery white fur. The animal I saw did not have a duck's bill or a plaid dog coat and was not twenty feet long. But aside from that, the resemblance was striking.

My mysterious animal seemed to have no interest in me as a person. Not at first, at least. It had no interest in my piece of sandwich either. The thing was mostly interested in my wound, which it walked up to and started licking. I was lying with my pant leg pulled up so the bite was exposed. My initial instinct was to shoo the animal away and try to protect myself. But the beast seemed so unthreatening, and the tongue felt so soothing that I just sat there and took my licks. After two or three minutes, I noticed that the swelling and discoloration had improved and that I felt much, much better.

After ten minutes or so, when the animal had satiated itself, it wandered back into the bushes. It was gone when I finally remembered my camera.

When I stood up a few minutes later, after briefly dozing again, my leg felt fine, my stomach felt fine, my head felt fine, and my temperature seemed back to normal. Even my mouth felt better. And the weather didn't feel nearly as hot. Of course it was now 4:30 p.m.

"Takes a licking and keeps on ticking," I said out loud, quoting an old Timex watch commercial. Then I started back up toward Pinnacles Pass, the Pinnacles Trail, and the Chisos Basin trailhead.

I know what you're thinking. The animal was a dream. Or a hallucination. Or a dog or a bobcat. And I might simply have fought off the snakebite on my own. You're probably right. Besides, as far as anyone I've talked to knows, there are no animals in Texas even remotely like the one I saw.

Then again, you never know. There are all sorts of strange animals in Texas.

PART 6

When I arrived back at the campground at 6:45, I learned that my wife had been frantic over my failure to arrive on time. All the park rangers were out looking for me when I came sauntering in. Somehow they had not spotted me during my return hike.

An emergency medical person examined the snakebite and said it didn't look very bad. He said my body had apparently done an excellent job of shaking off the venom. He put some antiseptic on the bite so that it wouldn't get infected, then sent me on my way.

I didn't mention to the medical person about the little animal that saved my life. I didn't mention it to Pat either. Or Jenny. I didn't figure they'd believe me. Besides, it's not up to me to persuade them that such animals actually exist. They'll run across their own Category Two, Three, or Four animals one of these days. Then they'll understand.

I also did not mention to my wife, or the Big Bend rangers, the conversation I had with the strange little animal. It happened just as the creature was leaving. It turned to me and said, in perfect English: "I'm happy to help out, but let's just keep this our little secret."

I figured they really wouldn't believe that.

TO VISIT

The hike: Pinnacles and Mount Emory Trails, Big Bend National Park, Texas

Distance: Four and a half miles (one-way)

Directions: From I-10 at Van Horn, 118 miles east of El Paso, take US 90 south for 136 miles to Marathon. In Marathon, follow US 385 south for sixty-nine miles into Big Bend National Park and on to the Panther Junction Visitor Center. Head west from Panther Junction for three miles, toward Terlingua and Presidio, to the Basin Junction, then go south for six and a half miles to the developed area in the Chisos Basin. The trailhead for the Pinnacles, South Rim, and Laguna Meadows Trails is located near the Chisos Basin store and ranger station.

9
Against Bears and Men

PART 1

I normally do not stop for a drink after a hike and I hadn't been in the Buckhorn Tavern in Yreka, California, since 1972. When my wife and I first moved out West, the Buckhorn had been a favorite hangout. On that particular day in 1994, I'd gone hiking in the area, finished early, and wasn't anxious to get home.

Driving though town, I found myself nostalgic for the good old days, and the next thing I knew, I was walking though the front door. Since I hadn't consumed alcohol since 1982, for me a bar drink consisted of club soda mixed with Rose's Lime Juice. That had not been the case in 1972.

Inside, the Buckhorn was just as dark as it had been twenty-two years earlier. And just as full of cigarette smoke. The main room consisted of a hardwood bar with bar stools, a long padded bench with tables along one wall, a dozen or so other tables, and hundreds of deer antlers mounted on the walls.

The Buckhorn had changed so little that Old Augie Atteberry, the Karuk Indian game tracker and shaman, still occupied his usual table in the corner of the main room, drinking lemonade and smoking a cigar. A swirl of smoke over Augie's head glowed slightly in the dim light. Augie recognized me, even though we hadn't talked in twenty-two years and were never particularly close. Still, I'd always enjoyed Augie and was surprised when he actually recognized me.

"Hey, Bernstein. What the hell are you doing here?"

I ended up sitting with Augie through three non-alcoholic drinks.

Augie Atteberry was a tiny man, perhaps five-foot-three, with silver hair in a ponytail almost down to his waist. He must have been pushing ninety, but he looked about the same as he had in the early 1970s. Of course in the dim light, it was difficult to assess such things.

The ancient man wore a San Francisco 49ers jacket, a black T-shirt with a Harley-Davidson logo, and a beaded necklace with an Indian motif that appeared to be some sort of religious amulet.

"What you up to these days?" Augie asked after we'd exchanged greetings.

"Well, for one thing, I wrote a guide book on day hikes in northern California."

"No kidding? I never took you for an outdoors guy. I figured all you did was sit around and drink."

"Not any more," I said, feeling a little defensive.

"I wish we had more time to talk," said Augie, "because there's hundreds of fantastic trails around here I could tell you about that aren't on the map."

"I'd love to hear about them," I said.

"So tell me," said Augie, "why do you only write about day hikes? Don't you like camping out?"

"Not really. I have kind of a bad back. I have a terrible time sleeping outdoors."

Augie smiled a relaxed smile, took a puff on his cigar, and looked me in the eyes.

"Ain't nothing wrong with your back," he announced.

"Yes there is," I insisted.

"If there is, it's all in your head. You don't look like a man with back problems."

"Trust me," I said. "I have a bad back when I try to sleep in tents."

"If you say so," said Augie. "But tell me this, you ever seen any bears on your hikes?"

"I've never seen a single bear on a hike," I confessed. Actually I'd always thought that was strange, considering that nearly everybody I talked to about hiking, most of whom had been on far fewer hikes than I, regularly encountered the ursine pests.

"You're afraid of bears, aren't you?" said Augie. "That's why you can't sleep when you camp out."

I nodded my head in sad assent. He had me.

"You need to get over it," said Augie. "The bears have been avoiding you because they know you don't want to see them. But one of these days, a bear is going to take offense at your attitude. Besides, you can't truly be in tune with nature if you are estranged from bears. It shuts out too much."

"I'd love to get over it," I said. "I keep telling myself that the fear is stupid."

"What you need to do," said Augie, setting his cigar in the ashtray and leaning forward so that his face was only a few inches from mine, "is subdue the spirit of the bear."

"Oh," I said, "is that all? And just how do I go about that?" Subduing the spirit of a bear did not sound fun. It did not sound safe either.

"The best way to explain it," said Augie, "is to compare it to a story in your *Bible,* the one where Jacob goes to see his brother Esau after many years."

"I know that story," I said. "Jacob cheated his brother out of his birthright, then ran away and hid for twenty years. Then he finally had to face him."

"And Jacob," said Augie, picking up the narrative, "was scared to death because Esau had sworn to kill him. Jacob realized that before he could face his brother, he must face himself. It says in the *Bible* that the night before Jacob was to see his brother, 'A man wrestled with him until the breaking of day.'"

Augie recited the rest of the passage, word for word:

Now when the man saw that he did not prevail over Jacob, he said, "Let me go."
But Jacob said, "I will not let you go unless you bless me."
And the man said, "What is your name?"
And he said, "Jacob."
And the man said, "Your name shall no longer be Jacob but Israel, for you have struggled against God and men and have prevailed."

"So what you're saying," I replied when Augie had finished, "is that all I have to do to capture the spirit of the bear, to secure the bear's blessing, is to struggle against bears and men and prevail? And if I do, the bear will bless me and change my name?"

"Something like that."

"Seems to me that it's much easier said than done. Besides, I can't see myself ever pinning a bear in an all-night wrestling match, even if I could induce one to take me on, which is insane."

"I understand what you're saying, but remember this is a spiritual wrestling match. And don't worry. The opportunity will come. You'll see."

PART 2

Old Augie Atteberry isn't a respected shaman for nothing. He knew what he was talking about, and he was absolutely right.

The Great Bernstein Bear Encounter took place a short five months after the chat with Augie, on a hiking trip to the Sycamore Canyon Wilderness of northern Arizona.

I went to Sycamore Canyon mostly because of a rampant case of cabin fever. I always get cabin fever in spring. It begins when the snow closes the mountain high country in late November or early December and ends when the snow melts in May or June. By March or April, I start to get extremely restless. Most of the time I simply endure it. But if the early-spring weather in Oregon is particularly bad, and the snowmelt is particularly slow, I've been known to take off for a few days to warmer climates, usually within a few days' drive. Over the years I've ended up in or around Palm Springs, Tucson, Las Vegas, and Ensenada, Mexico. Not to mention Disneyland, Knott's Berry Farm, and the San Diego Zoo with the wife and kids.

This time, I decided to make a trip by myself to Arizona to do some hiking in the Sycamore Canyon Wilderness. I'd seen much of the surrounding area—the Grand Canyon, Humphreys Peak, Montezuma Castle National Monument, Wupatki National Monument, Tuzigoot National Monument, Walnut Canyon National Monument, and my favorite, Oak Creek Canyon, with its twisty road and intense red sandstone cliffs and monoliths.

And always, in the middle of the map, like a big bleeding wound that demanded attention, miles from any paved road, sprawled the many-fingered, fifty-six-thousand-acre Sycamore Canyon Wilderness, better known as the "Little Grand Canyon."

I spent the first night at a campground in Valley of Fire State Park, a few miles east of Las Vegas. Valley of Fire is full of jumbled red-rock formations leading down to the Colorado River. Since I was fairly certain that the local bears were still in hibernation, I slept through the night in my tent, without a hint of back problems. I awoke to an awesome sunrise. The rocks grew redder and redder and redder, until I figuratively feared they would catch fire.

I arrived in Flagstaff, Arizona, at around noon, saying hello to the Grand Canyon on the way past and touring Sunset Crater National Monument, which I'd never visited before.

I'd chosen for my hike the southernmost and supposedly easiest trail into the Sycamore Canyon Wilderness, which followed Sycamore Creek upstream from its confluence with the Verde River to a place called Parsons Spring. The path, called the Parsons Trail, was supposed to be Sycamore Canyon's most popular. I'd read that it afforded the best views of the canyon and boasted the most water, the most clearly defined canyon walls, and the easiest auto access.

Assuming that the bears were still in hibernation, I again made the decision to backpack in and spend the night rather than stay in a motel or at one of the hundreds of campgrounds in the region. Since I planned to do some exploring on side trails, a centrally located campsite seemed like an excellent idea.

I arrived at the Parsons trailhead at about 3:00 in the afternoon. It was pretty easy to find. I was encouraged that all the dry washes crossed by the access road were indeed dry and that there was no indication of any impending storms that could cause the dry washes to fill up with water. Storms are not that uncommon in northern Arizona in March.

There were no other cars parked at the trailhead on that Wednesday afternoon, which meant I could count on a little solitude. The trailhead sat on a sagebrush-covered flat at the edge of a cliff with an impressive overlook of the lower canyon with its pink rock walls. From the trailhead I could see the first mile of tree-lined Sycamore Creek, to where it made a right-angle turn to the left.

The path dropped five hundred feet in the first third of a mile from the trailhead. It was very dusty and exposed until I reached bottom. Early on I passed through a gate with a sign asking hikers to keep it closed. The purpose of the gate, I assumed, was to keep the cattle I'd seen grazing on the surrounding hills out of the wilderness area. It also, I later decided, prevented the cattle grazing inside the wilderness— and there were a lot of them—from getting out.

Once the trail reached the creek, it pretty much hugged the water's edge, except for occasional forays where it cut across open (usually sandy) areas or over rock outcrops when the creekside became too twisty or rough. As I hiked, the scenery grew more and more lovely and the canyon walls drew closer and higher.

After a mile, where the canyon veered sharply left, the trail crossed the creek through ankle-deep water. Soon after, it arrived at Summer Spring, a popular swimming hole in summer, with a sandy beach where the creek widened and deepened at the base of a vertical red cliff. At Summer Spring the path crossed the creek a second time.

I checked the skyline as I forded the creek, to make sure there were still no storm clouds that could cause a flash flood and either cut off my return trip or kill me. I wasn't too worried about flash floods. As long as I knew that the bears were safely sleeping, these other potential dangers didn't concern me much.

The desert ecosystem in the canyon was fascinating. In addition to both black and eastern cottonwood, I observed Mexican walnut, Emory oak, ponderosa pine, velvet mesquite, and Arizona sycamore. Mesquite was the most common tree, scraggly little things no bigger than dogwoods and covered with thorns.

Not surprisingly, the star of the show—the largest and showiest of the trees—was the sycamore. Arizona sycamore looks much like the stately American sycamore found in urban front yards and native to the eastern United States, except its habitat is completely different. The Arizona tree adores desert streams such as Sycamore Canyon, where summer heat is intense but humid and winters are extremely mild.

I arrived at Parsons Spring after a leisurely two-hour stroll, which included four more stream crossings. The canyon widened out around the spring, which meant there was more potential cattle-grazing land than lower down.

Parsons Spring itself was a little emerald pool surrounded by reeds, sedges, and dense brush. It seemed to be a haven for hummingbirds and the happy songs of canyon wrens and hermit thrushes. Unlike Summer Spring, which I'd passed on the way in, there was no beach and you could not swim in it. In fact, when water is low, the actual spring is often difficult to locate because of the brush, although there are other swimmable pools nearby, in the creek below the spring.

For my night's lodging, I picked out a beautiful shady creekside location just below the spring. There I snacked on trail mix, set up my little dome tent beneath a large cottonwood, stowed my gear inside, and ventured out for a little more hiking before turning in for the night. I arrived at the spring at 4:45 in the afternoon, so there was still a little daylight left even though it was only March.

As I erected my tent and ate my snack, it was soon confirmed that, like many wilderness areas of the West, Sycamore Canyon was leased for cattle grazing. A bunch of cows filed past amid a cacophony of mooing and bell clanging. Apparently they were heading for another grazing site not quite so close to human intrusion. I worried that they might decide to come back in the middle of the night, bringing their mooing and clanging with them, so I was as rude as I could possibly be, shouting and waving my arms. Each time I shouted, they sped up their pace a little.

After getting settled and running off the cattle, I continued up Sycamore Creek for another one and a half miles to a large oxbow meander. It was quite a trek, past hidden side canyons and fern-filled grottoes. For the most part, the trail was either faint or nonexistent, but it would have been difficult to get lost. One side canyon, not too far from Parsons Spring, led to what looked like an impressive and easily reached vista point on the lower flank of Black Mountain. I decided to return in the morning and spend a couple of hours checking out this off-trail route.

On the hike back to my campsite, a quarter mile from my tent I came over a rise and observed a huge black bear sitting in a field. It was the first bear I'd ever encountered while hiking. Although it was a black bear, its color was actually a light cinnamon bordering on strawberry blond. But since it was obviously not a grizzly (I knew how to identify grizzly bears), it had to be a black bear. The thing weighed at least five hundred pounds.

Damn, I thought. They lied to me. The bears aren't in hibernation.

Or at least this one wasn't.

The bear wasn't doing much, just sitting there, puttering around and enjoying life. Were I in its position, I'd probably do exactly the same thing on a warm afternoon in early spring.

I stopped, backed up a little until the bear was out of view (which also meant that I was out of its view), and, with my heart pounding, pondered what to do. Since the thing was squatting smack in the middle of my intended route, there was no way around that did not involve an eyeball-to-eyeball confrontation. I waited several minutes, but the animal seemed settled in where it was, with no inclination to move anytime soon.

Finally, struggling to remember everything I'd ever heard about fending off bears, and mustering every ounce of courage, I shouted at the top of my lungs. Despite its immense size, the startled beast took off like a whippet at a dog track in the direction away from my voice.

Boy was I relieved.

Not until several minutes later, as I resumed my hike back to the tent, did it occur to me that during the five minutes in which I was aware of the bear and the bear was not aware of me, I had ample opportunity to get my camera out and take a picture. I could have taken a whole roll in fact. But the thought had never entered my head.

Back at the tent, I feasted on a dinner of canned beef stew and trail mix. Then I meticulously scoured my utensils in the creek, along with the empty stew can, to get rid of any food scent that might attract my ursine neighbor to come a-calling in the middle of the night.

Aside from taking numerous precautions, I tried not to think about the bear. Or about whether I would get any sleep that night.

Just before going to bed, I suspended my backpack with a nylon rope from a tree. Then I blew up my air mattress, unrolled my sleeping bag, and, as the shadow of night slowly moved from the canyon rim down across the valley, reluctantly crawled into my tent to try to get at least a little sleep.

I was not very hopeful. Usually my worry about bears is vague and unfocused. This time I had good reason to worry.

It did not help when, later that evening, the cows decided that they simply could not live without my scintillating company. Either that or I'd inadvertently camped in their favorite overnight spot. With the usual clanging and mooing announcing their return, they plopped themselves (literally) not far from my tent.

The problem, I soon ascertained as I snuggled up in my sleeping bag, was that cows tended to moo constantly and for no apparent reason. For animals that just stand around and eat most of the time, they sure seemed to have a lot to say. In any case, I already had enough on my mind. In addition to worrying about the bear, I had that hike in the

Summer Spring

morning up the steep red cliff, not to mention the 3.7-mile trek, with backpack, back to the car. A couple of hours' restful sleep would make life after sunrise much easier.

The cattle and I soon settled into a routine. It would be a quiet, still, wilderness night. Then somebody would start mooing. Then somebody else would start mooing. Then somebody else and somebody else, until my bovine neighbors had a full-scale cow chorus going. I'd endure it for a while then yell at them from inside my tent. I discovered that whenever I yelled, there would be instantaneous and total silence for twenty to thirty minutes.

PART 3

The cows eventually settled down for what I hoped would be the remainder of the night. But I still couldn't sleep and was still obsessing about the bear.

At about 3:00 a.m., in the midst of my tossing, turning, and fretting, I noticed that my head had somehow penetrated the rear wall of the tent and that I was looking up at the stars. I could feel the gentle night breeze on my face. It was very pleasant, and the stars were lovely, illuminating everything around me. Visibility was pretty good despite the darkness.

With my head poking through the tent, I recall reveling in the fresh air. At least I reveled until I saw a bear out of the corner of my eye, the same bear I'd seen in the field.

I quickly tried to pull my head back inside, but it was apparently stuck. As I struggled, growing ever more terrified, the bear came closer and closer, walking on all fours with long, slow strides. It approached to within three or four feet of where I lay. Then it leaned over, breathed on me with warm, sour-smelling breath, looked me squarely in the face, bared its fangs—and mooed. That was when I remembered the famous Bernstein anti-bear, anti-cow holler that had been so effective the previous day.

With supreme confidence, I opened my mouth and screamed, "Get out of here!"

The bear did not respond. It did not bat an eye. It was as though the animal had gone completely deaf. My foolproof holler was a dismal failure.

I was baffled and confused for a minute. Then it occurred to me that I was sleeping and had only dreamed my yell. I yelled again, and once more there was no response. The bear just stood there and stared at me. Eventually, though, I attracted two or three additional mooing bears, along with any number of cows, which were also mooing.

I became even more frightened when the bear pulled me the rest of the way out of the tent. I was naked, of course, because that's how I always sleep. The bear prodded, poked, dragged, growled, bit, and generally knocked me around like a rag doll. I lay on the ground curled up in a defensive ball, with my arms protecting my head and unable to breathe. I honestly feared I was about to die.

That's when I finally lost my temper. Spiritual battle or not, dream or not, this nonsense had gone on long enough. I angrily jumped to my feet, and with my uncovered and unprotected genitalia flapping in the night breeze, I kicked the bear in the rear end.

This time the bear, not I, curled up into a defensive ball on the ground. It looked up at me and growled the most plaintive, chilling growl I have ever heard. Then the animal got up and limped off into the night. Apparently the other bears, and cows, went with it, because I slept soundly from then on.

When I awoke for real, it was daylight and both my head and body were securely inside the tent. I was very tired, more tired than I should have been after three hours' sleep, and I felt extremely drained. But I was happy that morning had finally arrived, happy to be in the wilderness and looking forward to breakfast followed by a side hike up the beautiful red cliff to Black Mountain.

What a silly dream, I thought, chuckling inwardly as I went outside to enjoy the magnificent morning and fix my meal.

As I walked around the camp, I made a discovery that stifled any further chuckling. The nocturnal bear, it seemed, had been very real indeed. It left tracks around my campsite and clawed at the tree where the rope holding my pack was anchored. There were also cow tracks all around the camp that were not there when I went to bed.

Most of the tracks, both cow and bear, were concentrated around the rear of the tent, where I'd dreamed that my head had poked through the tent wall.

Suddenly I felt far more vulnerable. I could not be 100 percent certain that my yells had really been dream yells or that my kick had really been a dream kick. And the fatigue I felt was the kind of drained exhaustion you might experience after a toe-to-toe confrontation or a terrifying run-in.

In short, I felt like Jacob must have felt the morning after wrestling all night with an angel.

PART 4

After a breakfast of instant oatmeal, a carton of warm juice, and yet more trail mix, I folded my tent and rolled up my sleeping bag. Then I repeated the hike up Sycamore Creek that I'd scouted out the previous day, leading to the vantage point.

After scrambling up steep boulder fields, isolated forest pockets, and a couple of almost sheer rock faces, I surmounted the bench. Looking westward from the vista point, the entire Sycamore Canyon, seven miles across and twenty miles long, spread out below me. To the south lay Clarkburg and the farmlands of the Verde Valley. Behind me lay the gentle, pine-covered, six-thousand-foot summit of Black Mountain.

In the canyon far below, I could see the spot where my tent had been. A group of cows now lazed on the creekbank not far away.

As to the symbolic significance of my psychic, or possibly real, confrontation with the bear: Unlike the biblical Jacob, neither my name nor my personality was profoundly altered by the experience. I didn't notice any effect, in fact, until the next time I camped out, which wasn't until two years later. I discovered that I wasn't nearly as worried about bears as I used to be.

I now seem to encounter bears far more often than I used to, although still not very often. And so far, none of the bears have bothered me in any way.

I guess old Augie was right. As a result of the Sycamore Canyon experience, I somehow became more empathetic to the spirit of the bear and to other sources of vague dread in my life.

On the other hand, I now seem to be afraid of cows.

TO VISIT

The hike: Parsons Trail, Sycamore Canyon Wilderness, Clarkdale, Arizona

Distance: 3.7 miles (one-way), plus side trips

Directions: From I-40 at Flagstaff, go south on I-17 toward Phoenix. After five miles, take exit 337 to US 89-A and drive for forty-six miles through Oak Creek Canyon, Sedona, and Cottonwood. Just past Cottonwood, "Historic 89-A" goes straight while 89-A veers left. Historic 89-A takes you through Clarkdale. In Clarkdale, follow signs to Tuzigoot National Monument. Immediately after the road to the monument crosses the bridge over the Verde River, turn left onto Sycamore Canyon Road, which is paved for the first two miles. At mile five, you will start seeing signs saying you are on Road 131 and directing you to Sycamore Canyon. Proceed eleven miles from the turnoff to the Parsons trailhead.

Additional information: Road 131 is very rough in spots and crosses several dry washes with signs admonishing not to proceed if there is water in the washes. The best season to avoid flash floods is summer. The trailhead elevation, however, is only about two thousand feet, and a low-elevation canyon in Arizona is the last place you want to be in summer. When I visited Cottonwood in August 2002, the temperature was 107. It was even hotter in the canyon. Where the trail through the canyon approaches the creek, the humidity jumps way up. Away from the creek, where there is less shade, solar radiation reflects off the sandy pathway, greatly magnifying the heat. Bring plenty of water whenever you visit: There are grazing cattle in the vicinity, and the water in the creek is not safe to drink without treating.

10

Cryptozoology

PART 1

"Here's how I see it happening," I explained to Brian Boothby, my affable but always skeptical hiking companion, as we strode in full backpacks down the seemingly endless wilderness trail. "We'll get up real early one morning and the path will climb up onto a ridge, offering a panoramic view of a wide, dewy meadow below. At the edge of the meadow, we'll notice something large, furry, and black moving around."

"A bear, right?"

"We'll think it's a bear at first, but it will be walking on two legs. I'll put my camera on full zoom, snap a bunch of pictures, and we'll be instantly rich and famous."

"And love is a thing that can never go wrong, and I am the queen of Romania," said Brian.

Not many people in Grants Pass, Oregon, the town where Brian and I lived, were literary enough to be able to quote Dorothy Parker as a sarcastic comeback. That was one of the things I liked about him.

In fact, Brian was a mailman who walked seven miles a day on his route. He was in astonishingly good condition for our anticipated thirty-six-mile, three-day outing. Much better condition than I.

"I still say they're out there and they're watching us," I informed him for the hundredth time.

"And I still say you're crazy," said Brian, also for the hundredth time.

"I'm not crazy. We're going to see one and I'm going to get a photo, make a million bucks, and become famous."

"You're not going to photograph a bigfoot," Brian reiterated in exasperation. "You wanna know why?" He yelled the next sentence for emphasis. "Because there is no such thing as a bigfoot!"

I didn't really expect to photograph a bigfoot during the hike. I kept bringing up the possibility mainly because I enjoyed getting a rise out of Brian, whom I considered an intelligent and worthy adversary and friend. Not that I didn't hope to encounter a bigfoot. But I knew the chances were pretty slim. I would never admit that to Brian though.

There was ample opportunity to talk about bigfeet as we hiked because the trail's first eight miles, while extremely scenic, didn't really hit any highlights. It mostly made its way up the Stuart Fork of the Trinity River. Following a rather deep canyon, we saw only the river, which was actually a large, fast creek, and the forested slopes on either side. Only rarely did we catch brief glimpses up side creeks to one of the glistening white granite peaks for which northern California's vast Trinity Alps Wilderness, third-largest wilderness in the United States outside Alaska, is famous.

According to the map, the hike would get far more interesting after mile eight, when we passed the mouth of Deer Creek, entered Morris Meadows, and many of the Trinity Alps' highest and most beautiful peaks came into view. Beyond the meadow, the fifteen-mile trail began a fairly steep ascent to Emerald and Sapphire Lakes, our primary destination.

"I'll find a bigfoot one of these days," I assured my companion. "I've figured out exactly where to look."

"So have hundreds of other people," Brian pointed out. "And still nobody's ever proven they exist. I mean, you yourself have driven up and down Bluff Creek looking for bigfeet, including visiting the Roger Patterson site, and you haven't found so much as an extra-wide boot print."

Bluff Creek, like the Stuart Fork, is a tributary of northern California's Trinity River. It is located at the southern edge of the remote Siskiyou Wilderness between the towns of Somesbar and Hoopa. Bluff Creek is accessed by a low-quality dirt road. More bigfoot sightings have occurred on Bluff Creek than any place else. The famous 1967 Roger Patterson film, which remains the only unrefuted film ever taken of an alleged bigfoot, was shot along Bluff Creek.

"The trouble with you, Boothby," I said, "is that you have a closed mind. Even if you stepped on a bigfoot's toe, or a bigfoot stepped on your toe, your subconscious would probably register the animal only as a very large dog."

"And the trouble with you, Bernstein, is that you're an idiot."

"I still say we're in prime bigfoot habitat," I argued. That was, in fact, one reason I'd chosen the route. The other reason was a desire to visit Emerald and Sapphire Lakes, supposedly the two most exquisitely beautiful alpine glacial lakes in the world. On the desire to see the two lakes, at least, Brian and I were in total agreement.

"There's no such thing as prime bigfoot habitat," said Brian with an exasperated sigh. "An animal that doesn't exist can't have a habitat."

"A habitat of the mind," I suggested. I liked the concept. Then I explained to Brian, yet again, my theory about bigfoot habitat.

Based on past sightings, I have been able to map out precisely where in northern California and southern Oregon bigfeet might be found and where they probably will not be found. I am certain that bigfeet would not be found anywhere in the Mount Shasta, Yolla Bolly–Middle Eel, Castle Crags, Snow Mountain, Sky Lakes, and Mountain Lakes Wilderness Areas, all of which lie within one hundred miles of the Trinity Alps.

The Marble Mountain, Kalmiopsis, and Red Buttes Wilderness Areas, also within one hundred miles of the Trinity Alps, are "iffy" as far as the presence of bigfeet. The correct habitat is there—dense coastal forest, lots of rainfall, and tens of thousands of acres of remote, rugged backcountry, often with few trails—but the sightings aren't.

There are three northern California wilderness areas where I am positive that the fabled beasts are never far away. The conclusion is reinforced by the fact that I had never—not once—crossed a boundary of the Siskiyou, Russian, or Trinity Alps Wilderness Areas without being dogged at some point by the notion that somebody or something was watching me. And I'd hiked in those places on scores of occasions.

"If you've been in prime bigfoot habitat that many times," Brian noted, "you should have seen dozens of them by now. Hundreds. You should have invited a family of them home for dinner by now."

"You'd think so," I explained, "except for the Prime Rule of Bigfoot Hunting."

"Okay, I'll bite. What is the Prime Rule of Bigfoot Hunting?"

"The Prime Rule of Bigfoot Hunting," I explained, "is that if you purposely look for a bigfoot, you will never find one. To see a bigfoot, you have to be patient and hope it decides to come to you. That's how it has been with every person who's ever seen one. Or any other unverified mammal. And that's how it will probably be with me. Or with you and me."

"So we're screwed," said Brian. "Darn the luck."

I did not mention to Brian that I had made up the Prime Rule as we were talking.

According to the map, we were now approaching Morris Meadow. It meant that very shortly the valley would widen out and Sawtooth Ridge, a highlight of the Trinity Alps, would appear. I was anxious to see Sawtooth Ridge and Morris Meadow. Not as anxious as I was to see Emerald and Sapphire Lakes, but still pretty anxious.

I had one last point to make about bigfoot habitat before we turned our attention to more pressing matters. I told Brian that having hiked hundreds of miles of trails to the heart of bigfoot country's largest and most remote wilderness areas, it had become obvious to me that the paths only visit a minute fraction of the total backcountry, much of which is covered by rugged mountains and dense, giant forests fed by frequent coastal storms.

Could one hundred or so large, herbivorous, reasonably intelligent primates who didn't want to be discovered successfully hide out there? Hell, they could hide out in a single valley and never be discovered, if they picked the right valley. For example, in the western Trinity Alps— the immense two-thirds of the wilderness where hardly anybody ever goes—the North Fork of the New River drains fifteen thousand acres and has no trail access at all. It requires a thirty-mile drive up a logging road and a ten-mile hike just to reach the edge of the drainage, which is visited, on average, by fewer than one person every five years.

"All well and good," said Brian. "But it still seems to me that you're basing your belief solely on the fact that you can't disprove a negative—that you can never prove something's nonexistence, only its existence."

"And so we dreamers keep on dreaming," I replied.

PART 2

"Are there other nonexistent animals besides bigfeet that we need to worry about?" Brian asked as we made our way around the mouth of Deer Creek. "Six-foot-tall chipmunks, maybe, that speak Spanish?"

"Now you're talking," I laughed. "A photo of that would be worth way more than a plain old bigfoot. And, yes, there are other unverified mammals in the California Far North."

"And do you believe in them too?"

"Why not? Humans don't know everything."

"So what are some other unverified mammals, aside from giant chipmunks?"

"The only one I'm aware of is the California grizzly."

"The California grizzly isn't unverified; it's extinct."

"That's where you're wrong," I announced. "Or at least you might be wrong."

The authenticated facts, I explained, accepted by nearly every-body, are that the California grizzly was hunted to extinction following the gold rush of the 1850s and 1860s. The miners thought the bears were a nuisance, probably because grizzlies have a much greater ten-dency to attack and kill people than black bears.

By 1890, following thirty years of methodical slaughter, the Cali-fornia grizzly was no more. The last known grizzly, dubbed "Old Reel-foot" because of an unfortunate encounter with a leghold trap, roamed the Siskiyou Mountains along the California-Oregon line for forty years. In 1890 he was shot dead by a seventeen-year-old hunter. Old Reelfoot was stuffed and then displayed for many years in the county museum in Jacksonville, Oregon.

The thing is, in the bars and cafes of the most remote communi-ties of the California Far North—in places like Somesbar, Happy Camp, Hoopa, and Willow Creek—there are those who aren't so sure the Cali-fornia grizzly is extinct.

In 1971 Old Augie Atteberry, a Karuk Indian game tracker and sha-man, informed me of the Native American view of the California grizzly in no uncertain terms. At the time Augie was playing low-ball poker in a tavern in Yreka, California's second most-northern county seat.

"That stuff about there being no more grizzlies is crap," Augie announced while taking an immense puff off his big, acrid cigar. "My people—the Karuk, Yurok, and Hoopa—go a lot farther back into the forest than you white folks. We see grizzly all the time."

Augie Atteberry claimed that his father, also a game tracker and shaman, knew a chant that could summon the bigfeet. The creatures would never fully show themselves but, according to Augie, you could see them by the light of the campfire, moving round in the dark woods just out of view.

"So all he really saw was shadows," said Brian.

"I know," I said. "He also never bothered to explain exactly why his dad wanted to summon the bigfeet. So I'm a little skeptical myself."

"No you're not," said Brian. "You'll believe anything."

PART 3

As Brian and I entered Morris Meadow, we were treated to our first glimpse of Sawtooth Ridge, a jagged row of spires that abruptly rose three thousand feet above the meadow to the north and east, forcing the valley of the Stuart Fork into a 90-degree westward turn. The Stuart Fork and the valley ended at Emerald and Sapphire Lakes, six miles from where we stood. The white rock spires reminded me of marimbas. With a large enough mallet, you could have played songs on them.

The magnificent white ice-cream cone mountain that dominated the valley's west side, opposite Sawtooth Ridge, was called Sawtooth Mountain. I guess any formation with a jagged top was a candidate for the name back in the days when the area's only visitors were hunters. Verbally, they were not very creative.

Morris Meadow exceeded all expectations, and I was happy to be there. So, apparently, was Brian. So were a lot of other people, who suddenly materialized. In the eight miles from the trailhead, we hadn't encountered that many people. But in the meadow, humans swarmed everywhere we looked.

A hundred yards or so into the meadow, the path we'd been following for so long disappeared in the waist-high grass. We found that rather odd, considering the trail's high usage. The route broke into several faint way trails, which braided in and out of one another as we made our way across the grassy, mile-long expanse. We were briefly concerned about losing the trail, until we figured out that it didn't matter which path we took. They all converged at the far end.

All I knew was that I was actually in Morris Meadow, a place I'd wanted to visit for twenty years. And that each step took me closer to

Emerald and Sapphire Lakes, which I'd also wanted to visit for twenty years.

On the meadow's far end, the true path reasserted itself at a spot where a dense stand of giant Shasta red fir ventured out across the flat. In contrast to the open meadow's sunny glare, the forest was dark, silent, and musty smelling. Beneath the cathedral trees lay a low, green understory of fern, salal, huckleberry, trillium, and vanilla leaf.

The shadow of Sawtooth Peak was starting to move across the valley, but at 6:00 p.m. on a June evening, it was a long way from nightfall. It gets dark around 9:30 at that time of year. It was a little darker in the woods than it would have been at noon. But only a little.

Because we were tired and it was getting late, Brian and I began keeping an eye out for a suitable locale to put up our tent, build a campfire, and turn in for the night. However, the instant we entered the woods, I set what may have been the all-time record for neck-tingling, free-floating paranoia and the sensation of creatures peering at me. My skin tingled, and the pit of my stomach quivered like a can of paint on a mixing machine.

"There's something out there," I kept whispering.

"Leave me alone," Brian kept whispering back.

"I'm not kidding. It's a bigfoot, I swear."

"Okay, it's a bigfoot."

We walked the next quarter mile in silence. I had my camera out of its case with the strap around my neck, poised and ready, just in case. Not that there was enough light for a decent photo. I knew that any shot I took would default to the "flash" mode, which meant I had to be within fifteen feet of whatever I was photographing. While I desperately wanted to gaze upon my long-sought bigfoot, I wasn't sure I wanted to get quite that close.

In all my Bigfoot fantasizing, I had never considered lighting and focus. I always pictured the encounter in full sunlight, out in the open, with no tricky camera adjustments. I'd just aim and shoot.

Adjusting my backpack shoulder straps, and my determination, I took a deep breath and pressed ahead, keeping one hand on the camera. The sound of my breathing and Brian's was the only audible noise in the eerie jungle-forest. The duff litter on the trail surface absorbed the impact of our footsteps, while the trees and foliage absorbed the other sounds, including birdsong. The silence was absolute.

A few minutes later, as we rounded a curve in the path . . .

"What the hell is that?" Brian and I whispered in unison.

I stopped walking. Goose bumps rose on my forearms. My heart pounded in my chest. I'd have said something to Brian, but I couldn't talk. Brian saw it too, obviously, because he also stopped walking. He glanced at me with just as puzzled a look as I undoubtedly had. Then we both stared at the animal that walked silently along the trail—magnificent, sleek, and eerie—perhaps twenty feet ahead of us, moving in the same direction we were going.

I'd never seen anything like it before in my life. I'd never heard of anything like it before in my life.

It was definitely not a bigfoot. But beyond that, I hadn't the faintest idea what it was.

My first thought, after several seconds of confused and frantic flipping through the Rolodex in my mind that contained every fact I ever knew about mammals, was that it was a cougar. Except it was black, like a jaguar or panther. Cougars are a light tan.

Even if the animal had been a cougar, which it clearly was not, seeing one on a trail was highly unusual. Many lifelong hikers and hunters in the region have never seen a cougar in the wild. I'd been a little luckier. I once saw a mother and two cubs walk across a logging road I was driving on at the edge of the Salmon-Huckleberry Wilderness Area, near Mount Hood in north-central Oregon.

But this was not a cougar. It was the wrong color. It was very much the wrong color. It was as black as India ink. It wasn't a black panther or a jaguar either. The shape of its head was more cougar than panther. Besides, there are supposedly no black panthers in California or anywhere else in the United States, unless you count jaguarundis, which live in Texas. But jaguarundis are much smaller than the creature Brian and I saw, and Texas was two thousand miles away.

Saying nothing and keeping as quiet as possible, Brian and I watched the animal pad gracefully and silently along the path for ten seconds, which felt like a very long time. I moved my camera up to my eye then hesitated for a second. It occurred to me that if I took a flash shot, it would frighten the animal away. On the other hand, the beast was at the very edge of my fifteen-foot range; if I was going to get a photo, now was the time.

Slowly and firmly, I squeezed the button. The flash went off, and the shutter snapped.

And almost instantly, the animal disappeared. Most likely it simply slipped off into the underbrush. However, my perception, and Brian's, was that it had vanished.

The good news was that as soon as the animal vanished, the sense of a mysterious presence watching us also vanished. Nevertheless, we walked for another full mile, this time at Brian's insistence, before stopping for the night. Brian said he wanted to make sure we were far, far away from the prowling jungle carnivore we'd just seen.

The camping spot we picked seemed unthreatening and immensely comfortable. We spent the night alongside the Stuart Fork on a tree-shaded flat by a swimming hole. The primary topic of conversation as we relaxed, swam, and cooked dinner was the strange animal we'd seen.

"It was a black panther," Brian insisted.

"That's impossible," I countered. "I know for a fact that there are no black panthers in California."

"We're far more likely to run into a black panther than a bigfoot," said Brian, "because black panthers really exist. I say it was a black panther."

And so the argument raged.

PART 4

On the morning following our mysterious encounter, Brian and I awoke and took off for Emerald and Sapphire Lakes, a ten-mile round-trip hike. Rather than pack up the tent, we left it standing at the campsite, since we would pass it on the way back. By leaving the tent up, we could rest inside for an hour or so before leaving for Deer Creek Valley, where we planned to spend the next night.

We arrived at Emerald Lake at around 9:00 a.m. By now the Stuart Fork Trail was extremely steep and rocky. Hiking it was like climbing an endless stairway to heaven.

Emerald Lake covered forty-two acres and Sapphire Lake covered twenty-eight. Both were set in a deeply cut, perfectly formed alpine

Sapphire Lake

glacial basin. The basin appeared to have been carved into the white granite mountains by a giant ice-cream scoop.

If Emerald Lake was beautiful, which it was, Sapphire Lake was indescribable. The water was bluer, and the white rock walls on either side were steeper and higher. Because it was springtime, dozens of waterfalls rained over the smooth cliffs, fed by the abundant lingering snowfields above.

We ate lunch on the rocks by the shore of Sapphire Lake before hiking the five miles back to the little wooded flat where we'd left our tent and backpacks.

PART 5

One of the first things I did when I arrived home was phone the headquarters of Shasta-Trinity National Forest in Redding, California, which is in charge of the Trinity Alps Wilderness, and talk to their resident wildlife biologist. I had several questions for him, including one about black cougars. Or black panthers.

"As far as I know," the wildlife biologist replied, "North American cougars (*Felis concolor*) are all a light tan. The South American black jaguar might possibly range into the American Southwest but certainly not into northern California. The black leopard of Africa and Asia is obviously not found in the US. There's a Florida panther, but it's very small and more of a reddish brown. In fact, the only black mammal I can think of that's native to the Trinity Alps is the skunk."

The animal we saw definitely was not a skunk.

I spent the winter repeating the story to friends, or anybody else who would listen, about the fulfillment of my twenty-year quest, the magnificent lakes, and the strange and beautiful animal that was either a black panther or a very odd-looking cougar.

The photo I took of the cougar/panther turned out to be inconclusive. It showed an indistinct black form against an indistinct black background. It was not the stuff from which million-dollar deals with tabloid newspapers are made. I couldn't even get the photo printed in my hometown newspaper, which would have paid me ten bucks had they used it. They said it was too dark and blurry. So much for my millions.

PART 6

I met David Robbins at a book signing in a small bookstore in Grants Pass, Oregon, two years after my visit to Emerald and Sapphire Lakes. I was signing copies of my newly published volume on the Trinity Alps Wilderness, and he was signing copies of his latest novel. It was "Local Authors' Day," and four other writers also busily scrawled signatures and chatted among themselves between customers.

David is a talented, prolific, and underrated novelist. At the time I met him, he had two series going, cranking out a complete (if short) novel every month. His novels all involved mountain men and wilderness explorers. Despite having written more than two hundred books, he had neither wealth nor creative fulfillment to show for his efforts.

David and I quickly discovered that we had many things in common. One was that we were both bursting with brilliant ideas for deep and meaningful novels that we couldn't sell. We hit it off well enough that we arranged to meet for coffee a few days later. I did not mention to him that I don't drink coffee. I couldn't see myself saying "Let's meet for herbal tea" to a guy who wrote books about mountain men.

Our rendezvous took place at a Denny's restaurant up by the freeway interchange. We sat in a booth amid the aroma of bacon, eggs, coffee, and herbal tea. We were soon ensconced in a fascinating and wide-ranging conversation.

Ninety minutes into the discussion, as I was starting to think about leaving, David asked what I thought about bigfeet. I told him what I tell everybody, what I told Brian, that believing in bigfeet is sort of like believing in God. You can't prove it absolutely, but you can never quite rule it out. And just when you think you *can* rule it out, something unexplainable happens.

That was when David told me something I hadn't known before.

"I'm a member of the International Society of Cryptozoology," he said. "Our purpose is to study undocumented and unverified animals. Bigfeet are one of the animals that interest us."

"Bigfeet interest a lot of people," I said.

"There are actually a couple dozen species we're trying to gather information on," David explained. "Not just bigfeet. We're interested in animals that have been sighted by hikers or hunters, or sometimes loggers, but which no wildlife biologist or 'official' type has ever seen. Animals nobody has ever captured, killed, or photographed. Most are little subspecies of field mice and stuff like that. They're almost all nocturnal."

"That makes sense," I said. "I've always wondered how scientists ever became aware of the existence of something like the ringtail, for example. Ringtails are completely nocturnal, very timid, and there aren't very many of them. I've sure never seen one. All I have is the word of biologists. What else is on your society's list?"

"Let's see. There's the California grizzly, and the . . ."

"What about black cougars?"

David leaned forward with considerable interest, looking a little skeptical but also excited.

"What do you know about black cougars?" he inquired.

"Are they on your list?"

"Absolutely. Reports of black cougars are considered more plausible than bigfoot reports, even though they don't occur nearly as often.

The animals seem to be confined entirely to the Trinity Alps Wilderness, where they're sighted once every four or five years, usually by backpackers traveling cross-country, away from the established trails. No Forest Service worker or scientist has ever seen one, and most don't even know about them. We think they are genetic aberrations from normal parents, like a reverse albino. But they could be a distinct variety or subspecies. Nobody knows for sure because we haven't seen enough of them."

"Well then," I said, "do I have a story for you."

PART 7

The evening following my meeting at Denny's with David Robbins, I excitedly called Brian Boothby to tell him what I'd just learned about black cougars. I figured he'd be extremely interested.

"You're crazy, Bernstein," said Brian after listening to my narrative. "I don't remember seeing any black cougars. The one we saw was tan. And believe me, I wouldn't forget something like that. Next you'll be telling me we saw a bigfoot on the hike."

I have no explanation for Brian's sudden memory lapse. However, I distinctly remember discussing the animal's coloration at length with Brian at the time of the sighting and arguing for hours about whether it was a black panther or merely an off-color cougar. He remembers none of that conversation and insists rather adamantly that all we saw was a regular old tan cougar.

I guess when you're dealing with mythical beasts, memory lapses can happen.

TO VISIT

The hike: Stuart Fork Trail, Trinity Alps Wilderness, Shasta-Trinity National Forest, Trinity Center, California

Distance: Fifteen miles (one-way) to Sapphire Lake

Directions: Take CA 3 north from Weaverville to Trinity Alps Road near the Stuart Fork Bridge. Follow Trinity Alps Road three miles to the Stuart Fork trailhead.

Mad Deer

PART 1

I suppose I should have taken it as a bad omen when Brian Boothby and I saw a rattlesnake at the turnoff to the Deer Creek Trail. We were in the center of northern California's Trinity Alps Wilderness, where the Deer Creek Trail branched off from the Stuart Fork Trail, eight miles from the Stuart Fork trailhead from which we had hiked the previous day.

But we barely noticed the snake. It wasn't very impressive, just a shy baby that warned us well in advance and did its best to get out of our way. The little guy quickly slithered off into the tall grass as we approached. We didn't pause or walk a wide arc around it or anything. We just kept on hiking up the trail.

I was too busy making wisecracks about the name of the trail we'd just turned onto to worry about bad omens or infant rattlers. The trail led to Deer Creek Valley, Deer Creek Camp, Deer Creek Lake, Deer Creek Mountain, and Deer Creek Pass—and of course Deer Creek.

Since deer are about the most harmless animal ever to tread the surface of the globe, Brian and I looked forward to a pleasant and uneventful couple days on the Deer Creek Trail. What could possibly happen on a path named for such a benign, passive, and boring creature as the ordinary, everyday, run-of-the-mill, dime-a-dozen, seen-one-seen-them-all, Pacific Northwest Columbian black-tailed deer?

What I did not mention to Brian was that although the rest of the world seemed smitten with the notion of adorable little Bambis, I always found them slightly annoying. Their passivity somehow struck a nerve. Every time I saw a deer flee in terror, as they invariably did, I felt a wave of disgust. I knew my reaction made no sense—that deer are wise to flee and are merely acting out their genetic programming. As nearly as I could figure, my hostility had to do with the passivity I occasionally saw in my own personality. It was probably all very Freudian.

We started up the Deer Creek Trail at about 4:00 in the afternoon. At that time of year, the end of June, it didn't get dark until after 9:00 pm. So we had plenty of daylight left. The only fly in the ointment of our itinerary was that we were both extremely tired after lugging back-packs for two days and twenty-four miles.

Our destination that evening was Deer Creek Camp. Most of the day had been taken up visiting Emerald and Sapphire Lakes, fifteen miles from the Stuart Fork trailhead and two of the most beautiful high-mountain lakes on the planet. No matter how the day might end, it had already gone down in my personal history as one of the most memorable.

According to the Forest Service map, the route ahead of us on the Deer Creek Trail was fairly daunting. Deer Creek Camp lay four miles distant. Beyond that, it was two miles, with a two-thousand-foot elevation gain, to Deer Lake and Deer Creek Pass, then four miles over Stonewall Pass, Little Stonewall Pass, and Red Mountain Pass, then a final six miles to the Stoney Ridge trailhead. The latter was one of the least used in the wilderness but we had dropped off a car there on our way to the Stuart Fork trailhead. All three passes exceeded 7,500 feet in elevation, and the trail's total length came to sixteen miles.

Almost from the first step, the Deer Creek Trail felt uncomfortable. For one thing, there was that rattlesnake at the trailhead. For another, there was the total absence of people. The Stuart Fork Trail was among the most popular paths in the Trinity Alps. Hiking the Stuart Fork was like hiking the hajj in Mecca. Among California wilderness aficiona-dos, the Stuart Fork Trail is legendary. As a result, it is decidedly not a haven for seekers of solitude. We ran into people every few minutes, most of them talkative and friendly, as someone on a once-in-a-lifetime outing ought to be.

But the sense of spooky loneliness evoked by the Deer Creek Trail wasn't just because we had the place to ourselves. I'd been the only hiker on hundreds of trails and almost always felt perfectly comfort-able. Deer Creek was different. It felt as though we were trespassing, as though everyone but us had the good sense to stay away.

"I don't like this place," I said to Brian.

"Neither do I," Brian admitted. "But we're tired and it's late. I'm sure we'll feel better after we stop for the night."

"I hope so," I said.

Something else that distinguished the Deer Creek Trail from the Stuart Fork Trail was the lack of trees. Meadows and open areas dotted many of the region's valleys, but they invariably alternated with forest stands, and it was the forests not the meadows that usually dominated. In contrast, Deer Creek Valley had no forests. Not even an occasional clump of pines. Slopes of cured-out grass pockmarked with low, spine-laden bushes extended from the creek to the craggy peaks on either side of the valley. And everywhere there was the sickening-sweet smell of snowbrush, a fairly ugly shrub whose leaves are sticky to the touch. During our late June visit, we would have expected the grass to be a brilliant emerald green, as it had been on the Stuart Fork, just one valley away. But it wasn't. It was yellow, dry, and apparently dead.

The trail itself wasn't that bad though. The general trend was uphill, but the rise was manageable. As we walked I identified for Brian the wildflower and brush species. In addition to grass and snowbrush, I pointed out Indian paintbrush, low delphinium, lupine, oxeye daisy, green manzanita, whitethorn ceanothus, and a couple dozen other species.

"I'm impressed," said Brian. "For a barren place, there sure are a lot of different wildflower and shrub species."

"Except for one," I replied. "I would have expected to run into tons of deerbrush ceanothus in a place like this. But so far, I haven't seen any at all."

PART 2

Deer Creek Camp was one of the loneliest and most beautiful places I have ever experienced. Even cynical old Brian was impressed. The approach started a half mile away, where the creek, the valley, the trail, and the defining ridge all made a 90-degree turn southward. Prior to the turn, these landmarks had all been oriented east to west. All Brian and I could see during our initial eastward march was Sawtooth Ridge to the north and an unnamed mountain slope to the south. At the southward bend, the quality of the vista ratcheted up several hundred degrees.

At the turn, Deer Creek's dramatic source popped into view like the opening curtain at a Broadway play. Three glorious mountains, one white, one black, and one red, lined up in a row at the valley head. The white summit, composed of granite, was 8,400-foot Gibson Peak, one of the highest in the Trinity Alps. The black schist mountain in the center was Deer Creek Mountain, while the mountain of red serpentinite was Siligo Peak.

Deer Creek Pass, the highest point on our route, lay in the gap between Gibson Peak and Deer Creek Mountain. The pass was approximately two miles distant and two thousand feet higher in elevation. It did not comfort us that we could see large patches of snow high up on the mountainside, level with the pass. We couldn't tell whether there was snow in the pass itself or not.

"Be sure to get a photo," Brian instructed as the three mountains began glowing red in the low-angled, late-afternoon light. I quickly complied. Twenty minutes later, our little valley was wrapped in shadow, even though it wouldn't be fully dark for another two and a half hours.

"That's some shot," I commented, pointing my brand new Nikon at the peaks and fiddling with the lens settings. "Maybe the best of the whole trip."

Deer Creek Camp occupied a large, open flat on the valley bottom with a stone fire ring and room for a couple tents. The first thing Brian and I did after I took the photo was sit down for a well-deserved rest. Or, I should say, we collapsed in exhaustion. It took nearly forty-five minutes to get up the energy to put up the tent and make dinner. There was no hurry though.

I dined on canned beef stew, trail mix, and a cold Pop-Tart. Brian treated himself to freeze-dried beef stroganoff. While we cooked on my little propane stove, I noticed a deer—a tiny, passive-looking doe—wandering around outside the camp, maybe five hundred feet away. At the time I thought it was kind of charming . . . and perfectly appropriate considering the name of the place.

"Wow," I said, "look at the deer."

"Cool," said Brian.

As we ate, the animal gradually moved in closer to us, almost to the edge of the campsite area.

"It's probably hungry," I said.

"Probably," said Brian. "But I read somewhere that you're not supposed to feed deer human food or it could poison them."

"I read the same thing," I said. That was when I noticed that there were now three deer outside our camp and that they had all moved in a little closer. I smiled and continued eating beef stew out of a can.

The next time I looked up, in response to a rustling in the bushes nearby, there were twenty deer at the edge of the camp, including four immense bucks. They were all staring at us. Even though the gallery of animal eyes sent a shiver down my neck, I was willing to give them the benefit of the doubt. These were deer, for heaven's sake, the world's most unthreatening mammal.

"Shoo!" I hollered, waving my arms in the air.

The deer scattered. If anything, they scattered a little too quickly. One instant, there were dozens of them milling around. The next instant, there were none.

"Good riddance," I said to Brian. "They were starting to bug me."

After dinner, Brian took a quick, soapless bath in the creek to relax, clean up, and cool off. I did the same thing when he was done. Brian used the creek to wash off the shirt he'd worn that day, which was drenched with perspiration. He figured to wear it the next day too. We saw no deer the entire time.

To dry the shirt, Brian stretched a clothesline between a bush and a dwarf, solitary pine tree. He draped the shirt over the clothesline, hoping it would be dry by morning. By now the shadow of the adjacent mountain ridge had worked its way completely across the valley. It was about 8:30 p.m., which meant we had perhaps half an hour of daylight left.

After getting dressed again, Brian and I sat around the fire ring, nibbling on trail mix. As we sat, a large buck with massive, six-pronged antlers suddenly appeared. This time it was inside the camp. It was the first deer we'd seen in a while and the first to actually enter the camp. The animal made a beeline for Brian's shirt, which it began chewing on.

I thought the deer munching on Brian's shirt was funny. Brian did not.

"It probably wants salt," I explained. "Deer have a huge craving for salt. It's like cocaine to them."

"Well, it can't have my salt," Brian said as the animal continued dining on his shirt. And to the deer, Brian yelled, "Scram! Get outta here!" It did not have the same effect as when I'd shooed the animals off earlier. Brian's words went completely unheeded. Finally he picked up a small stick and tossed it at the preoccupied beast, hitting it lightly on its flank.

The deer took off all right. But it took Brian's shirt with it. We looked all over for the shirt that evening and searched again briefly the next morning. But we never did find it.

Following the attempt to locate Brian's shirt, we spent the last few minutes of daylight enjoying the remoteness and beauty of our campsite and trying to relax.

As we sat, the deer gradually returned—all twenty of them. At least that was how many I estimated. They were constantly moving around, so an accurate census was difficult. For all I knew, there were fifty deer. Or a thousand. They kept walking, silently, around and around the campsite, like the army of Joshua surrounding Jericho before sounding the trumpets and moving in for the kill.

I tried to assure myself, and Brian, that the animals were just deer, doing what deer do. All they probably wanted was salt, which we did not have, or food, which we could not give them in quantity.

As the deer circled, their ring grew gradually smaller and tighter. They would move closer and closer until they were at the very edge of

Gibson Peak, Deer Creek Mountain, and Siligo Peak from Deer Creek Camp

the fifty-foot-diameter area that made up the campsite. Then one of us, Brian or myself, would holler at them to go away and they'd back off a couple hundred feet. A few minutes later they'd be circling again, and the noose would again draw tighter and tighter.

And then it was time for Brian and me to turn in for the night.

PART 3

Despite our extreme fatigue, for the second consecutive night neither Brian nor I slept very well. We went to bed shortly past dark, after shooing the animals off several more times. It was a warm night, so I stripped down to my underpants and T-shirt. Brian, a little more formal than I, had brought pajamas.

Immediately before I sealed us into Brian's two-person nylon dome tent for the night, I urinated on the ground fifteen feet away, near some bitter cherry bushes. It was the closest thing the site offered to a restroom. While I was at it, I yelled at the deer again, which had become part of our routine. I couldn't see them in the dark, but I could hear rustling in the bushes not far away. I hoped they would eventually decide to go to bed and leave us alone. Or wander off and haunt some other hapless campers.

More likely, Brian and I figured as we lay inside the tent, the deer would either circle all night, start nosing around the camp looking for food as soon as we disappeared into the tent, or turn into demons and eat us when the moon rose.

None of the three scenarios was very conducive to sleep, which we desperately needed. The idea of toting my backpack over three snow-covered, 7,500-foot passes without having slept for two nights in a row was as terrifying as any imagined deer scenario.

After I returned to the tent from the bitter cherry bush, Brian went outside and urinated. Then he too climbed inside and zippered the door shut.

Then we were alone, just Brian and I and the warm wilderness night. And twenty demented, unpredictable deer. My down mummy sleeping bag, which offered protection to 30 below zero, proved way too hot. I tried crawling inside it briefly but soon found myself sweating like a wrung-out sponge.

Sweating was bad, not only because it made it harder to sleep but also because the presence of salt inside the tent might excite the deer.

Brian also lay on top of his sleeping bag rather than climb inside.

"Maybe the deer will react to our urine the way they do to coyote or cougar urine," I suggested. Coyotes and cougars are territorial predators that urinate to mark the boundaries of their domain for other predators. Nonpredatory animals such as deer show the utmost respect for these markers.

For a long time after going to bed, Brian and I didn't hear or see anything except an occasional rustling in the bushes, which could just as easily have been a breeze as a deer. Lying on top of my sleeping bag and looking up through a small mosquito-netting window in the ceiling, I could see the Milky Way, an exceptionally mundane name for the spiral arm of our celestial galaxy.

Brian and I talked for a while about the day's activities, our wives, and our jobs. We did not mention the deer, possibly on the theory that if we refused to acknowledge them, they would disappear.

For a while the strategy seemed to work. Early in the evening, I came within a hair of dozing off. Then the moon came up. It was a bright, full moon, almost the intensity of daylight. The kind of moon that drives lunatics and vampires to full fury.

I don't know if it was the rising moon that touched off the deer or not. All I know is that with the moonrise, anything that moved outside the tent was projected in shadow on the feeble layer of nylon that protected us from outside threat.

I first noticed the moving shadows when a gentle breeze shook the scraggly pine tree. Looking up at the tent wall through the darkness, the shadowy motion resembled the claw hands of a witch grasping at our tiny shelter. The sight made my stomach lurch and triggered a brief squirt of adrenaline until I figured out what it was.

A while later, when the rustling noises outside began increasing in frequency and volume, I attributed them to the wind—until I saw the shadow of a deer on the side of the tent, projected to twice the size of a grizzly bear. This time there was no question: Unlike the pine branch witch, this definitely was no tree branch.

Sweat or no sweat, I climbed into my sleeping bag and pulled it over my head. I did not mention to Brian what I'd seen. I hadn't heard from him in a while, and if he was asleep I saw no reason to disturb him. On glimpsing the deer shadow, however, I knew that my own night's sleep was pretty much shot.

"Did you see that?" Brian whispered.

"Yeah. Our friends are back."

"Get the hell out of here!" Brian hollered at them. And the shadow dutifully trotted off.

But not for long.

As they had done during dinner, the deer shadows began circling our camp in an endless procession, drawing gradually closer. Hollering caused them to back off at first, but they gradually got used to it and began ignoring us. After a while the circle around our tent was so tight, we could hear the deer brushing against the nylon with a soft swoosh.

This went on for hours. We debated packing up and leaving but decided against it. We might find our way out of the valley and up to Deer Creek Lake by the light of the full moon. However, the tent, as frail as it was, represented our only defense. Once outside, there was no telling what might happen.

At around 2:00 a.m., lying huddled in my sleeping bag watching the shadows go around and around and around, I reached my limit. Rage, fatigue, frustration, and confusion welled up inside me.

"GET THE HELL OUT OF HERE!" I screamed. I jumped out of my sleeping bag, rose to my knees, and began pounding the side of the tent with my fists. "GET OUT, GET OUT, GET OUT!" Once I started, I couldn't stop. I was vaguely aware of Brian trying to calm me down, but it was just too much. I continued yelling for ten minutes.

Fortunately, Brian's tent was pretty strong. I came close to knocking it over or ripping it, but in the end no harm was done. I only wished my pounding had made a little more noise. It made virtually none, although I'm pretty sure that a couple of my blows had contacted the side of a deer.

"Feel better?" Brian asked when I finally calmed down.

"I guess," I whispered.

I couldn't say whether the deer ever returned that night. They sure didn't hang around long during my little outburst. When it was over, I fell asleep within minutes. According to Brian, they did not return.

I was glad to have helped out.

Brian and I didn't talk much that morning. We woke up around 7:00, gobbled down a quick breakfast, packed our belongings, looked around one last time for the shirt, and departed. Or I should say, got the hell out.

The deer not only completely disregarded our line of urine but we also observed that every spot where Brian and I relieved ourselves had been pawed at and disturbed. One explanation for the deer's lack of respect for our line was that they had become confused as to the established order of things, wherein humans are normally the predators and deer are the prey. More likely, the deer had eaten the urine for its salt content. Those fellows sure did fancy their salt.

A half hour after waking up, we started up the steep trail to Deer Creek Lake and Deer Creek Pass. I was still pretty tired and not looking forward to the massive expenditure of energy I knew would be required that day, but I felt confident I'd make it.

After a while we reached a point high above the valley beside a beautiful spot where Deer Creek cascaded down the gray rock face. Pausing for the first time to look back, we could see Deer Creek Camp below us in the distance.

I'd estimate that there were a hundred deer milling around the spot where we'd camped. From our vantage point, they looked more like buffalo on the Great Plains. It was probably my imagination, but it seemed to me as though the deer were doing a dance, presumably in celebration of having driven out the two intruders who refused to give them salt or food.

PART 4

Deer Lake was as lovely as anticipated—a shallow, clear, ten-acre pool in a small, smooth, treeless basin surrounded by the three jagged, multicolored peaks. What I liked most about Deer Creek Lake was that it completely lacked the mystical aura, the feeling of otherworldliness, that we'd felt in Deer Creek Valley. The universe, to our great relief, felt normal again.

There were actually people at Deer Creek Lake. A bunch of them. They were there because the side trail from Long Canyon joined the Deer Creek Trail just over the pass. Also, the popular Four Lakes Loop, which Brian and I decided not to visit, took off at Deer Lake. It was only a six-mile stroll from the Long Canyon trailhead to Deer Creek Lake. Brian and I had hiked fifteen miles from the Stuart Fork Trail parking lot to reach Deer Lake, not counting the twelve-mile side trip to Emerald and Sapphire Lakes.

Despite the access to Deer Lake provided by Long Canyon, I was surprised to encounter so much humanity. I just wished some of them had shown up at Deer Creek Camp the previous night.

Nobody to whom Brian and I spoke at Deer Creek Lake had been to Deer Creek Camp or had the slightest intention of ever going there. I got the impression that the other hikers thought we were a little screwy for taking the route we took, which they regarded as a godforsaken trail to nowhere.

We managed to negotiate all the passes, scrambling in the snow at each one, and arrived at the Stoney Ridge trailhead without further incident, happy but exhausted. Especially exhausted.

A few days later I anxiously picked up my six boxes of slides from the photo processor. Soon after, alone in the living room with the shades drawn, I projected them onto the wall. The Emerald and Sapphire Lake shots were sublime, as were Echo Lake and Siligo Meadow. The Deer Lake shots were delightful.

The only photos that did not live up to expectations were the Deer Creek Camp shots. The first time through, I forgot to look for the slide that Brian and I had predicted would be the best of the entire trip. I had to back up and look a second time before figuring out which photo it was. The photo failed to capture the dramatic steepness of the mountain rise, and the glorious late-afternoon colors were all washed out.

I couldn't find any shots at all with deer in them.

A few days after returning home, I phoned the Shasta-Trinity National Forest headquarters in Redding, California, which is in charge of the Trinity Alps Wilderness, and spoke with their resident wildlife biologist about the Stuart Fork and Deer Creek Trails.

To my question about unusual deer behavior at Deer Creek Camp, the guy replied, "I've camped at Deer Creek Camp and have never seen any deer there at all. The legend is that they all vanished fifty years ago when a gang of poachers, right at Deer Creek Camp, massacred over two hundred deer in a few hours. Nobody has seen a single deer in Deer Creek Valley since then."

TO VISIT

The hike: Deer Creek Trail, Trinity Alps Wilderness, Shasta-Trinity National Forest, Trinity Center, California

Length: Sixteen miles (one-way), plus an eight-mile hike to the trailhead

Directions: From Weaverville, California, on US 299, take CA 3 north to Trinity Alps Road near the Stuart Fork Bridge. Follow Trinity Alps Road three miles west to the Stuart Fork trailhead. Hike the Stuart Fork Trail eight miles to the junction with the Deer Creek Trail. Exit either via the Long Canyon trailhead or the Stoney Ridge trailhead. The latter route takes you past Echo Lake, one of the most exquisite lakes in the wilderness.

/2

Black Butte Miracle

PART 1

It's a recurrent theme in my life: Whatever I like, my children, bless their evil little hearts, instinctively hate. And whatever I fanatically love, my children despise. It's a fundamental law of nature, a template for Creation.

This has nowhere been truer than in my abortive efforts over the years to take my children hiking. I hike a lot and frequently observe other parents hiking with young children. The families always seem so happy, their kids marching proudly along with their little backpacks and water bottles.

Hiking would appear to be the perfect family bonding activity. It's a fantastic opportunity to instill all sorts of wonderful values about nature and conservation. As an added bonus, you get your kids away, however briefly, from TV and automobiles and electronics and other terrible influences. It's just you and your beloved offspring, their adoring eyes looking to you for leadership and instruction.

At least that's how it seems to be with everyone else's children.

My children, alas, were whiners when I took them hiking. Had they whined because they were tired or hungry, I could have understood it. Had they whined because they'd stoically worked their sweet little buns off and deserved a rest, I'd have been delighted to accommodate them. But they didn't. They whined because they could. Because they knew it irritated me. They started whining with the very first step and continued until the blessed relief of our parked car finally came into view.

"Daddy, I'm tired." (Never "Mommy, I'm tired.")

"Daddy, this is too hard."

"Are we almost there, Daddy?"

"Can we go home now, Daddy?"

"Daddy, my feet hurt."

"Daddy, I'm thirsty."

"Daddy, I have to go to the bathroom."

184

"Carry me, Daddy."

In fairness, the above was only true when my children, my three beautiful, angelic daughters, were little. Things improved considerably when they reached their teens and adulthood. Adult to adult, they love hitting the dirt defile with their doddering dad. Or at least they now have the good sense to say they do, whether it's true or not. But in their preteen years, they were miserable company best left at home.

In retrospect, if I'd had any brains, I'd have done just that—left them at home. But I kept passing all those families on the trail—the ones straight out of the family-togetherness commercials you see on TV—and I rationalized that if those people could manipulate their children into being enthusiastic and cooperative, there was no reason I couldn't. I was a patient, loving parent, and for the most part, my children did not hate my company. Inspired by the passing families, I'd bravely try again. Only to be disappointed yet again.

I never expected their gratitude or anything. I just hoped that after at least one of the outings, I'd get the feeling when we arrive home that they just might possibly have had a good time. Or at least that they didn't have an awful time. Alas, even on the rare occasions when they didn't whine every second of the hike, I never sensed that they'd had much fun.

Over the years I developed several techniques, some rather pathetic, to counter the whining. When the kids were little, I would agree to carry them for a specified number of minutes if they would walk for a specified number of minutes without griping. As they got bigger, the carrying time diminished and the time required to earn the reward grew longer. After age seven or so, when they got up into the forty-to-fifty-pound weight range, carrying them even a short distance became out of the question.

When they got older, a popular gambit involved bribery. I'd pay them for not whining, usually so much per minute. Their earnings would drop to zero the instant they said anything negative. They almost never ended up with any money.

Somewhere along the line, for reasons I can't explain, some of my love of the outdoors managed to sink in with the two older children, Jennifer and Sara. Sara, in fact, wrote a chapter in one of my hiking guidebooks. It was very well written and a completely different perspective from anything I ever wrote.

All of which brings us to Anna, my youngest child, born when I was almost forty. Early on I was determined that Anna, of all my children, would be the heir to the Bernstein hiking legacy, that I'd find a way to make her love hiking without having to wait until she was grown up.

The dream started to fall apart the very first time I took Anna hiking, when she was just six months old. My wife and I hiked to the top of Mount Baldy, a small peak just outside the town where we lived. I carried Anna in an infant's backpack seat. In addition to constant fussing and squirming, Anna spent every instant of the trip pulling my hair, gouging her fingers into my ears, or poking my eyes out.

As it turned out, that was a good day in the saga of Anna the Hiker. As a hiker she was even more whiney and exasperating than her sisters. That's why I was shocked when, during a drive through northern California, Anna actually asked me to take her hiking. She was ten at the time and had never asked to be taken hiking before. Most of the time she went to great lengths to avoid being taken hiking. In fact, none of my children had ever asked to be taken hiking. Not once, ever.

At the time of Anna's startling request, we were heading south on I-5 near Mount Shasta. Shasta is an immense, solitary volcano, the major landmark of the California Far North and one of the world's most beautiful mountains.

Where the interstate crests atop a small pass, a large, barren, steep-sided cinder cone rises almost straight up from the side of the road. The formation is called Black Butte and is 6,200 feet high, which is 2,500 feet higher than the freeway but nearly eight thousand feet lower than Mount Shasta, five miles away.

Something in Black Butte sparked Anna's imagination. Maybe it reminded her of a movie she'd seen on the Disney Channel. Maybe it was that she could not only see the entire mountain but also the entire trail from the freeway. Maybe it was because from the backseat of the car, the path didn't appear that difficult. Whatever her motivation, whatever momentary spell came over her, I quickly agreed to take her.

Besides, I'd never been on the Black Butte Trail and always thought it looked pretty interesting. With its barren volcanic starkness, to me Black Butte evoked images of the terrible wasteland in the realm of the Mordor, in the last chapters of the *Lord of the Rings* trilogy.

"Please, Daddy," Anna said. "Pleeeeease take me up Black Butte."

Anna and I agreed to return in a couple of weeks. It was mid-June at the time, and Black Butte, unlike most other high-mountain trails in the region, was just about snow free. So there was nothing to stop us.

At least nothing that I could have anticipated.

PART 2

Good hiking shoes for children are hard to find. Lots of kids' shoes look like hiking shoes, but they're too often all show and no substance, designed to make youngsters and adults think they've purchased the real thing. Not that there aren't excellent children's hiking shoes to be had. There are lots of them. But when it comes to buying shoes for their children, too many parents are reluctant to spend money because the items will be outgrown in a few months. So they end up purchasing cheapies that look like real hiking shoes but may not be.

If I've learned anything about hiking with children, it is that shelling out a little extra money on shoes is an excellent investment. You needn't purchase a fancy boot either. A good, well-made, well-fitting gym shoe, walking shoe, or cross-trainer will do nicely, although athletic shoes can be even more expensive than hiking boots.

When Anna and I left for our eagerly anticipated ascent of Black Butte, on a sunny October day with the temperature in the sixties, the last thing I worried about was her shoes. She had on a pair of simple, well-broken-in, kids' cloth-top sneakers. The kind she always wore. I had on the usual leather-top sneakers that I always wore. My shoes cost eighty bucks. Hers cost eight. I hadn't anticipated that her shoes would become a problem.

Following directions on the official *Shasta-Trinity National Forest Recreational Opportunity Guide* for the Black Butte Trail, I easily located the little trailhead parking area and Anna and I started walking. After a brief, level jaunt through the woods, we emerged on the flank of the volcanic cone, on the section of trail seen from the freeway. The segment was very steep, rocky, and exposed.

It wasn't quite as exposed as I thought it would be, though. As seen from a car on the freeway, the impression of Black Butte is of a giant gravel pile devoid of vegetation and hostile to all life. Up close the steep gravel slopes support a fair quantity of pine trees, sun-loving shrubs, and wildflowers. There are more than enough trees to land you into the shade every now and then.

Anna, bless her heart, didn't start complaining until we were almost one and a half miles into the two-and-a-half-mile hike to the summit, three-quarters of the way up the long, steep traverse of the mountain's main flank. I'd purposely gone very slowly to that point, so Anna wouldn't tire too quickly. I figured if I beat her to the punch by suggesting rest breaks, she'd have less to gripe about. We'd stopped and rested at least twice when the complaining began. That's not counting short breaks.

As we neared the end of the long initial pitch, Anna started in. As it turned out, her complaint was very legitimate.

"Daddy," my beautiful young offspring announced in an angelic voice, "my shoes hurt."

"You mean your feet hurt," I corrected. "Shoes are inanimate objects that have no feeling."

"Don't be stupid, Daddy. You know what I mean."

After a few more steps and several dozen more complaints, I stopped to have a look. None of my usual "brave-soldier-stiff-upper-lip" exhortations had worked (they never did), and she seemed genuinely uncomfortable.

She explained that the seams on the back of her tennis shoes were rubbing on the back of her heels. On inspection, I observed that there were no blisters yet but that the area in question on her cute little feet was indeed an angry red. If I'd brought my trusty Buck knife (which had been mysteriously lost or stolen five years earlier), I'd have simply sliced off the offending shoe part. But I didn't have a trusty Buck knife.

It was actually kind of a grim situation. We were considerably more than halfway up the trail, so even if we turned back, Anna was facing a lengthy trek and a situation that could only get worse.

I stood there trying to act reassuring and in control, trying to figure out what to do. But I couldn't think of a thing. Finally I decided to check my pockets to see if anything therein inspired an idea. It was a long shot, because I don't usually carry much in my pockets. A little bit of cash, a wallet, and a watch—that's about it.

My hand landed on my checkbook, in the back pocket of my jeans. I wasn't sure why I'd brought the checkbook. Normally I leave it in the car because of the extra weight. I've never once written a check while on a hike.

Grinning triumphantly and basking in the blinding aura of my brilliance, I deftly removed the check pad and register from the plastic cover. Then I ripped the cover in half, lengthwise along the fold. I had to bite it to get a tear going but it eventually came apart pretty evenly.

I inserted one half of the check book cover in each of Anna's shoes, lining the inserts up so they reached from under the back of her foot, up the rear of her shoe, perfectly and comfortably covering the part that was rubbing against her heel.

There were no further complaints from Anna, about either hurting shoes or hurting feet. The only problem was that I had to adjust the inserts every five or ten minutes because they kept trying to either work their way out of the shoe or slide off center. A small price to pay.

Not long after the shoe incident, we arrived at the part of the trail not visible from the interstate. Having surmounted the peak's conical flank, the path made a sharp switchback and then entered a narrow canyon between the main summit and two small subpeaks. There was almost no vegetation in the canyon, except for a few brave saxifrages (rock-breaking wildflowers). Mostly the canyon contained giant heaps of ash, pumice, and lava rock in a brilliant color display ranging from pink to purple to gray to white. It was a terrific place, if you like multicolored rocks and don't like plants.

The little canyon posed few impediments to my rapidly tiring child. On the far end, the path made a second switchback and began climbing the mountain's ultimate summit. This final section was much steeper than any segment heretofore, but I could tell from the map that we were less than half a mile from the top.

At the second switchback, Anna and I had a long rest and a long debate. She wanted to turn back, and I wanted to continue to the summit. After much persuasion, to my great relief Anna agreed to give it one more shot. So we plodded on, Anna dragging herself painfully with every step. I was beginning to poop out myself, but I didn't tell Anna that.

The last part of the trail approaching the summit passed through some sheltered areas containing lots of pine trees and therefore lots of shade. Then, finally—grimy, sweaty, out of breath, and exhausted—we arrived on top.

To our surprise, the summit teemed with hiking humanity, even though we hadn't seen a single other person during the rest of the trek. Since there was only room for one person at a time on the summit, we had to wait our turn.

The actual peak was a small, steep-sided rock outcrop about three feet square. The view was tremendous. You could see Mount Shasta, Mount McLoughlin, Mount Eddy, the entire Marble Mountain range, most of the Trinity Alps, and Castle Crags. Not to mention the entire length of I-5 from Siskiyou Summit in Oregon to somewhere north of Redding.

I took a picture of Anna at the summit, and she took one of me. She looked adorable in her long brown pigtails, T-shirt, shorts, eight-dollar tennis shoes, and little day pack. I made a point to elaborately congratulate Anna on her accomplishment. I told her to smile for the photo, and although she tried valiantly, she just didn't have a smile in her.

I understood.

"Do we have to hike all the way back down, Daddy?" she asked.

"I'm afraid so," I replied.

"I'm not sure I can make it."

"You'll make it. It's much easier than the hike up. Besides, what choice do you have?"

PART 3

"Couldn't you call a helicopter or something?" Anna suggested as we started on the journey back to the car.

"Wouldn't you know it?" I replied. "I plum forgot my two-way radio."

That was in the days before people started carrying cell phones on hikes, in the distant pioneer era of the early 1990s.

I explained to my daughter that even if we called a helicopter, there would be no place for it to land. And even if it could land, they'd charge us thousands of dollars. So our best plan was to face the music and get it over with.

As I explained all this, I tried to walk as fast as possible. Anna seemed to do better when I engaged her in conversation than when

I left her to her private thoughts. Her private thoughts all seemed to center on how much her feet hurt.

I could tell, though, that her complaints weren't idle and that she was genuinely exhausted. I was well aware that my daughter was not an active or athletic type. That's why I'd been trying to go slowly and take it easy. I briefly tried carrying her, but she weighed seventy pounds; if I did that for too long, I would be the one needing a rescue helicopter.

The truth was that no amount of rest short of several hours in bed would resuscitate poor little Anna or restore her spirits. Unfortunately, it was starting to get late, and we didn't have time for many more lengthy respites.

Despite her complaints, Anna managed to plod on somehow until we arrived at the exact same spot where I'd put the inserts into her shoes. They were still doing their job, by the way. Rather well, considering. I'd gotten so adept at shoving them back into her shoes every few minutes that I could do it without either of us breaking stride. Anna hadn't complained about her feet since I'd constructed the inserts. Thank heaven for small miracles.

At the windswept pine where I'd worked the miracle of the checkbook inserts, Anna stopped, sat down, and announced that she wasn't going any farther; that this was the end of the line, that she'd had it. She informed me that she was fully prepared to spend the rest of her life at this spot regardless of the consequences. She made it clear that she wasn't just talking about a long rest either. She was not taking another step, no matter what I did or said.

"So there," she concluded, with her arms folded in front of her and the most singularly determined look I'd ever seen on her face. She was not kidding.

I had no idea what to do. I wanted the trip to be fun and memorable. If I yelled, argued, or forced her, it would ruin the experience. And yet we couldn't just stay there. Spending the night was out of the question because even though it was a warm late-spring day, nights could get pretty chilly that time of year at that elevation. Besides, we had no food left. Not to mention my wife would get frantic if we failed to return home.

I decided just to wait, hoping that once Anna got a little rest, she'd realize how foolish she was being and start walking again. Twenty min-

Anna, refusing to budge on Black Butte

utes later, though, she was as resolute as ever. And I was getting angry but trying not to show it.

That's when the second miracle occurred. In all my years of hiking, over hundreds of pathways, I'd never seen anything like it from a hiking trail.

I first observed the miracle out of the corner of my eye and didn't think much about it. I hadn't noticed it at all on the way up. As it was, it took a few minutes for the vision to penetrate my awareness. Yet there it was, an aura of light, a shimmering yellow rainbow in the distance at the base of the mountain. It beckoned to us like the star in the east had beckoned to the Magi.

The Golden Arches: It was the McDonald's restaurant in Weed.

"I'll be darned," I said, trying to sound nonchalant. "You can see McDonald's from here. I've never seen a McDonald's from a trail before. It must be a sign."

"Of course it's a sign. It's a McDonald's sign. I want to go to McDonald's. Can we, Daddy, when we're done hiking?"

"Of course. It's only a ten-minute drive from the trailhead."

"Goody. Thank you, Daddy."

With a perfect child's grin, Anna bolted ahead of me down the trail, like a jackrabbit in a headlight.

We quickly made it to the car, with me praising the Almighty Creator of the Universe, and the Golden Arches, with every step. Soon after, Anna was feasting on a Happy Meal in air-conditioned, tile-floored comfort, and I was enjoying a Filet-O-Fish and a strawberry shake.

PART 4

Anna became a vegetarian soon after the McDonald's episode, although she claims that the Weed McDonald's had nothing to do with it. Still, whenever I tell the story of Black Butte in Anna's presence, she always closes with the comment, "I can't believe we ended up at McDonald's."

The caveat came three days later. Back then I used to write up some of my hikes for the little Grant Pass newspaper. They used a photo of Anna with my story, the one where she was sitting on the Black Butte summit with I-5 far below in the distance. If you had a magnifying glass, you could barely make out the Weed McDonald's just over her right shoulder.

Everyone in Anna's class at school, including her teacher, made a big deal out of the article and photo. A lot of people did comment, though, that while it was an adorable picture, Anna didn't look very happy.

"She wasn't very happy at the time," I explained to them. "But she cheered up later on."

TO VISIT

The hike: Black Butte Trail, Shasta-Trinity National Forest, Mount Shasta City, California

Distance: Two and a half miles (one-way)

Directions: Take I-5 in northern California to exit 738 for central Mount Shasta City. Proceed through town, following signs to the Everitt Memorial Highway (up West Lake, left on North Mount Shasta Blvd., right on East Alma, right on Rockfellow, and left on Everitt). At mile 2.2 on the

Everitt Memorial Highway, turn left onto gravel Penny Pines Road (CR 41N18). Penny Pines makes a hard left after 0.1 mile and a 90-degree right one mile later. After another 0.3 mile, go right at the fork; continue for 1.2 miles and turn left at the power line. It is then another 0.7 mile to the trailhead parking area. Don't worry—there are signs.

For the Weed McDonald's, get back on I-5 and continue north for seven miles to the first Weed exit (exit 745).

13

A Voice Crying in the Wilderness

PART 1

This story is about a conversation I once had with God and about a lesson God taught me about patience. The irony is that I'm not even sure I believe in God. And yet, from time to time, God talks to me and I talk to God. That is possible because of what I call "Paradox Theory," a theory I invented.

The Basic Rule of Paradox Theory is this: "For every truth in the universe, its exact opposite is also true." Admittedly, this theory is not very useful in applying scientific method or understanding most Western religions. However, Kabalistic Jews, Buddhists, Hindus, Taoists, Native Americans, Animists, and Earth Mothers, for the most part, find it perfectly logical. Or at least a few of them do.

Of course there is a prime corollary to the Basic Rule, which states that the Basic Rule also applies to the Basic Rule. But we won't go into that.

The point is that it is possible to believe in God with all your heart and soul and at the same time not believe in God, with all the force and conviction of a die-hard skeptic. I submit, in fact, that a lot of people regard God exactly as I just described, although most will not admit their skepticism.

And no, I do not hear voices when God talks to me. At least not audible voices. Later in the story, when I use phrases like "God said," I really mean that thoughts were formed in my head. Sort of.

PART 2

The deepest canyon in the United States is called Hells Canyon. It is two thousand feet deeper than the Grand Canyon, which is only one mile deep. Unfortunately, visiting Hells Canyon is far more difficult than a trip to the Grand Canyon. Hells Canyon occupies a remote stretch of the Snake River along the Idaho-Oregon border.

When I say "remote," I'm not kidding. Hat Point, the only spot on the canyon rim accessible by car, is reached by a twenty-four-mile-long dirt road full of ruts, steep grades, narrow twists, turns, bumps, grinds, and bottomless drop-offs.

I'd wanted to see Hells Canyon ever since I first heard of it in college in Michigan in the late 1960s. But somehow, despite living in Oregon for twenty years, I never made it. I especially liked the idea of driving six hundred miles without leaving the state. Gold Hill, where I live, is located in the state's extreme southwest corner. Hat Point occupies a mountaintop in the state's extreme northeast corner.

My wife, Patricia, and I finally made it to Hat Point in October 1987. Back then we went on road trips all the time. The problem on every trip was (and still is) that I have a touch of Attention Deficit Hyperactivity Disorder (ADHD) that makes me impatient and easily stressed.

On this particular journey, I planned to leave at 7:00 a.m. and arrive in La Grande, the nearest city to Hat Point, at around 6:00 p.m., with short visits to the Painted Hills and John Day Fossil Beds. Pat, however, managed to putter around until 7:20. My goal was to arrive in La Grande while there were still motel rooms available. When I travel, I get a schedule fixed in my head, and I am never comfortable until I arrive at my destination and know everything is all right.

"Will you relax," my wife kept saying over and over. "You're ruining the trip with all your rushing."

I nearly panicked when a carefully selected shortcut through the Blue Mountains from John Day to La Grande turned out to take much longer than I had estimated. We lost nearly twenty more minutes, in addition to the twenty minutes we lost at the beginning of the trip and the forty-five minutes we lost at a gift shop in Mitchell, near the Painted Hills.

We pulled into La Grande at 5:30 p.m., a half hour earlier than my targeted arrival time. I don't know how that happened. We departed for the Wallowa Valley, Hells Canyon, and Hat Point the next morning.

Somewhere along the route from La Grande to Joseph, we entered the magnificent Wallowa Valley and the Wallowa Mountains came into view, abruptly rising up like the Front Range of the Colorado Rockies. Deep glacial canyons cut the range, with old lateral moraines appearing as huge elongated gravel piles spilling out onto the flat valley floor.

The Wallowas are considered the most rugged peaks in Oregon. They rise to 9,832 feet, with several peaks over 9,500 feet. The Wallowa and Blue Mountains are the only ranges of the Rocky Mountains to enter Oregon.

PART 3

From Wallowa Lake, outside Joseph, we drove forty miles up a canyon lined with brown volcanic rimrock. A stream called Little Sheep Creek ran along the canyon bottom. The road took us to the tiny village of Imnaha. There we started up the dreaded twenty-four miles of gravel and dirt to Hat Point. The road wasn't nearly as bad as rumored. It had a few rough spots, especially near the beginning, but many back roads where I live are far worse.

For the first seventeen miles, the road from Imnaha to Hat Point peered down into the canyon of the Imnaha River, of which Little Sheep Creek is a tributary. The Imnaha Canyon is spectacular in its own right, with the Wallowas rising on the other side. Were it not dramatically overshadowed by the adjacent Hells Canyon, Imnaha Canyon would rank among Oregon's most scenic drives.

Beyond mile seventeen the road arrived at the top of a sort of mesa, leveled off, and began a broad, 180-degree sweep around to the Hells Canyon side. Supposedly that's where the real scenery lay. Not that there was anything wrong with the Imnaha/Wallowa side.

I couldn't wait to get to the Hells Canyon side, even though Pat kept telling me to slow down. Personally, I thought thirty to forty miles per hour was plenty cautious. But she wanted me to go no more than five miles an hour. The road was very narrow and the drop-offs were frighteningly steep, with no guardrails and a long, long way to the bottom. But I was in a hurry, and I've never been much good at going slowly. As the road finally made its way around to the Snake River and Hells Canyon side of the rim, Pat and I grew more and more excited.

There was one slight problem. On the Hells Canyon side of the rim, the canyon was filled to the brim with dense, white fog. It had snowed in the Wallowas the day before, and the weather remained blustery and overcast. Since the elevation at Hat Point was 6,900 feet, fog and lack of visibility could eventually turn out to be the least of our problems.

At mile fourteen, with ten miles still to go, it began snowing. It snowed on and off all the way to Hat Point, mostly in the form of flurries that, to our relief, didn't stick to the ground.

We pulled into the small gravel Hat Point parking lot feeling exceedingly grateful to have made it. Our only concern was that thus far, we hadn't seen the slightest trace of Hells Canyon.

Hat Point turned out to be a lovely little flat with a fire lookout tower and a short trail leading through the woods to an observation deck. The setting was a grassy meadow dotted with artistically placed clumps of subalpine fir and mountain hemlock. Both are high-elevation trees adapted to biting wind, bitter cold, and tons of snow.

I poked around taking pictures of the lookout while Pat walked down to the observation deck—a little wooden patio with a split-rail fence around it, glued to the canyon rim. When I finally walked the three-hundred-foot trail to the observation deck, she was on her way back to the car to get warm. It had stopped snowing by then, but it was still windy and cold.

"Don't waste your time," my wife warned. "The canyon is completely fogged in and you can't see a thing."

My heart sank as I arrived at the observation deck and confirmed that she was correct. White mist swirled everywhere, hanging heavily in the frigid, damp air. The view of the canyon was limited to a few feet of gray lava rock on either side of the platform.

I felt like crying. After eighteen years and six hundred miles, I could not permit my quest to go unfulfilled. I had to see Hells Canyon. I just had to.

Despite my stoic determination, I felt discouraged. The thick, heavy fog appeared to have settled in for an extended duration and was not about to lift anytime soon. Short of suddenly acquiring X-ray vision, or waiting a week, I could think of no reasonable solution to the problem.

Then, for no apparent reason, a sentence from the *Old Testament* popped into my head. Now you must understand that I am not a religious person. I am certainly not a *Bible*-quoting type.

The quote that popped into my head was this: "Keep your mind on the Lord." I looked it up when I got home and found that it was from Isaiah 26:3.

It seemed like a reasonable suggestion.

"How about it, God?" I said out loud. "Will you help me out?"

Almost immediately after I made my short request, a peacefulness descended on me. And a feeling of absolute confidence that the fog would lift shortly.

I paced back and forth on the platform gathering my will and strength, then I reared up like Moses at the shore of the Red Sea.

"OK, God," I commanded, "part the fog."

I gestured my mightiest Charlton Heston gesture. Then I peered once again into the empty whiteness.

Then God, or whoever it was, spoke unto Art Bernstein: "Wait upon the Lord," I was instructed. I later verified that the phrase was from Isaiah 40:31.

OK, I thought, *if God wants me to wait, I'll jolly well wait.* "Waiting" consisted of counting to one hundred, then commanding the fog to part once more. Needless to say, nothing happened.

"Come on," I pleaded, out loud, feeling a little stupid for talking to the air and glad that no other people were around. "I promised Pat she could shop in Joseph, and we need to get back."

I counted to one hundred a second time, much more slowly, pacing all the while. When I was done, I peered as hard as I could into the formless void to see if something, anything, was materializing through the haze.

I saw only a formless void.

"Wait," the voice in my head repeated. And I waited. Ten minutes. Fifteen minutes. Twenty minutes. I thought I'd go nuts. I couldn't stand the tedium.

Am I missing something? I wondered. *Is there something else I need to do? Some formula?* I waited a couple more minutes, trying to reassure myself while hunching down in my jacket against the wind.

"Go get your wife," said the voice, finally. "If I'm going to part the fog, I need witnesses."

"She's not that interested," I replied. "And it's too cold for her to wait out here. And it's a long walk back to the car. And I might miss something if I leave. And . . ."

"Get your wife," the voice repeated.

I continued to stall. Fortunately the voice talking to me resolved the issue by getting my wife for me.

"Hi, Art."

Hearing Pat's voice behind me, I turned to greet her so that my back faced the canyon.

"Hi," I answered. "Sorry to take so long, but I was hoping the fog would lift enough to let me see down to the bottom. No such luck though."

"What are you talking about?" she said, as though I'd lost my mind, an all-too-familiar look. "The view is gorgeous."

I turned back toward the gorge. It was as though the fog had been slit with a knife. A mile or more below, we could see with perfect clarity the churning riffles of the Snake River. The hole in the fog, perhaps an eighth of a mile wide, enabled us to look down our side of the canyon to the river, then halfway up the far wall on the Idaho side. It was worth every second of my forty-minute wait.

"Wow," I whispered. That was the best I could muster. I squeezed my wife's hand, and we both stared until the hole closed up five minutes later, never to reopen during our visit.

TO VISIT

The hike: Hells Canyon National Recreation Area, Oregon

Distance: One hundred yards (The trail is no longer there.)

Directions: First get to Joseph, Oregon, on the Wallow River plain at the foot of the Wallowa Mountains. To reach Joseph, take OR 82 east from I-84 at La Grande. After seventy miles, in Joseph follow the paved Little Sheep Creek Highway left toward Imnaha, forty miles away. Hat Point Road #4240 (also called Sheepy Ridge Road) begins in Imnaha. It's twenty-two miles to the Memaloose Guard Station and landing strip. Turn right at Memaloose onto Spur 315 and proceed two more miles to Hat Point.

The Misplaced Mountain

PART 1

"Well, then," said my wife, Patricia, with only a slight hint of regret, "I guess it's over."

When she said that, we were sitting opposite each other on oak chairs in the office of J. Wendell Thayer, family therapist. The room smelled of lemon furniture polish, which I presumed was regularly and liberally applied to the oak table, chairs, and desk. No amount of polish would wipe away the years of accumulated tarnish on Pat and my relationship.

With Pat's proclamation in Dr. Thayer's office, twenty-nine years of marriage—half a lifetime of shared joy, heartache, and life events—went down the tubes. The year 2000 had been bad all the way around, and I remember sitting in that office with a knot in the pit of my stomach, hoping that the Third Millennium would eventually get better because it couldn't get much worse.

The marriage had always been shaky, and over the years the situation had steadily deteriorated. Now, finally, there was no other recourse. The time had come for us both to move on.

I reacted by doing what I often do in reaction to stress and sadness. I selected a beautiful, remote place that I'd always wanted to visit, drove by myself for two or three days, and went hiking there. On this occasion I picked Great Basin National Park in eastern Nevada.

I never dreamed I would end up losing an entire twelve-thousand-foot mountain during the hike. It was especially embarrassing because, as an experienced hiker, I pride myself on my directional sense and ability to find my way. I never get lost.

PART 2

The 11,922-foot-high Nevada peak that I misplaced was called Pyramid Peak, the fourth-highest summit in Nevada's Great Basin National Park. At 13,063 feet, Wheeler Peak, three miles north of Pyramid

Peak, is the park's highest summit. Wheeler Peak is also Nevada's highest mountain entirely inside the state.

Wheeler ranks well up among America's most beautiful mountains. I've always had a particular fondness for barren mountains that jut starkly up out of the middle of the desert. By those standards, Wheeler Peak and Great Basin National Park have it all: great starkness, great jutting height, and, above all, great beauty adorned with lots of surrounding desert, barren slopes, active glaciers, alpine lakes, aspen groves, piñon and juniper groves at lower elevations, Engelmann spruce and subalpine fir in the more sheltered pockets, and limber pines at tree line. On the highest, most exposed slopes, there are populations of bristlecone pine, Earth's longest-lived species. Plus there is Lehman Cave, one of the nation's better limestone caverns.

In 2000 it had been eighteen years since my last visit to the area, when I'd climbed Wheeler Peak. This time I decided to check out the path to Baker Lake, which supposedly occupies a spectacular, steep-walled cirque basin. And if I made it to Baker Lake, I figured I might as well climb Pyramid Peak, which rises directly above Baker Lake to the southeast.

On a Saturday morning in July, I got into my car and headed south and east to Reno and Fallon, Nevada. I then lit out across fabled US 50, the "loneliest road in America." US 50 across Nevada fit my mood perfectly. Especially the 250 miles from Fallon to Ely, near the Utah line. Only two towns disrupt the loneliness, Austin and Eureka, both mining towns from the nineteenth century built on mountainsides. Austin looks down on the Reese River valley, which Mark Twain wrote about in his book *Roughing It.*

I did not think much about Patricia or the divorce as I drove, although I worried that I might. In fact, any troubles in my life were quickly left far, far behind as I sped ever-forward in my fragile little world of protected unreality.

After eating dinner in the gambling casino in Ely, I rented a motel room for the night. In the morning, after a greasy breakfast at the same casino, I drove to the park. Wheeler Peak came into view a few miles past Ely, looking far higher, steeper, and more lovely than any mountain I'd passed thus far.

Inside the park, I pulled into Baker Creek Campground at 8:00 a.m. to use the facilities and fill my water bottles. The Baker Creek trailhead, where I planned to hike, is a mile past the campground. I hit the pathway at 9:00 a.m. My backpack contained a day's worth of food, a tent, a sleeping bag, a camera, and sundry other goodies necessary for an overnight campout.

My intended route included the six-mile hike up Baker Creek to Baker Lake, where I would spend the night. At daybreak the next morning, I planned to leave my backpack at the lake and make the difficult two-mile journey up to Johnson Pass. From the pass I would walk off-trail for a final mile, along the supposedly smooth and treeless ridge, to the top of Pyramid Peak. Then I would return to Baker Lake, gather my belongings, hike back down to the car, and spend the night at Baker Creek Campground.

The trail to the lake proved relaxing and scenic, even though it climbed 2,600 feet in six miles. I marveled at how hiker-friendly this particular mountain range seemed to be, how even the most difficult trails seem to reach out, welcome, and offer comfort. Other mountain ranges often feel foreboding, as though the peaks were letting you visit as an indulgence and you really were not welcome.

The path began in a series of broad, open slopes covered with sagebrush, scattered mountain mahogany bushes, and piñon pines. After a mile the path found Baker Creek, which it followed for the next two miles. Many welcome level pitches greeted me in this section.

At mile three the path began climbing a series of steep talus slopes and glacial moraines, with breathtaking glimpses into the cirque basins above. After four miles the path passed the remains of an old cabin. It then swung away from the creek as it continued its ascent of the rocky moraines for two more miles. Beginning at the second mile, most of the path was in the shade, with quaking aspen in the upland areas and mixed conifers closer to the creek.

A mile before I arrived at the lake, the trail offered a view into the yellow rock cirque basin immediately adjacent to the Baker Lake basin. The adjacent basin had no lake at the bottom, just a green meadow and an aspen grove. Above the basin, I could see Johnson Pass and Pyramid Peak. To climb Pyramid Peak, I had to follow a trail from Baker Lake into this basin and then ascend a nearly vertical slope to

Johnson Pass. The route looked extremely difficult, and according to the map, it rose 1,500 feet in one mile. But the route from the pass to the actual summit appeared pretty easy.

After four hours, I arrived at Baker Lake, a ten-acre gem at the base of some absolutely vertical yellow cliffs rising up behind a third of the lakeshore. The rest of the shore, where there were no cliffs, was forested with small conifers. The lake's water level fluctuated greatly, so only about half the rocky lakebed, the portion closest to the cliffs, contained water.

I didn't want to leave Baker Lake. There was nobody else there, and I found the beauty and serenity overwhelming. I set up my tent, relaxed, cooked a meal, and generally puttered around until dark.

One thing I failed to accomplish during my puttering, although I tried, was locate the trail from Baker Lake to Johnson Pass, the one I needed to follow to climb Pyramid Peak. The trail was shown on the map, but a park ranger had warned me that the path was difficult to find. He had suggested that I look for rock cairns at the lake's southeast end, but I saw none. Although I could find no trace of a trail leading away from Baker Lake, I discovered that if I climbed over a small talus slope at the edge of the Baker Lake cirque, I could see every place that the missing trail was supposed to lead, from Baker Lake to the adjacent treeless basin and up to the pass.

PART 3

The next morning at 7:30, I again hit the dirt pathway, this time carrying only a canteen and a small day pack. I never did find the spot where the trail to Johnson Pass leaves Baker Lake, but, as I said, the route was obvious. Thirty-five minutes later, in the green meadow in the basin below the pass and adjacent to Baker Lake, I finally picked up the path, which I followed for a second mile to the ridgetop. That second mile, as expected, bordered on horrible. Not only was it extremely steep but there wasn't a single tree or square inch of shade. A section in the middle wound through a series of rock outcrops that I found somewhat terrifying. I couldn't see Baker Lake during the ascent to Johnson Pass, but I kept expecting it to pop into view at any minute as I gained altitude.

Pyramid Peak

Halfway up the slope, amid the dust and grit, with my forehead, T-shirt, and jacket drenched in perspiration, it occurred to me that I'd left my camera in my backpack, back at the lake. So my intrepid scaling of Pyramid Peak would be recorded only in memory, not on film. Going back and retrieving the camera was out of the question.

At 9:00 a.m., I stood atop barren, featureless Johnson Pass, elevation 11,260 feet, where the trail crossed over the ridge. I was pretty hungry when I hit the pass, and more than a little tired, so when I noticed a gnarled old limber pine all by itself beside the trail, offering a postage-stamp-size patch of shade, the only shade for miles, I sat down, gobbled a few handfuls of trail mix, and took a few large gulps of water. Then I leaned back and closed my eyes, intending to resume walking in two or three minutes.

PART 4

I must have fallen asleep. At least that was my immediate thought when I woke up. I noted from my watch that an hour had passed. No big deal. I still had all day.

I stood up, gathered my gear, and looked around. Below me, I was pleased that I could finally see Baker Lake. It was the first time I'd been able to see it since leaving the Baker Lake basin. Baker Lake is on the left, or north, when you stand on the ridgetop and face Pyramid Peak, so I immediately oriented myself in that direction. And there was the summit, the object of my endeavor, a mile away, looking very large and pyramidal.

The peak was a smooth, treeless dome composed entirely of gravel and scree slopes. Half a dozen other peaks in the vicinity had just about the same look and were nearly as high, but I'd studied the map pretty carefully, so there wasn't any question in my mind that this was indeed Pyramid Peak. It was the one rising directly up from the pass with Baker Lake on the left.

Climbing Pyramid Peak took about half an hour. Maybe less. The view from the 11,922-foot summit was not quite as impressive as the view from Wheeler Peak had been, years earlier, but it was stunning nevertheless. And a lot less crowded. I could see Wheeler Peak, the rest of the Snake Range, and the surrounding desert.

There is something about standing on a mountaintop that you poured out your personal sweat to reach that is more satisfying than just about anything else in the world. No wonder some people get addicted to it.

Half an hour later I was back at Baker Lake. It sort of occurred to me as I hiked, in the dark periphery of my awareness, that the trip from the summit to the lake seemed a lot shorter than the trip from the lake to the summit. Part of the reason, I assumed, was that I was now going downhill, not uphill. Still, I had no explanation as to why the path now led directly to the lake instead of first going through the adjacent basin. At any rate, I was too tired to allow such trivia to penetrate too far into my consciousness. Mostly I just wanted to get back to my campsite.

PART 5

When I arrived back at Baker Lake, it seemed different than it had a few hours earlier. At first I attributed it to the changed lighting. But the differences really didn't begin to click in my brain until I discovered that all my gear was missing. I panicked and began searching for my campsite but couldn't find any spot that looked even remotely like it.

I combed the lakeshore in rapid, frantic circles, muttering under my breath and praying for some sort of clue to magically set things right. The idea of my camera and all my camping gear being stolen was unacceptable.

It was only after I sat down on a boulder to collect my thoughts and composure that it dawned on me that during my ascent of Pyramid Peak, I'd seen no evidence of the other nearby lake, Johnson Lake. In fact, I'd forgotten all about Johnson Lake, although it was very prominent on the map, in a basin immediately south of Johnson Pass.

When I'd faced Pyramid Peak up on the pass, Johnson Lake should have been visible to my right, with Johnson Peak, only thirty feet lower than Pyramid Peak, rising immediately behind me. On reaching the Pyramid Peak summit, I should have been able to see Johnson Peak behind me and several more eleven-thousand-foot-plus summits in front of me. Instead I had found myself looking abruptly down on the desert.

Slowly I figured out what happened. What cinched it was the sudden realization that when you climb Pyramid Peak, Wheeler Peak should be easily visible on your left. In fact, it had been on my right. Why I failed to notice that—and dozens of other clues that I was turned around 180 degrees and climbing the wrong mountain—is something I will never fully understand or be able to explain.

Apparently, when I awoke from my nap, I'd started walking in the wrong direction, toward Johnson Peak instead of Pyramid Peak. I should have been tipped off by the presence of Johnson Lake, easily visible on my right. Except I had mistaken it for Baker Lake and had climbed the wrong peak.

That also explained why I could not find my gear.

Chuckling to myself at my stupidity, I hiked back up to the pass and back down to the little side basin and Baker Lake—the real Baker Lake—where my stuff awaited exactly where I'd left it.

I debated climbing Pyramid Peak as I passed it on the pass but decided that one mountain a day was enough. Besides, I had already completely lost interest in Pyramid Peak. Johnson Peak, the one I actually climbed, was now *my* mountain, the one I frequently thought about and described to all my friends.

I had moved on.

And that was the lesson of Pyramid Peak.

TO VISIT

The hike: Baker Creek Trail to Baker Lake and Pyramid Peak, Great Basin National Park, Nevada

Distance: Baker Lake, six miles one-way; Johnson Pass, nine miles one-way

Directions: Take US 50 from Carson City or Sacramento to Ely. Or take US 50A from Fallon, east of Reno, and then US 50 to Ely. (It is 325 miles from Reno to Ely.) Fifty-seven miles past Ely, still on US 50, turn right (south) onto NV 487 toward Baker, five miles away. At Baker, NV 488 heads west, arriving at the Great Basin National Park Visitor Center and Lehman Cave entrance after six miles. Just before the visitor center, take the gravel road left for three miles to Baker Creek Campground and for one more mile to the Baker Lake trailhead.

15

Henry the Warrior

PREFACE

Although this story is fictional, it is rooted in truth. Many years ago, a youth club member did die tragically on the Caribou Lakes Trail in northern California. However, the Junior Boy Rangers of California are a complete figment of my imagination, and the story is not intended in any way to be critical of the thousands of caring individuals who work for youth programs such as the Boy Scouts, Girl Scouts, and Camp Fire. I have been deeply involved with both Boy Scouts and Camp Fire and greatly admire both organizations.

In fact, this story is really not about children or youth programs at all. As with all stories worth reading—and I hope this falls into that category—the characters are intended as archetypes and the story as an allegory.

PROLOGUE

In the very heart of the Trinity Alps Wilderness—the third-largest unit of the US Wilderness Preservation System outside Alaska—twelve miles from the nearest road on an extremely hot, exposed, steep, and sublimely scenic segment of the Caribou Lake Trail, a half mile from where the path crests spectacularly at the top of Sawtooth Ridge, there stands a small stone monument with a bronze plaque. The plaque's inscription says: "This trail segment is dedicated to the memory of Henry W. Evashevski, the world's greatest Junior Boy Ranger."

That's all it says. There are no dates, and it does not explain what a Junior Boy Ranger is or exactly why Henry W. Evashevski was the greatest of them all.

PART 1

"Guess what, Grandpa," said my eleven-year-old grandson, Brandon, as we sat watching TV at his parents' house in Mount Shasta, California. "I joined the Boy Scouts."

"That's fantastic," I said. "I hope you enjoy it. I used to be a Boy Scout, you know."

"You did not," he said. "You're too fat."

"I wasn't fat back then," I replied. "And I'm not that fat now. Besides, in this day and age, there must be dozens of overweight kids in your troop."

"There are a few."

"I hope nobody makes fun of them."

"Maybe a little, once in a while."

"Do the leaders make fun of them?"

"Of course not. Leaders are supposed to be nice to everybody."

"That's good." I said. "It's not nice to make fun of people."

"I know that," said Brandon, rolling his eyes. "Did you ever go hiking when you were a Boy Scout? Our troop goes hiking a lot."

"A little. I grew up in Detroit, where there are hardly any trails. I imagine it's a lot different living in Mount Shasta. Would you like to hear a story I know about a group of hikers about your age?"

"Sure," said Brandon.

"Great," I said, leaning back on the couch. "The story is about the Junior Boy Rangers of California, a group that no longer exists. A guy I used to know at the Forest Service up in Weaverville told it to me. It happened in 1948, on a trail in what is now the Trinity Alps Wilderness."

With Brandon listening intently, I began telling the story.

PART 2

"Come on, Mom," said Henry, sitting on his bed and looking up from the book he was reading, *Native Tribes of the American Northwest.* "Don't make me join the Junior Boy Rangers. I'm not Junior Boy Ranger material."

Henry's mother, Helen Evashevski, a slightly chubby but neatly dressed women in her forties, stood in the doorway of his bedroom.

"Why not?" she asked. "What do you have to lose? Maybe you'll make some friends."

"Or maybe the kids from school will make fun of me even more. Nobody wants to be my friend at school. Why would they want to be friends at the Junior Boy Rangers?"

"At least give it a try. The Junior Boy Rangers do all sorts of things that boys like to do, like hunting, going hiking, and playing games. If you had a dad, he would do those things with you. But I never could."

"And I'll look ridiculous and they'll I call me 'fatso' and laugh at me and nothing will change."

"Instead of sitting alone in your room or at the library studying about Indians and Hiawatha, you can learn about Indians with boys your age."

"Someday I'll move away from this stupid town and become a real anthropologist so I can do nothing all day but study about Indians. Maybe I'll go to Michigan or Minnesota, where Hiawatha lived. From what I've read, the Junior Boy Rangers don't know anything at all about Indians. They just use a lot of made-up words that are supposed to sound like Indian words."

"I don't know why you're so down on Weaverville. It's been very good to us. I have a wonderful job with the county, and we own our little house."

"Weaverville has been awful to us. I don't have any friends, and you don't have any real friends. When I leave, I'm taking you with me."

"Whatever you say. But please, for me, just go to one meeting. That's all I ask. Just one."

"All right, all right," said Henry. "I'll go if you insist. But I'll probably regret it."

"You're a good boy," his mother said. "I just know that once the other boys get to know you, they'll also realize what a good boy you are."

"I doubt it," said Henry, going back to his book.

Henry's one and only Junior Boy Ranger meeting took place at the Weaverville Middle School, the same school Henry trudged six blocks to every weekday except in summer. Going back voluntarily, during off-hours, was not something he looked forward to doing.

"Have a wonderful time," said his mom as she dropped him off in front of the school amid a hoard of adolescent boys in black uniforms with white bandanas bearing the slogan "Loyalty Is My Honor." The children shouted, hit, tripped, and pushed one another as they made their way into the gym. Henry could think of few things worse than being alone in the middle of a crowd of noisy adolescent boys.

"I know this is going to be a fabulous experience for you," Henry's mother concluded before driving away.

Taking a deep breath, unsure whether he'd prefer to be noticed or not noticed, Henry entered the gym. He wore a brand-new uniform his mother had purchased when she signed him up for the group—before her discussion with him, it turned out.

Henry felt bad about his mother spending her hard-earned money on something in which he had so little interest. He hoped he'd like the Junior Boy Rangers—and more important, that the Junior Boy Rangers would like him—if only to justify his mother's expenditure.

As he entered the gym, Henry's main worry was that the other boys would consider him presumptuous, or too new a member, to wear a uniform. And that they'd tease him because of it.

That didn't happen. If anybody had a problem with Henry's uniform, they didn't say anything. In fact, nobody spoke to Henry at all. None of the kids and none of the leaders. It was as though he were invisible, as though he didn't exist.

After a few minutes, a balding, gray-haired man with terrible posture and bad teeth called the meeting to order. He was wearing a uniform similar to Henry's except that it was full of medals and badges, most of which looked homemade.

If this guy is in charge of the troop, Henry thought, he sure doesn't sound very friendly. He reminded Henry of a dictator as he stood on the stage, shouting into a tinny-sounding microphone. He barked out orders and kept threatening to punish people if they didn't settle down.

"I'm counting to ten," the leader warned in a near-scream. "And anybody who isn't sitting down gets the gauntlet. One, two, three . . ."

Henry gathered that the kids were supposed to sit cross-legged on the floor, which made sense because there weren't any chairs. As the man began counting, Henry looked around for a place to sit. There wasn't anybody in particular he wanted to sit near—or not sit near.

". . . four, five, six, seven . . ."

As Henry was deciding where to sit, he wondered what "gets the gauntlet" meant. He figured it had something to do with a medieval military ritual called running the gauntlet, in which a rule breaker, usually a deserter, was forced to run between two rows of soldiers who struck him with clubs or broadswords as he passed. The victim was not intended to survive. To Henry's relief, he did not see any broadswords.

". . . eight, nine, TEN. You there, fat boy," said the guy on the stage. "I said sit down. You think I'm kidding?"

Henry looked around to see who the unlucky person was that the leader was yelling at. It seemed to him that dozens of boys were not yet seated.

The guy was talking to him, Henry.

"I apologize," said Henry, quickly plopping himself onto the floor as he felt his face flush red with embarrassment.

"Looks like we have our first gauntleteer," said the leader with a grin. The other kids found this hilarious. The man *had* to be kidding about the gauntlet thing, though, Henry reasoned. After all, it was his first meeting. Nobody had even said "hello" to him yet. And the offense was so minor.

They weren't kidding.

Running the Junior Boy Ranger gauntlet, fortunately, was not quite the same as running a medieval army gauntlet. The other kids all stood in a line with their legs spread apart. The "victim," in this case Henry, was instructed to crawl through the tunnel of legs as fast as he could while each person in line whacked him with their hand on his rear end as he passed.

"Go on, son," the guy on the stage barked as Henry stood facing the row of boys, trying to decide whether to cry or run away. "We ain't got all day."

It never occurred to Henry to refuse to go through the tunnel. One simply did not question teachers or youth group leaders in 1948. With shame and resignation, he did as he was told. Slowly he dropped to his knees. Then he started crawling as fast as he could, which wasn't very fast. The slaps on the bottom didn't hurt particularly. He was well padded. What hurt the most was that nobody cared that this punishment was inflicted during the first five minutes of his first meeting, when he desperately needed to feel welcomed.

Afterwards, Henry debated walking out of the meeting. He'd much rather be by himself, outside in the pleasant autumn air; in the dark where nobody could see the "fat boy." But he didn't. He owed his mother that much. Besides, if he went outside, they might make him run the gauntlet again.

The rest of the meeting was pretty boring. They talked about upcoming activities, none of which sounded very interesting. The troop was going to spend a day planting trees for the Forest Service. And they were having a candy sale to raise money. And they planned a father-son banquet (a lot of good *that* was going to do Henry). Finally, they announced that instead of the usual October Camporee, the troop was going on a three-day backpacking trip into the Trinity Alps.

None of those events sounded remotely interesting—least of all a thirty-six-mile hiking trip into the Trinity Alps with a full backpack. A fellow would have to be crazy to go on a trip like that.

PART 3

The closest Henry ever came in his entire life to yelling at his mother was the day she arrived home with a brand-new backpack. Henry hadn't bothered to share the details of the meeting with her, least of all the part about running the gauntlet. He told her everything had gone well and that he had talked to a few of the other kids. His mother seemed pleased. The look on her face was worth the lie.

Henry hadn't shared anything whatsoever with his mother about the backpacking trip. Not one word. The troop must have mailed her a newsletter or something, because she found out anyhow. Henry's heart sank when he saw the brand-new backpack, a big green apparatus covered with pockets and zippers and straps and clips. It must have cost a fortune. She had also purchased a belt canteen, a cooking kit, a sleeping bag, and a pile of additional camping paraphernalia.

"I can't carry all this stuff for thirty-six miles," said Henry.

"You worry too much," his mom replied. "I'm sure the leaders will take that into consideration and not go too fast."

Henry thought about that a minute. From what he'd observed, it seemed that "consideration" was not a strong suit of the Junior Boy Rangers.

"I still don't want to go," he mumbled. "I'll never make it."

"Of course you will. I talked to that nice Mr. DelaGrange, and he assured me you'd be fine as long as you had a good attitude. He said that he and the boys will make sure you don't get too far behind."

Horace DelaGrange was the balding guy with bad posture who had made Henry run the gauntlet. Henry despised him, to put it mildly. One thing Henry knew about Horace DelaGrange was that when he said, "I'll make sure he doesn't get too far behind," it meant something very different from what his mother had in mind.

Preparing for the trip was actually kind of fun. The troop had sent home a list of things to bring: dehydrated food, snacks, toilet paper, three days' clothing, a towel, and so forth. Henry especially liked preparing and packing the snacks. He purchased a half dozen Clark bars and a bag of malt balls.

"Extra energy," he explained to his mother with a grin. "Also, it might come in handy if we need to do some trading with the Indians."

The night before the trip, Henry listened to the weather report on the radio, desperately hoping that the trip would be canceled due to rain. No such luck. The report called for sunshine and unseasonably high temperatures, with a high of 110 degrees in Redding and 102 degrees in Weaverville. At seven thousand feet elevation, Henry estimated that the high temperature in the Trinity Alps would be 90 or 95.

On the morning of the big trek, Henry rode from Weaverville to the trailhead in a van owned by one of the parents. The driver was Mr. Heck, a big, pleasant sawmill worker. He was the father of Trout Heck, whom Henry recognized from school but had never spoken to. Trout's mother came along, too, and his little sister, Amy. Also present was Evan Grofe, another schoolmate of Henry's that he had never spoken to.

Trout's mother said "hello" to Henry when the group pulled up in the van in the driveway of his mother's house. Henry received the greeting with a grunt and a nod. Just before Henry got in, while he and Mr.

Heck were outside loading Henry's backpack behind the van's tailgate door, Henry overheard Evan whisper to Trout, "What's he doing here? He'll never keep up."

"Shhhh," Henry heard Trout reply. "My mother asked Mr. Dela-Grange the same thing. He told her there was nothing to worry about."

"I still say he'll never keep up. If we have to constantly wait for him, we'll be gone a week. Besides, he's a total creep."

"Will you shut up?" Henry heard Trout whisper. "He'll hear you."

After a farewell hug and kiss from his mother, Henry got into the van. His parting words to her were, "Not in front of everybody. It's embarrassing."

Henry rode in the third seat with Trout's sister. Amy didn't say anything to Henry during the journey, and Henry didn't say anything to Amy. Or to anybody else. Nobody talked to Henry until they arrived at the trailhead, at the end of a dirt road in a tree-shaded Forest Service campground along a pretty little stream.

"We're here," Trout Heck's father announced. Henry climbed slowly out of the van, feeling like a condemned prisoner about to take his last walk. Except in this case, the last walk was thirty-six miles long.

The night before, when Henry had tried on the backpack, it seemed pretty heavy. Today it seemed ten times heavier. Henry thought about changing his mind and returning to Weaverville with the Hecks. But he didn't.

According to the flyer sent home by the troop—the one containing the list of things to bring—they would walk twelve miles the first day, to Portuguese Camp. The flyer said that the trail to Portuguese Camp was easy and "almost level." After a night at Portuguese Camp, they'd make their way to Emerald and Sapphire Lakes, three miles away. Then they'd return to camp, gather their gear, and hike up to Caribou Lake, three miles from Portuguese Camp and three thousand feet higher.

The trail segment from Portuguese Camp to Caribou Lake was described in the flyer as "difficult." But the flyer also said, "we'll go slowly" and "not push the boys too hard." After a night at Caribou Lake, the outing's final day would be spent making the fifteen-mile journey back to the trailhead.

As Henry began the hike, he experienced a moment of despair. He didn't see how he could possibly carry the huge, heavy, awkward pack twelve miles in one day. He doubted if he could walk twelve miles in a day even without a pack.

A few dozen yards into the journey, Henry was perspiring like a lawn sprinkler, barely able to catch his breath and worried that he would have a heart attack. He dared not tell this to anybody, however. Least of all Mr. DelaGrange, who he knew would only snarl at him to quit complaining if he knew what was good for him.

Henry held off complaining as long as he could. He knew what was good for him. And he knew what was not good for him.

The twelve miles to Portuguese Camp, as predicted, were fairly level as hikes go. From Henry's perspective, if this was the easy part, he had good reason to dread the hard part later on.

Five minutes into the trip, Henry had become the last person in line among the twenty-five boys and six adults. Within twenty minutes, everyone else had vanished from sight. Because of his frequent stops, Henry assumed that the other kids were getting farther and farther ahead. It occurred to him that if he got far enough behind, he'd meet everyone else coming back.

Henry liked the idea. He liked being by himself too. It sure beat being made fun of and yelled at. But he also knew that if he failed to show up at camp, they'd come looking for him. And they wouldn't be very pleasant when they found him. Henry's best bet, therefore, was to try to stay as close to the group as possible.

At mile four, the route passed a side trail that supposedly led three miles up an adjacent canyon to Alpine Lake. From the junction on the main trail, you could look up the side canyon, which framed a beautiful snow-white mountain far in the distance. The mountain was white not because of snow—it was too late in the season for that—but because of the white granite rock that looked very much like snow.

Henry's concern that he wouldn't make it to Portuguese Camp by dark was allayed when he arrived at the junction with the side trail and some of the Junior Boy Rangers were still there, having walked down to see the river crossing. If everyone else arrived at the camp at 3:00 p.m. and he showed up at 3:30 or 4:00, it wouldn't be so bad.

The part of the hike that Henry enjoyed least was every half hour or so, when Mr. DelaGrange would come to check on him. It was always Mr. DelaGrange, never one of the parents or other troop leaders. Mr. DelaGrange never had anything encouraging or pleasant to say. He invariably seemed angry about the inconvenience. He had promised Henry's mother that he would personally look after her son, and he intended to keep his word.

Henry would have preferred that Mr. DelaGrange not keep his word.

Once, when Henry was sitting on a fallen log catching his breath and looking at a particularly beautiful waterfall, Mr. DelaGrange called him a "big fat slug" and a "worthless, lazy pig." And always, he would end by warning Henry that he'd "better shape up" or they would leave him behind.

As always, Henry apologized and said he'd try harder. He did observe, however, that hoisting the agonizing weight of the backpack and forcing himself to start walking again was much more difficult when he was crying.

At mile eight, four miles from Portuguese Camp, Henry arrived at Morris Meadow—an immense, flat expanse of cured-out, waist-high grass. To the left, a row of elegant white mountains rose up. To the right and also straight ahead lay Sawtooth Ridge, a precipitous, nearly vertical rock wall three thousand feet high with a jagged top.

As Henry stood at the lower end of Morris Meadow and stared up at Sawtooth Ridge, he tried not to think about the fact that the following day, he would be expected to climb to the top of that ridge, carrying a full pack.

There was plenty to see in Morris Meadow. The first thing Henry encountered was the turnoff for the Deer Creek Trail. Mr. DelaGrange had mentioned this turnoff to him and told him to be sure to go straight ahead and stay on the Stuart Fork. Henry did as he was told. Henry always did as he was told.

Mr. DelaGrange also warned about rattlesnakes.

"Morris Meadow is loaded with rattlesnakes," he said. "So watch where you step, and listen for rattling noises. If you get bit, don't worry. With all that blubber you got, any venom would get too diluted to do much harm."

Henry laughed, even though he didn't find Mr. DelaGrange's joke very funny. He laughed because Mr. DelaGrange laughed, and he didn't want to appear rude.

Henry arrived at Morris Meadow at around 2:00 p.m. It meant that the first day's hike, to Portuguese Camp, was two-thirds over and he had miraculously survived. To be sure, his leg muscles ached and his chest was sore from all the panting. And he had a headache. And he'd consumed a couple gallons of water (he'd brought along iodine purification tablets so he could refill his canteen out of the numerous side creeks he passed). And he was exhausted beyond words. And his shoulders hurt from the backpack straps' constant gouging.

But all in all, Henry was proud of himself. He'd covered eight miles in six hours, and there were six more hours of daylight in which to cover the last four miles.

He was going to make it.

While walking through the high grass of the meadow, reveling in the glory of his almost-accomplishment, Henry heard a rustling in the grass near his feet. Then he felt a slight sting on his ankle, just above his sock top. Immediately after, it occurred to Henry that he'd also heard a rattling noise. Or at least he might have heard a rattling noise. Henry stopped, took off his pack and examined his ankle. There were two small puncture wounds there, each with a tiny droplet of blood.

It was obviously a rattlesnake bite. Henry immediately concluded that he was going to die. Fingers trembling, he desperately squeezed at the spot on his ankle to see if he could force the venom out. There was no way he could suck the spot because he couldn't get his mouth within three feet of his ankle, and he was extremely reluctant to cut the spot with a knife.

Luckily, Mr. DelaGrange showed up just then. He examined Henry's ankle and concluded that while it might indeed have been a snake-bite, no venom had been injected. The spot had swelled slightly after ten minutes, but Henry felt about the same as he felt before the bite, which wasn't very good.

"I guess I just can't trust you by yourself," said Mr. DelaGrange. "I'll have to stay back here with you until we get to the camp. I hope you're satisfied."

Henry was not satisfied.

According to Mr. DelaGrange, the best thing to do for a snakebite was move around as much as possible so that your metabolism would speed up and detoxify the poison faster. Actually, Henry recalled reading the exact opposite, that it was better to keep still. With your heart beating more slowly, the poison would not spread around your body as fast and the kidneys would have more time to filter it out.

Henry did not share this information. One simply did not contradict Mr. DelaGrange.

Henry slowly put his pack back on and began trudging up the path. He limped a little at first because it hurt where he'd been bitten. But the slight pain soon went away. Henry concluded that Mr. DelaGrange was correct, that little or no venom had been injected and that he'd be OK. He would not die in Morris Meadow of a rattlesnake bite. It was a great relief.

Henry wished Mr. DelaGrange would go away. Mr. DelaGrange tried to walk beside Henry but kept pulling ahead. Every few minutes he'd stop and wait for Henry, making a comment such as, "Man, I never saw anybody go so slow in my life. What the hell did you come on this trip for anyhow?"

Henry had been asking himself the same question many, many times.

PART 4

Henry showed up at Portuguese Camp with Mr. DelaGrange at 4:15 p.m. He was the last person to arrive. Henry was pleased to learn that he was not the troop's only slow hiker. When he arrived, the faster hikers were teasing a couple of other boys about how long they'd taken. The boys being teased were glad to see Henry because it drew attention away from themselves. Fast and slow alike all proceeded to unite in harassing Henry.

Henry was not the troop's only overweight person either. But he was definitely the most overweight. For reasons Henry could not explain, nobody made fun of the other chubby kids. They only made fun of Henry. The other fat kids made fun of Henry too. Henry figured that they saw him as an example of what could happen if they didn't shape up. Nobody wanted to end up like Henry.

Aside from being overrun with Junior Boy Rangers, Portuguese Camp was one of the most beautiful places Henry had ever seen. The little camp was located on a small flat by a creek, shaded by white firs and lodgepole pines. The creek was actually the upper reaches of the Stuart Fork. White granite rock slopes rose steeply up on either side of the creek.

Between the two chalk-white canyon walls ran the clearest sapphire-blue water that Henry had ever seen. It was lined with large boulders that looked like giant marshmallows. Somebody had built a low dam of rocks and cobbles to form a small swimming hole. When Henry arrived, one of the first things that attracted his attention was ten or fifteen naked boys splashing, shrieking, and laughing in the pool.

There was not enough money in the world to induce Henry to appear naked in front of those boys, let alone go swimming with them. He did manage a sponge bath later on when it was almost dark, in a secluded spot several hundred feet upstream from the camp.

As the group set up camp and prepared dinner, one of the boys actually talked to Henry. Except for the teasing and Mr. DelaGrange's haranguing, nobody had spoken to Henry at the meeting and nobody had spoken to him during the hike.

The person who talked to Henry was Trout Heck.

"Glad you finally made it," said Trout, pausing briefly in front of Henry, who was sitting by himself on a log, eating dinner. Trout was on his way from one cluster of kids to another. "I was worried about you."

"Thanks. I got bit by a rattlesnake."

"Seriously? How come you didn't die?"

"Beats me. I don't think it was a very bad bite. Wanna see?"

Henry showed Trout his barely visible double puncture wounds.

"I'll be damned," said Trout. Then he left to join his friends. Henry overheard Trout telling the other kids about the snakebite. He debated going over and joining them. They would never actually invite him, of course. Boys that age did not do such things. But Henry remained where he was.

After dinner, the leaders brought out a bunch of marshmallows, graham crackers, and Hershey bars. Everyone roasted the marshmallows in the campfire and made them into s'mores, a camping classic. Henry loved s'mores. He ate four of them. Evan Grofe ate six. Henry also ate two more Clark bars.

Then it came time to go to bed. Henry did not have a tent, and none of the other boys wanted to share their tent with him. Since Henry was frightened of sleeping out in the open, Mr. DelaGrange finally said he could share his tent. "But try not to hog the whole thing or you'll be out on your ass," he added.

Predictably, sharing a tent with Mr. DelaGrange was a nightmare. Henry was so tense that despite being exhausted, he didn't sleep for one second. He wasn't the only person who didn't get much sleep. He heard other kids talking and laughing in their tents until 3:00 a.m.

At 4:00 a.m., Henry dragged his sleeping bag out of Mr. Dela-Grange's tent and laid it a couple feet from the entrance. He fell instantly asleep. When the bugle blew reveille at 8:00 a.m., all the kids bounded joyously and loudly out of their tents. Henry wondered where all their energy came from, since most had accomplished only four or five hours sleep. He also wondered what kind of idiot would carry a bugle in his backpack for twelve miles just to blow reveille.

Henry was still exhausted when reveille blew. Even Mr. Dela-Grange tripping over him didn't elicit much more than a mumble. Henry tried to make himself get up but kept falling back asleep. The poking and prodding of leaders and other boys every few minutes had no effect. Even the heavenly aroma of pancakes, scrambled eggs, hash browns, and sausage cooked in an iron skillet over a campfire had no effect.

When Henry woke up for good, everyone else was gone. He panicked for a second, thinking they'd deserted him. But when he saw the tents and gear still there, he figured the others were all at Emerald and Sapphire Lakes. He vaguely remembered someone telling him the troop was leaving, that they would be back in three or four hours and that he should stay near camp and not get into trouble.

Henry had a fine time by himself. He went swimming naked, climbed around on the rocks, and even fished a little. The troop returned around noon.

At around 2:00 p.m., everyone, including Henry, departed for Caribou Lake. Henry had never seen such a steep trail. Not that he'd seen many trails. To make things worse, most of the route was out in the open, with no forest cover, and it all faced south, the hottest, sunniest direction. Henry figured the temperature was at least 90 degrees. But it was only two and a half miles to the ridgetop. After the twelve miles he had walked the previous day, how difficult could that be?

Henry fell back into his position in the rear almost immediately, although this time he stayed close enough to the rest of the troop that he could see that some of the other kids were also struggling. In fact, everybody was struggling. Even Mr. DelaGrange. Even Trout Heck.

Henry struggled the most. He thought it would have been a wise idea for the leaders to suddenly announce that they were not going to Caribou Lake after all but instead were returning to Portuguese Camp.

No such luck.

Henry's queasiness started after about fifteen minutes of hiking. As he slowly plodded up the endless switchbacks, perspiring and panting, the queasiness worsened. It was like a police siren far off in the distance, coming closer and closer. Pretty soon it was deafening and there was no escape.

Henry tried to keep going but quickly discovered that hiking and nausea were incompatible. After a mile, he vomited but didn't tell anybody. There was nobody to tell. So he rested a few minutes, caught his breath, and started hiking again.

The nausea soon returned, this time accompanied by dizziness. Henry felt feverish, too, but figured it might just be the heat.

A mile and a half into the hike, Henry fell over. His knees simply buckled, as though some unseen prankster had pulled the tangible universe out from under him. One minute he was walking, head and shoulders slouched down, gasping for air. The next minute, he was sleeping peacefully on the ground.

And a couple minutes after that, he vomited for a second time. And a third and fourth time.

Henry had no idea how long he was unconscious. Opening his eyes slightly, an act he found surprisingly exhausting, he looked around for shade. The only shade he could see were a few flecks of cool gray at the base of a large, rangy mountain mahogany bush, fifteen feet from where he lay.

He nearly had a heart attack crawling on his ample belly to the ten-foot-high shrub. The maneuver took several minutes and he arrived queasy, panting, and unable to move one more inch. It was almost as though he was paralyzed. Or nearly paralyzed.

Then he just lay there on his side and groaned. Wave after wave of the most violent nausea Henry could possibly imagine assaulted his midsection, like lines of Lakota warriors sweeping down on horseback from a hilltop. With each successive wave, Henry vomited. The vomit ended up in an ever-enlarging puddle beside Henry's head, from which he was unable to move away.

Henry was now certain that he had a fever. He estimated his body temperature at about five hundred degrees. He also had a pretty bad headache.

That was when Mr. DelaGrange showed up, accompanied by Evan Grofe and another one of the leaders; a short, stupid man named Mooney.

"Leave it to old Henry," said Mr. DelaGrange in disgust on discovering Henry's plight. "What's wrong now?"

"I don't feel well," Henry whispered.

"You never feel well. It's only half a mile to the top and another half mile to the lake. Now you get yourself up and quit being a baby."

"I can't."

"Of course you can."

"I think I have a temperature. And I've thrown up a whole bunch of times."

"Maybe he's really sick," Mooney commented.

"Sick, my ass," said Mr. DelaGrange. "Besides, he can't stay here even if he is sick. And I'm not about to carry him. You wanna carry him?"

"If he's got heat stroke," said Mooney, "we shouldn't move him. You can die from heat stroke. Didn't he get bit by a snake yesterday?"

"He doesn't have heat stroke," said Mr. DelaGrange, sounding exasperated. "If he did, somebody would have to hike all the way back to the trailhead and send for a helicopter. But he doesn't. He has heat exhaustion. We all have heat exhaustion. In case you haven't noticed, it's very hot out. Henry has it the worst because he's the fattest. The treatment for heat exhaustion is to rest, catch your breath, and drink some water. It's not the least bit life threatening."

Henry was relieved to hear that.

"What's the difference between heat stroke and heat exhaustion?" asked Evan Grofe.

"With heat stroke," explained Mr. DelaGrange, "you look pale and feel cold and clammy. With heat exhaustion, you turn red and feel feverish."

As it happened, Henry had read about heat stroke and heat exhaustion. He would have sworn it was the other way around; that heat stroke was red and feverish and heat exhaustion was cold and clammy. But as usual, he didn't argue with Mr. DelaGrange. Nobody argued with Mr. DelaGrange.

"So what should we do?" Mooney asked.

"Beats me," said Mr. DelaGrange. "All I know is, he's a mama's boy and it ain't gonna do no good to coddle him. You think you'll be able to get up any time soon, Henry?"

"I guess so," Henry whispered.

Henry did not think he'd be able to get up any time soon. But that was not the answer he believed Mr. DelaGrange wanted to hear.

"Good. When you feel up to it, we'll see you at Caribou Lake. Otherwise, we'll catch you on the way back, tomorrow morning."

"You mean you'd really leave me here overnight?" Henry made one last, panicked effort to stand. But his legs just wouldn't work. He'd never had his legs not work before. At least the nausea had eased up a little.

"I suspect you'll be along in a little while, young fellow," said Mr. DelaGrange, winking at Mooney. "If not, have a pleasant night. See you later."

Henry wanted to beg them not to go. But no words came out of his mouth as Mr. DelaGrange and the others walked away. Henry didn't have the energy to call out after them. Besides, his record at persuading these people to do favors for him, any favors, was pretty dismal.

Mr. DelaGrange did leave his canteen with Henry because Henry's canteen was nearly empty. Mr. DelaGrange's canteen was half full. Mr. DelaGrange also took Henry's backpack off him and stood it against the bush, within what should have been easy reach.

Then Henry was alone. Alone, terrified, and sick. But mostly alone.

PART 5

Henry spent the next few hours drifting in and out of consciousness. He tried several times and failed to stand up and start hiking again.

The nausea abated a little, only to be replaced by the worst headache Henry could possibly imagine. It felt as though two pickup trucks were colliding head on, over and over and over, inside his brain. The sun was blinding, and the burning, dripping sweat invariably found its way into his eyes. His mouth way pretty dry too. But that was the least of his problems.

On two occasions, Henry was able to reach his canteen and take a drink. He also succeeded in sliding his supine body a couple feet away from the vomit puddle so that he wasn't lying right in it. It stunk to high heaven. And he managed to get his pillow out of his backpack and under his head, which made his situation much more comfortable. He worried whether he'd be able to get his sleeping bag out when night came. And he worried a lot about whether he'd be eaten by bears or cougars if he slept out in the open.

But mostly, Henry dozed.

Henry attempted to eat several times, but getting at his food was just too overwhelming. Finally, late in the afternoon he managed to extricate the bag of malt balls in his backpack. Or what was left of it. He reached in the sack, took a giant handful, and dropped the candy into his mouth. He missed on his first attempt, and the malt balls landed all over his face and neck and rolled down the inside of his shirt. The second time, he was right on target.

Fifteen minutes after eating the malt balls, Henry woke up with an awful taste in his mouth. He'd fallen asleep without fully swallowing the food and it had just sat there, half chewed. There wasn't much saliva to wash it down. The little bit of food that did manage to make it to Henry's stomach was soon barfed back up.

As the hours slowly passed, Henry kept hoping the Junior Boy Rangers would return. He also kept hoping that when the sun got low and it cooled off a little, he'd start to feel better. Or at least feel less like his head and body were pressure cookers about to explode. But the headache kept getting worse. And his legs continued to lie uselessly at the end of his body like giant sofa pillows. And still nobody came. Finally it was too late in the day to hike the last mile to Caribou Lake. Henry was not about to attempt the hike to Caribou Lake by himself in the dark.

And then it was night.

When the sun dipped behind the mountain and the last rays of daylight disappeared, it became very cold very fast. It was October, after all, and Henry was dressed in a T-shirt on an exposed mountainside at an elevation of 7,500 feet. His last valiant act of movement was to extricate his sleeping bag from his pack. There was no way he could get it spread out and crawl inside, but he did manage to unroll the bag and wrap it around his shoulders. It was a lot warmer than just the T-shirt.

He'd probably have frozen to death without the sleeping bag.

Despite the rapidly falling temperature, Henry still felt feverish. And the headache would not go away. He was unable to stay awake for more than a few minutes at a time or to sleep for more than a few minutes at a time. Most of his "awake" minutes were spent in semiconscious delirium.

Henry did have an interesting dream during the night. He dreamed that Hiawatha came by on the trail. It was not the first time he'd dreamed about meeting Hiawatha.

It was nice to see Hiawatha again, tall and noble in the silvery light of the full moon, dressed in buckskin with his black hair billowing in the breeze.

"My goodness, Henry," said Hiawatha, standing beside the youngster and looking down at him. "What's wrong?"

"I don't know. They left me here. Can you help me?"

"I'll try. Would you like some of my strength? Some of my courage? Some of my spirit?"

"If you don't mind," said Henry.

"I'll give it a shot," said Hiawatha. He took an arrow out of the beaded quiver dangling from his back, pressed the chipped-stone tip against Henry's forehead, and made an elaborate ceremony of closing his eyes and concentrating. Henry felt a rush of energy flow from Hiawatha through the arrow into his body. He felt himself grow stronger and stronger.

He tried to stand, but still his legs would not work. And still his head throbbed. And still he longed for the quiet release of sleep.

Of course he already was sleeping.

To make matters worse, poor Hiawatha now looked noticeably smaller and weaker. What had been a robust warrior was now slouched, haggard, and emaciated. Henry felt guilty about having done that to his friend.

"You need more than I have to give," said Hiawatha. "I'm sorry."

"Thank you for trying," said Henry.

"Any time," said Hiawatha. "I'm going to leave you now to find a friend of mine and see if she can assist you. Her name is Kateri, and her magic is greater than mine. Or at least different."

Henry knew of Kateri. She was a Mohawk of the Iroquois tribe who lived in New York State in the 1600s, or what would become New York State. She was the daughter of a chief and the only Native American ever to make it through the initial stages of Catholic sainthood. But Kateri had lived in New York and Hiawatha had lived in the upper Midwest. What would they be doing in California? Then Henry realized it was a dream. Hiawatha had not visited Henry. And Kateri would not visit Henry.

When Henry woke from his dream, it was starting to get light—about 6:00 a.m., Henry estimated. The good news was that his headache felt much better and he was a little more alert. The bad news was that he still couldn't move his legs. In fact, his arms also seemed paralyzed, which meant he couldn't reach the water or food. All he could do was lie on the ground on his side under the mountain mahogany bush.

The mountain mahogany bush, it turned out, provided shade on Henry's side only in the afternoon. In the morning the shade was on the other side of the bush. It was still pretty chilly out, but there wasn't a cloud anywhere and the day was building up to be another scorcher. Before long, the sun would again be bearing relentlessly down on Henry.

Henry could see the Caribou Lake Trail as it meandered up toward the lake and ridgecrest. The morning smelled fresh and dewy, and Henry would have started hiking to Caribou Lake in an instant—if only he could move.

Another appendage Henry could no longer move was his head, at least not much. He was able to wiggle it slightly from side to side only with great effort. Up and down were out of the question. He could not shade his eyes with his hands or prevent the sun from shining directly into them. Henry had no doubt that the sun in his eyes would grow much more uncomfortable as the day wore on. Unless, of course, the Junior Boy Rangers came and rescued him.

At around 7:00 a.m., Henry noticed somebody walking down the trail from the direction of Caribou Lake, the only direction he could see. He hoped it was the Junior Boy Ranger troop.

The person hiking down the trail was not a Junior Boy Ranger but a young woman. She was the first hiker Henry had seen on the trail since Mr. DelaGrange, Mooney, and Evan Grofe the previous afternoon. Unless you count Hiawatha. However, this person was real.

The young woman was tall, slender, and lovely. She was dressed in hiking boots, Levi's, and a nylon windbreaker. Her long black hair was gathered into a pair of shimmering pigtails. She carried no backpack but wore a beaded pouch around her waist. There was also a large beaded amulet around her neck.

Henry got the impression that the woman was Native American.

"Wow, kid," said the woman on seeing Henry, "what happened to you? You look terrible."

"I don't know. I got sick yesterday and they left me here."

"Bummer. You say some people abandoned you? All by yourself? That's mind-blowing."

"Could you help me out?"

"Sure. What can I do for you?"

"If you could get me a drink, that would be a good start. My canteen's right over there. Then, if you don't mind, somebody needs to tell the people I'm with that I'm very sick and not getting any better. They're up at Caribou Lake."

The woman walked over to Henry, sat down with her legs crossed, and gently lifted his head onto her lap. She positioned herself so that the shade of her body sheltered and cooled Henry's face.

The woman smelled wonderful, like lilacs, soaproot, wild gentian, spring meadows, and chocolate cake on his birthday. She gently caressed his forehead and cheeks, and then she took the canteen, lifted Henry's head so he could drink, and held the container to the young man's lips. Henry managed four or five swallows before she took it away.

"You'll make yourself sick if you drink too much," she said.

"I'm already sick," Henry whispered.

After a minute or two, the woman gave Henry another few sips, then a few more. Henry hadn't realized how parched his mouth had been. When he was done drinking, the woman poured some water onto a handkerchief and wiped Henry's forehead and eyes. It felt cool and soothing.

"Your face is badly sunburned. I still can't believe those people just abandoned you."

"What's your name," said Henry, "if you don't mind my asking?"

"Why would I mind? My name's Katie. What's your name?"

"Henry."

"You're a cool guy, Henry. I'm pleased to meet you."

"And I'm happy to meet you," said Henry, welling with pride that this beautiful woman had somehow taken a fancy to him. "Are you Native American?"

"Is it that obvious? Yes I am. I'm a Mohawk. Full-blooded. From upstate New York. Ithaca, to be exact."

"Isn't Ithaca on Lake Cayuga, the name of another Iroquois tribe?"

"Wow! How did you know that? You're pretty smart, aren't you?"

"And you're pretty far from home."

"I guess I am. I travel a lot."

"Well, I'm glad you're here."

"I'm glad I'm here too."

"I was wondering," said Henry. "If you don't mind, could you possibly hike back up to Caribou Lake and tell the people to come and get me?"

"I could," said Katie, still sitting with Henry's head in her lap and caressing his forehead. "I could even help you get there. The question is, is that really what you want? I get the feeling that you don't care much for them. They sure haven't treated you very well."

"To be honest," said Henry, after pondering Katie's words, "I don't ever want to see another Junior Boy Ranger as long as I live. Least of all those guys. What I really want is to go home, to my mother's house. To sleep in my own bed. After that, I'd like to make sure Hiawatha is OK."

"I beg your pardon?"

"Never mind. You asked what I really wanted. I guess what I really want is to travel, like you. But I'd like to do it without carrying all this fat around and having everyone make fun of me."

"Where would you go?"

"That's easy. Northern Minnesota and upper Michigan."

"Because that's where Hiawatha lives?"

"That's where Hiawatha lived," Henry corrected.

"You're a right-on kid, Henry. And you know what? I think I can help you. No lie. I can get you to Caribou Lake and your mother's house. And even to northern Minnesota and upper Michigan. Would you like that, Henry?"

"Would I?" For the first time in days, possibly the first time ever, Henry was starting to feel excited about his future. Provided, of course, that this strange and wonderful person wasn't just concocting a story to make him feel better. Or that she wasn't just another dream.

No, Henry decided, that was not possible. For the first time since leaving home two days earlier, Henry smiled. And Katie smiled back.

"Before we get started, I need to explain a few things," said Katie. "First of all, I'll be using Chimariko rituals and prayers because this is Chimariko country. Since my magic is Mohawk, it might lose a little in translation. Probably not, but it could happen. Consider this your consumer warning. Shall I go ahead? If you don't want me to, that's perfectly groovy. You're the boss."

"Go ahead. I want you to."

The first step in Katie's ritual was to prop Henry up against the mountain mahogany bush so that he was in a sitting position. Then she took some beads from her waist pouch. Henry recognized them as black and red warrior beads. She placed the beads around Henry's neck, took a couple steps back, and began chanting, her face looking upward to the heavens.

The chant was loud, clear, and magnificent as it resonated off the majestic mountain summits. It gave Henry goose bumps. He had no idea what she was saying, but it evoked all sorts of emotions, most of them having to do with strength, dignity, and freedom.

"Congratulations," said Katie when she had finished singing. "You are now a Chimariko warrior. That means you are worthy of receiving the gift."

"Wow," said Henry. To his amazement, he actually felt a little like a warrior.

Then Katie took a brown feather out of her pouch, waved it in the air, and began chanting again. This song was even more beautiful than the last.

After a few minutes, Henry noticed a magnificent bald eagle soaring gracefully, far overhead. The great bird circled around Katie in tighter and tighter orbits. Then it landed on Katie's shoulder.

"Now," Katie announced, "there's only one more step. Chimariko warriors have been doing this for generations as part of their initiation ritual. You ready?"

"Ready as I'll ever be," said Henry, his heart pounding with excitement and curiosity.

Katie leaned forward, spoke some words in a language Henry didn't understand, and touched Henry's forehead with the feather.

Instantly Henry felt a flow of energy, of power, of life. And suddenly he was looking down at his own limp, dust-covered, pale, lumpy, slumped-over body leaning against the mountain mahogany bush. It looked awful. It took Henry a couple minutes to realize that he was now seeing through the eyes of the eagle.

"Now fly, young Henry," said Katie, lifting Henry the Eagle onto her hand and throwing him upward into the air. "May you be the great warrior you were meant to be. And may you never again suffer pain, neglect, or humiliation from uncaring humans."

Henry flew away. He was surprised and amazed at how easy it was. He didn't need any lessons or anything. He just seemed to know. He circled upward until he could see Caribou Lake, beautiful and blue, wedged between a green meadow and a bright red mountain summit. The Junior Boy Rangers were camped along the shore. They were cooking a communal breakfast in the same cast-iron skillet in which breakfast had been cooked the day before.

Even from a thousand feet in the air, Henry could smell the sizzling sausage and bubbling pancakes. His newly acquired, greatly improved sense of smell was overwhelming and would take a little getting used to. Likewise for his newly acquired visual acuity. It was like waking up one day and discovering you were Superman, with all his superpowers.

On seeing the troop camped by the lake, Henry briefly thought about forgetting all this eagle stuff and rejoining them. But he didn't. That probably wasn't an option anyhow. He swooped low over the camp for a better look.

"Hey, everybody," Henry heard Mr. DelaGrange shout. "A bald eagle. Will you look at that!"

Mr. DelaGrange was the person standing at the skillet, cooking breakfast for everyone.

"Wow!" "Ooh!" "Cool!" the kids all replied. They were admiring him, Henry, the fat kid nobody liked. He flew several wide circles and did a couple wing dips. The Junior Boy Rangers were duly impressed. If they only knew.

Then Henry swooped down over the encampment. At first he wasn't sure he could pull it off. Then he reminded himself that he was an eagle. And he could do anything any other eagle could do.

When Henry was directly above the skillet, he relieved himself. The telltale "plop" confirmed that he'd hit his target. Then he began climbing for a second run, which was also followed by a low swoop. This time, his bomb landed squarely on top of Mr. DelaGrange's balding head.

A warrior must be able to shoot straight and true.

Then Henry left. It was his last contact ever with the Junior Boy Rangers of California.

Henry flew diagonally across the Trinity Alps toward Weaverville. He soared over the top of Granite Peak, then Monument Peak, then over the forested foothills and cleared ranches until he came to Weaverville, in the canyon of the Trinity River.

Henry was glad for the opportunity to say good-bye to his mother, although there was a definite communication problem. All his poor mother could comprehend was that for some reason, a bald eagle had landed in her front yard while she was mowing the lawn. She was impressed, of course, even though she failed to grasp the significance. After all, how often does a bald eagle land on your front yard?

Henry realized that his mother would never make the connection between her son and the eagle. But he didn't care. Seeing his mother one last time made him feel a lot better about leaving.

Having said his good-byes, Henry set out for northern Minnesota, the Big Sea Water, and Hiawatha. He felt an obligation to return Hiawatha's spirit, the one Hiawatha had so generously loaned him. Also, he hoped Hiawatha could restore his human form, although that was only a minor consideration. Most of all, Henry just wanted to live in peace among the Ojibwas, even if he had to do it perched in a tree.

PART 6

At 9:30 a.m., the troop arrived at the spot where they'd left Henry. Mr. DelaGrange had been a little worried when Henry didn't show up at Caribou Lake but figured his least-favorite Junior Boy Ranger was just being his usual fat, lazy self. He wouldn't put it past Henry to hike all the way back down to Portuguese Camp, even if it scared everybody to death, rather than climb the final half mile to the ridgetop.

The one thing that never entered Mr. DelaGrange's mind, not even for a second, was that Henry's complaints were true. That simply was not possible.

When the Junior Boy Rangers arrived at the spot where Mr. Dela-Grange had left Henry, they were horrified to discover that Henry was still there. In fact, he'd only moved about twenty feet.

They didn't notice him at first. Then one of the kids asked, "What's that?"

The child pointed to a mound alongside the trail. They hadn't seen it on the way up. On closer inspection, the mound turned out to be a rock pile, two feet high, two feet wide, and five feet long, which someone had built very recently. On top of the rock pile was a beaded deerskin blanket, weighted down with rocks on the edges so it wouldn't blow away. Beneath the blanket, in peaceful repose, lay the lifeless body of Henry Wadsworth Evashevski. In one hand Henry clutched a bow and arrow. In the other he held an eagle feather. Around his neck there was a string of red and black beads.

Later a tribal shaman called in by the Trinity County Sheriff's Department explained that the rock pile was a traditional Chimariko funerary platform and that Henry's remains had been disposed of according to Chimariko custom. Henry apparently had been given a warrior's funeral.

Henry's body was carried out of the wilderness on a pack mule by a Forest Service employee. The funerary platform was dismantled. According to the Chimariko shaman, the spirit of the deceased ascends within the first twenty-four hours. After that, it's OK to bury the body in the ground.

According to the county coroner, Henry died of complications arising from severe heat stroke, possibly exacerbated by rattlesnake venom. The coroner confided that Henry must have suffered terribly and that he could have been saved had he gotten medical attention, or at least been brought out of the sun, up until a couple hours before his death, which the coroner estimated occurred at around 7:30 a.m. The coroner did not tell Henry's mother the part about Henry having suffered.

Helen Evashevski was devastated by the death of her son, especially when she heard how preventable it had been. A substantial legal settlement did little to mollify her grief. Neither did the criminal charges brought against Mr. DelaGrange by the sheriff's department. He was ultimately acquitted.

The mysterious blanket, beads, feather, and bow and arrow found on Henry's body did mollify her grief. She was grateful, knowing that somebody at least had taken the trouble to properly tend to her son.

In the aftermath of Henry's death, the Weaverville Junior Boy Rangers were disbanded and all their leaders, including Horace DelaGrange, were barred from ever again being associated with the organization. The entire statewide Junior Boy Rangers organization was dissolved shortly after due to dwindling membership, unfavorable publicity, and financial problems arising from Mrs. Evashevski's damages claim. A Boy Scout troop replaced the Junior Boy Rangers in Weaverville.

Henry was given a lavish second funeral at the Catholic church in Weaverville. Everyone from Henry's school showed up. At the service, many of his classmates and some of the Junior Boy Rangers got up and told how much they liked Henry and how much fun he was to be around.

It made Helen Evashevski very proud.

Two years after Henry's death, the local Boy Scout Council, headquartered in Redding, named a property they had purchased for him. It became the Henry Wadsworth Evashevski Boy Scout Camp. Fifteen years after that, at Helen Evashevski's urging, members of Henry's old Junior Boy Rangers group, now grown up, placed the monument and plaque alongside the Caribou Lake Trail where Henry's body had been found. Henry, the worst Junior Boy Ranger who ever lived, would have been amused by all the fuss.

But once again, it made Helen very proud.

They never did find out who built the funerary platform and performed the Chimariko warrior ceremony, but it probably doesn't matter.

"Besides," said my grandson Brandon, "that's a secret between Henry and Kateri, and it's nobody else's business."

TO VISIT
The hike: Caribou Lake Trail from the Stuart Fork Trail, Trinity Center, California (Trinity Alps Wilderness, Shasta-Trinity National Forest)
Distance: Two and a half miles one-way, plus twelve miles from the Stuart Fork trailhead to the Caribou Lake trailhead, near Portuguese Camp
Directions: Take CA 3 north from Weaverville to Trinity Alps Road near the Stuart Fork Bridge. Drive three more miles to the Stuart Fork trailhead.

16

Swift, Immediate, and Violent

PART 1

In my experience, 99 percent of the time the wilderness is quiet, serene, and predictable—and absolutely nothing happens. On the rare occasions when things do happen, they are usually swift (meaning fast moving, like a diving osprey), immediate (of extremely short duration, like a twig snapping in two), and violent. And then the quiet, peace, and solitude descend once again. That's how nature is. That's how nature works. Most of the time.

This is not an offhand opinion but a conclusion based on more than six hundred hikes during a long career as a professional hiking guide writer. If my hikes averaged five hours each, that's 180,000 minutes of hiking. Of those 180,000 minutes, I have spent a total of ten minutes witnessing flash floods, three minutes observing bears, thirty seconds dodging rattlesnakes, ten seconds in the presence of foxes, five seconds watching cougars vanish into the underbrush, and less than one second watching lightning strike.

These things happen so rarely, and so briefly, that one can easily get lulled into complacency and forget that 99 percent is not 100 percent.

On October 5, 2005, it took less than one second for me to break my leg while hiking five miles up a wilderness trail, setting up a chain of events that put me in serious danger of death and changed my perception of life, death, God, and eternity forever.

PART 2

In July 2006 I married an amazing and wonderful woman named Lynn. The beautiful, all-denim ceremony took place indoors (it was 106 degrees out) in a tiny synagogue in Ashland, Oregon. My best man was Lynn's teenage son, David. His toast, during the reception following the ceremony, was especially memorable.

"I guess Art asked me to be his best man," he said holding up his glass, "because I was the one who went for help when he broke his leg on the Union Peak Trail, and he keeps telling everyone that I saved his life. What he fails to mention is that the accident occurred shortly after he confided in me that he planned to marry my mother."

He was joking of course. We had no such conversation. But it drew a huge laugh. David was being modest. He did save my life that day.

Two years after the wedding, David graduated from South Medford High School. To graduate from high school in Medford, Oregon, you need to research and write a "Senior Project." David based his Senior Project on the incident alluded to in the toast—my broken leg five miles up Crater Lake National Park's Union Peak Trail, his amazing run for help, and my ultimate rescue by a National Park Service Search and Rescue Team.

His senior project was titled *Wilderness Preparedness, Survival and Rescue.* In the first section he described the events on Union Peak in detail. The section was called "How Not to Prepare for a Hike."

PART 3

I first met Lynn in the Medford airport in September 2002 while flying to New York for my Aunt Blanche's funeral. Lynn was flying back to New York after visiting a friend. Even though Lynn had spent her entire life in and around New York City, she loved the Western wilderness and was anxious to visit every trail I wanted to show her.

Mostly I found her amazingly easy to talk to. We frequently discussed things that I had never before admitted to anybody.

On one date in particular, after she moved to Medford in October 2003, we had rented and watched a movie called *Love and Death*, starring Woody Allen and Diane Keaton. It had to do with Allen's character being conscripted to fight in the Napoleonic Wars on the side of Russia while being in love with Keaton's character.

"Not his best movie," I said afterwards as we snuggled in the dark on the couch.

"It was OK. A little pretentious, maybe."

"I was disappointed," I concluded. "Years ago I read an interview with Woody Allen where he said that the only two things he fears in life are love and death. I thought maybe the movie would offer some genuine insights into that."

"Do you fear love and death?" Lynn asked softly.

"I don't fear love," I said, giving her a squeeze. "But I imagine everyone fears death."

"I don't. I believe in Heaven. Don't you?"

"I wish I did. I want to. But I just can't make myself. There's not one scintilla of proof, or even a scintilla of flimsy evidence, that there's an afterlife. There have been times during my life when I worried about death constantly, about never again having a moment of conscious awareness for all eternity. It's not a comforting thought."

"And now?"

"I'm still not happy about it. But a few years ago I had a conversation at a cocktail party with a friend who was dying. I asked if he was afraid, and he said absolutely not. He said that in his observation, people who are inordinately afraid of death are actually afraid of life. That helped quite a bit, but I still worry about death far too much."

"Do you believe in God?"

"I think so. But you know me; I wrestle with everything, like Jacob wrestled with the angel. In the end he defeats the angel and the angel names him 'Israel,' which means 'God Wrestler.' That's me, the God Wrestler."

"I love you," was her only comment. A minute later, we were both asleep.

I was about six when I first pondered what death felt like and its utter inevitability, and I didn't like it. I remember playing with a Hopalong Cassidy cap gun in our back yard one warm summer day in 1949 and frightening myself over the eternal question that has plagued all humankind since they acquired the ability to think about the future. It occurred to me that perhaps you dream when you die. That, I thought, would make death much more tolerable.

Of course I was unaware, being only six, of the many metaphysical and cosmological theories—some propounded by the world's greatest thinkers—which held that life itself is nothing but an elaborate, extended dream, or that our existence on Earth is all in the mind of our Creator, with no physical reality.

"Yeah, that's the ticket," I said to myself. "You dream when you die." I liked the idea and excitedly ran into the house to check it out with my mother, who was sitting at the dining room table drinking coffee, smoking, and reading a newspaper.

"Mommy, do you dream when you die?"

"No," she replied, without looking up.

PART 4

I'm not sure why I chose the Union Peak Trail at Crater Lake National Park for our hiking sojourn on that cool October day in 2005. Perhaps it was because even after living near Crater Lake for thirty-five years, I have never grown tired of it. Perhaps it was because Lynn, who would be accompanying me, preferred trails that weren't too steep but had a little length to them.

The Union Peak Trail was ideal on both counts. The five-and-a-half-mile route leads to an extremely remote corner of Crater Lake National Park. The path rises gently for five miles and then soars nine hundred feet in a half mile in one of the steepest, most difficult and exhausting trail pitches you're likely to find anywhere.

I didn't tell Lynn about the horrendously steep part, only about the long, gentle part. I figured she would have no problem with the easy five miles. And even if she chose to sit out the final half mile, I knew that the view of the immense white pyramid at the end of the trail would be incredible. As I later discovered, it's a view seen by very few people, including most National Park Service employees.

Most visitors to Crater Lake National Park are aware of Union Peak only as the big, white, rocky summit that briefly looms in the distance at mile sixty-eight on OR 62 as you approach the park from the west. You come around a bend and there it is, poking majestically above the trees. A few seconds later you round another bend and the peak vanishes, never to return to view on any paved road.

To climb Union Peak, you park at the southbound Pacific Crest Trail trailhead on OR 62, a mile from the park's south entrance station. From the sweet-smelling, mosquito-ridden, little lodgepole pine flat, you hike south on the Pacific Crest Trail (PCT) for three miles, then west on the Union Peak Trail for two and a half miles. And there you are.

As it turned out, I was extremely lucky to be in a national park that day, at a trailhead only one mile from an entrance station. Had I been five miles up a Forest Service trail, which had been the case on 90 percent of my previous hikes, there's no telling how things might have turned out. Things would also have been worse—far worse—had I been alone, which had also been the case on 90 percent of my hikes before I met Lynn.

As we planned the trip, the only thing that bothered me was the report of "snow at higher elevations" that had occurred two days earlier. I worried that at seven thousand feet elevation, the trail might be blanketed with snow. But since then it had been quite warm (for October) and sunny, if very cool at night. On the day of our hike, the world was bright, shining, and fragrantly autumnal. The high temperature in Medford, Oregon, the nearest city to Crater Lake, was predicted to reach around 70 degrees Fahrenheit. The previous night, the Medford temperature had dropped to 34 degrees. But Medford's elevation is only 1,500 feet. At seven thousand feet, temperatures on Union Peak would be much cooler. That's why I took the precaution of wearing a light windbreaker instead of just a T-shirt.

Just before dinner the evening before the hike, I was sitting in the living room of Lynn's apartment in Medford watching TV. Lynn was in the adjacent kitchen cooking. Neither of her teenage sons, Eric and David, was home at the time.

"Can I ask David if he wants to come hiking with us tomorrow?" she said as the scent of wok-fried chicken wafted across the room. David was fifteen and a bright, inquisitive, active, and very athletic tenth grader whom I liked a lot.

One of David's many activities was the high school cross-country track team. I viewed his track achievements with some parental (or impending step-parental) pride but also as an activity that felt a little alien to my own life experiences. I always tended to be just the opposite of David—clumsy, slow, and a terrible athlete. Although I didn't often admit it, I chose hiking as my preferred exercise because, yes, it was challenging, aesthetic, and varied but also because you could go at your own pace and nobody cared if you did not look sleek and elegant as you walked.

On two or three previous hikes with David, he had walked on ahead by himself and reached the end of the trail long before his mother and I showed up. Still, he seemed to enjoy the treks, although like most high schoolers, he tended to have a rather full schedule.

"Sure," I said to Lynn without looking up from the TV. "Ask him."

To our delight and surprise, David said yes.

PART 5

It was a beautiful, sunny autumn morning, around 10:00 a.m., when we arrived at the southbound trailhead for the Pacific Crest Trail in Crater Lake National Park. Even though summer was over and winter was well on its way, you could still smell the fragrant balsam sap of the Shasta red firs and the pine sap of the lodgepole and western white pines. It was a truly great day for hiking.

Lynn and I love hiking but make it a point not to get too fanatical about it. We go only on day hikes, turn back if we get overtired or bored, and mostly just enjoy ourselves. Preparation for these easy outings had gotten to be a habit that we rushed though without much thought or planning: We brought lunch, snacks, drinking water, and a little extra clothing just in case. We had cell phones but knew they probably would not work in the middle of a national park.

The truth was that in thirty-five years, nothing really bad had ever happened to me on a hike. I'd never needed a compass, knife, hatchet, or tourniquet. Not even matches, except when camping out overnight, which I had not done in years. Even on my extremely rare overnight outings, I usually fixed cold meals so that I wouldn't attract bears or have to mess with things like camp stoves. I had a few Band-Aids tucked inside a flap in my wallet, but they were old and funky from having been there for years. I think Lynn carried some gauze pads, adhesive tape, and Neosporin in the little day pack she carried, but I wouldn't bet on it.

In six hundred hikes, I'd sprained an ankle once and reduced the swelling by dunking the ankle in a creek. I had managed to walk out four miles with little difficulty. The ankle quickly went numb and stopped hurting until I got to the car, then it hurt like mad all the way home. I had it X-rayed a few days later, but they found nothing. The doctor prescribed an Ace bandage and a few Tylenol.

I also fell and bonked by forehead on a rock once while hiking and got stung on the neck by a bald hornet—both hurt like hell for a few minutes but did no lasting harm. I dropped a boulder on my foot once, but that, too, caused no real damage.

And that was about it as far as my experience with hiking injuries.

In short, despite being a supposed "expert" in outdoors lore, I had gotten decidedly complacent about basic safety and allowed myself to gradually slide into woeful and dangerous unpreparedness, which is the exact opposite of what I try to teach readers in my hiking books. Since I was also, theoretically, in charge of the safety of Lynn and David, my laxity was inexcusable.

Still, what could happen? We'd walk in, stare at the pyramid for a while, eat our lunch, and walk out. It was a hike like any other hike, and easier than most.

The path's first two miles inscribed a straight line through the woods. It crossed no creeks, there were no noticeable landmarks, and little sunlight penetrated to the forest floor or onto our bodies. The woods seemed dark, humid, and chilly, even for an old-growth, closed-canopy understory. I found the darkness a little unusual, since lodge-pole pine, which constituted about 30 percent of the forest trees, tend to allow in a fair amount of light. After a mile or so, we started encountering a few very gentle hills, with easy ups and downs. Otherwise, the boring, featureless expanse continued.

David spent most of the first couple miles bounding far ahead and then waiting for us to catch up. Lynn kept yelling at him to slow down and wait for us. But holding David to our pace was like trying to rein in a ferret.

An hour into the hike, Lynn announced that she wasn't feeling well and wanted to go back to the truck. David and I offered to go with her, but she insisted that we continue without her. After assuring us that her sudden illness was nothing serious, she turned around and headed back down the trail.

A few minutes later, at the top of a small, densely wooded rise, David and I encountered the sign for the side trail to Union Peak, an etched metal square bolted to a metal post with an arrow pointing to the right that said UNION PEAK—3 MILES. I was a little surprised at encountering the side trail so soon. We'd been hiking on the PCT for only about an hour, and I calculated that we'd gone about two and a half miles. Also, most trail guides I'd read, including my own, claimed that it was three miles, not two and a half, up the PCT to the junction with the Union Peak Trail. I knew from having hiked the same path a decade earlier that the junction lay in the middle of a large, unforested pumice flat. We had not yet arrived at the pumice flat. Also, on my last trip, it had been two and a half miles, not three miles, from the PCT junction to Union Peak.

After a moment of confusion, I announced to David that apparently the Union Peak Trail had been rerouted since the last time I'd hiked it.

"Are you sure?" he inquired.

"Positive," I replied. "Most likely they decided to run the trail along the ridgecrest. On the old trail, you walked along the bottom of the ridge past the pyramid, then doubled back on a very steep upgrade to reach the pyramid's base. I remember wondering at the time why the trail didn't just follow the ridge. I guess somebody at the Park Service thought the same thing. The distances seem to be the same either way, though—five and a half miles—only now it's two and a half and three miles instead of three miles and two and a half."

We hung a quick right onto the Union Peak Trail, and it wasn't long before we found ourselves out of the woods, walking along the crest of a narrow, grassy ridge with excellent views to the north and south. The route occasionally dipped off the ridge into the dense forest and then wandered back to the ridge, which was dotted with stunted, wind-swept, fresh-smelling mountain hemlock and whitebark pine. It was gorgeous. Even David, who is not prone to eloquence about aesthetics, thought the scenery was spectacular.

"Nice," he commented at one particularly breathtaking vista point.

"Yeah," I replied.

David was about five-foot-seven and growing like a beanstalk, a handsome kid with crew cut hair and a ready, sincere smile. Lanky almost to the point of skinny, he walked with an easy lope apparently unfazed by upgrades, distances, or any other stressor.

Unlike David, I was not in the best shape of my life. Not even close. A year and a half earlier, I'd contracted pneumonia and nearly coughed myself to death. My lungs still weren't quite back to normal. I'd also gained weight as a result of the illness, which I could not seem to lose. Although I was fit enough to tackle this particular trail, I had no intention of attempting the ultra-steep rock pyramid at the end. I'd climbed the pyramid the last time I'd hiked this trail and knew it was monstrous. However, I expected that David would have no problem whatsoever.

David and I didn't talk much as we hiked along the ridge, but I noticed that he no longer wandered far ahead, as he had done when his mother was with us. Whenever my overweight, sixty-two-year-old body lumbered up one of the steeper spots, David would stand just ahead of me, looking on solicitously to make sure I was OK. He wasn't obtrusive or impatient, and he probably wasn't even aware that he was doing it.

For the most part, the path along the ridge held a remarkably even grade with few steep spots. It was always uphill, but it was mostly an easy uphill.

From the ridge we could see for miles north and south. However, the one thing we could not see was the pyramid of Union Peak that marked the final destination and end of the trail. A few miles north of the ridge, we could see the peaks on the south side of the Crater Lake rim—Mount Scott, Garfield Peak, and Cloudcap. You could see Llao Rock poking up from the lake's north rim, but you could not see the actual lake.

The south side view was just as interesting. We peered squarely into the Seven Lakes basin at the core of the Sky Lakes Wilderness Area, about eight miles away. Rising behind the basin was Devil's Peak. The various glacial cirque basins of the Seven Lakes basin could be seen merging, then swooping down over a steep incline into the valley of the Middle Fork of the Rogue River—the longest, deepest, and most dramatic glacially carved canyon in Oregon—which ran to the south and west of our ridgetop vantage point. I'd hiked up the Middle Fork twice over the years and down it once.

"Neat," said David as I explained all this to him.

A few minutes later, two miles onto the Union Peak Trail and four and a half miles into the hike, the summit finally revealed itself—big, bold, and brassy, glistening in the bright autumn sunshine. It was very near, only about a half mile away, very large and very white. With its immense size, I was amazed that we had not been able to see it until then.

"We have to climb that?" said David.

"You can. I don't plan to."

"Cool," said David. "I'll try not to take too long."

While passing a barren little flat just before the start of the rise that sloped directly onto and up the nine-hundred-foot pyramid, I noticed a pile of sticks and small logs on the left.

"That's where the old trail meets the new trail," I said, gesturing toward the narrow path that could be seen emerging on the far side of the brush pile. David glanced over but didn't say anything, and we kept walking. Beyond the little flat, the path wound back and forth a couple times up some loose scree slopes, then took off up the white granite rock.

When we arrived at the actual rock face, I walked for six or seven minutes, found myself gasping for air, and sat down. At my urging, David scampered on ahead like a happy, curious chipmunk. The trail up the pyramid was extremely steep, exceeding a 45-degree angle in spots, but it was relatively shady due to the towering rock face and the scattered, gnarled, windswept trees that somehow anchored themselves in the multiplicity of cracks and crevices.

Had it been July instead of October, I'm sure the path would have been far less shady and much more exhausting. In October, though, the sun never gets directly overhead. Still, it was a difficult climb.

I sat for five minutes, walked for five minutes, sat for ten minutes, walked for three minutes, and so forth. After David had been gone forty-five minutes, I began to worry a little that he should be returning by now. Soon after, to my amazement, I actually found myself approaching the summit. That was when David finally reappeared, scrambling down the path as it wound high above me.

"Damn," he said, stopping to catch his breath. "Those last few hundred feet were a bitch."

Union Peak as seen from Mount Scott Trail. The author broke his leg in the clearing just to the right of the pyramid.

"I know," I said. "The trail disappears and you have to scramble up the rock face. I assume you made it OK."

"Yeah," he said. "I was starting to get out of breath, but it was great. You want me to wait while you go to the top? It's not that far."

"Nah," I said, amazed that David had actually gotten tired. "I've been there before." As we started back down, I added, "You can relax now. The worst is over."

That turned out to be one of the least accurate statements I've ever made.

PART 6

As we climbed back down, David became a lot more talkative. I told him about my previous experience coming down off the pyramid. Rounding a tight bend ten years earlier, I'd accidentally brushed against a large boulder, maybe a foot in diameter, and knocked it squarely onto my foot. It hit so hard that it bounced. I was sure my foot was smashed to smithereens, but it was completely unharmed; the rock didn't even leave a bruise.

"Have you ever had a broken bone?" David asked as we scurried down the loose scree fields piled up against the pyramid's base.

"Never," I said, "although I've fallen a million times and had a couple of badly sprained ankles."

"I've never had a broken bone either," he said as we reached the bottom of the pyramid and stepped out onto the little level flat where the old trail came in, marking the end of the pyramid and the upper end of the ridge.

At that instant—that very instant—my left foot shot out from under me, slipping on the exposed, tightly compacted, rock-hard soil that was covered with a few loose sand granules. Smooth rock thinly covered with sand granules, as I well knew, can be extremely treacherous.

Simultaneously, the tip of my low-top New Balance walking shoe caught on some unseen microspeck. My foot buckled backward under me, propelling me suddenly forward. I landed spread-eagle, face down on the ground, hitting very hard—as though I'd been body slammed by a five-hundred-pound sumo wrestler.

The part that bothered me most was a soft, muffled "pop" that emanated from my left ankle halfway through the fall. It was a sickening noise, and I was pretty sure I knew what it was. I knew absolutely that it was not good. In fact, it was very bad. Sitting up, I looked at my ankle and saw that my entire foot was now displaced sideways by about an inch and was no longer firmly anchored to the end of my leg.

"You OK?" asked David.

"I don't think so. I heard a 'pop,' and I seem to have dislocated my foot."

"That sucks. Your foot sure doesn't look very good. It looks like a trout dangling from a fishing line."

"Yeah, but it also seems to be slowly slipping back into place."

The conversation after the accident took about a minute, during which I could actually see my foot slowly moving back into proper alignment. Still, I was not optimistic.

The last time I'd sprained an ankle on a hike, I walked four miles on it. But I hadn't heard a "pop" that time, and my foot hadn't been dislocated.

"I'll be real surprised if you can walk on that," said David.

With the foot now appearing a little less dislocated, David reached out a hand and helped me stand up. Leaning on David, the first tentative step was relatively painless. So was the second step. I began to feel a tiny bit hopeful.

The third step reminded me of the old *Star Trek* episode where Captain Kirk and the *Enterprise* crew are on this planet whose rulers have attached metal collars around their necks. The crew gets zapped every time they do something wrong—and getting zapped sends them writhing on the ground screaming in agony.

In short, after the third step, I found myself writhing on the ground screaming in agony. The pain hadn't lasted very long, but it felt as though I'd been struck by lightning.

"What can I do?" asked David, looking concerned but surprisingly calm.

"I don't know," I said. "Maybe we could rig up a crutch."

The only suitable deadwood was about three hundred feet straight downhill, at the farthest edge of the clearing. David ran down, picked out a sun-bleached length of wood with a side branch sticking out about four feet up, and brought it back. It was perfect.

I quickly discovered that walking on a single crutch is not easy. Even leaning on David, I kept losing my balance and ending up on the ground. Or I would accidentally put weight on the ankle, it would hurt like hell for an instant, and I would end up on the ground. Even when I didn't end up on the ground, I made such slow progress, and each step was so labored and exhausting, that it would have taken an hour just to cover the hundred feet or so to where our path exited the little open flat on its long journey back to the trailhead. I didn't think about it then, but I was starting to go into shock. Not to mention that I was exhausted from my workout on the pyramid.

"This is no good," I said. "Maybe you should just go for help."

"I can do that. Should we splint the ankle first?"

David broke up the crutch by holding it with one hand and stomping on it and fashioned two splints. I tied them in place, one on either side of my bad ankle, with David's T-shirt that he had ripped into cloth lengths. It was an excellent splint, but I still couldn't walk.

"I should probably find someplace a little more sheltered to wait," I said, eying a small clump of trees at the edge of the flat on the side away from the summit, about one hundred feet away. Leaning on David, I tried walking again, but after falling three more times, I decided instead to crawl to the clump of trees.

That proved to be even worse than trying to walk, because the same decomposed granite sand-granules-over-rock that had caused my tumble now poked their little crystal knifepoints into the palms of my hands. I made it to the trees, but it was extremely painful; my palms were starting to bleed by the time I got there. I could not have gone much farther.

"Do you have any matches to start a fire?" I asked David. "I didn't bring any, and once the sun dips behind the pyramid, it could get awfully cold up here. If the summit is 7,700 feet and we're nine hundred feet lower, that puts us at 6,800 feet. And from the barrenness and stunted trees, I would guess that this ridge can get very windy."

"I didn't bring any matches. Sorry. I can leave you my sweatshirt, a sandwich, my watch, and a bottle of water. But I should probably take my other water bottle with me. I plan to run all the way."

"You're going to run the entire five miles?"

"Sure. I've run five miles before, tons of times."

"But you've never run five miles after climbing a mountain."

"Yeah, but this will be mostly downhill. It shouldn't take long. At ten minutes a mile, it'll take fifty minutes—an hour at the most, although I've run a mile in five minutes."

I did not mention to David that my personal best time for one mile was nine minutes.

As we spoke, David's watch informed us that it was 2:30 in the afternoon, which meant we had perhaps four hours of daylight left.

"OK," I said, dubious but having no choice. "But be careful. I sure wish our cell phones worked."

"Don't worry about a thing," said David as he turned away. "Just stay where you are, don't go too far from the trail, and try to keep warm and calm. I'll get you out of this."

And then he was gone and I was alone.

PART 7

I didn't know it at the time, but when David makes a statement like "Don't worry, I'll get you out of this," it's not just a statement but a sacred obligation. Here is the story, later told to me, about the adventures of David and Lynn in their attempt to have me rescued before I died of exposure. David ran and ran and ran, as fast as he reasonably could, and arrived back at the trailhead in only forty-five minutes. He stopped only once, at the junction, to take a drink.

Lynn, meanwhile, having sat in the car for almost four hours, started feeling much better and figured that David and I would be showing up any time, so she began walking up the trail to meet us. She'd walked for ten minutes when David showed up, sweaty and out of breath.

"What's wrong? Where's Art?" she asked.

"He's about five miles up. I'm pretty sure he broke his leg. He said that if he has to spend the night up there, he could freeze to death. Otherwise, he seems OK. He's alert and seems to be thinking clearly."

"OK then," said Lynn, "let's find some help."

Mother and son got into their white Toyota pickup and drove one mile to the park's south entrance toll station, where a pleasant-looking woman in her fifties sat in the booth stopping cars, collecting tolls, and passing out brochures.

"My boyfriend broke his leg or something on the Union Creek Trail and he's stranded," Lynn told the woman. "What should I do?"

"Pull over and wait," said the woman, "and don't worry. We're all well trained for this kind of thing."

From the truck, Lynn and David could see the woman talking on the radio. A few minutes later, a Park Service vehicle showed up and the lady pointed Lynn and David out to the driver. The pair followed the Park Service vehicle to the park headquarters area, three miles up the highway and then through a maze of narrow roads and rustic stone buildings to a small, unobtrusive door with a sign that said DISPATCH. Lynn, David, and the driver went inside to a cluttered little office that smelled of adhesive tape and stale coffee. Lynn told the person at the desk, a rugged-looking man with an immense square chin, who was dressed in a ranger uniform, what had happened.

"Most of our regular search-and-rescue people have left for the season," Lynn was informed by the man, whose name was Mike. "So

I'll have to call around for volunteers. That may take an hour or two. Meantime, can we get you anything? Sandwiches, soda pop, candy bars?"

Lynn and David accepted the offer, and the food showed up an hour or so later. As it turned out, there were three regular search-and-rescue members still on duty, including an emergency medical technician. In addition, three volunteers were quickly rounded up. Rounding out the group—they needed ten to twelve persons—proved a little more difficult, as everyone else had to drive in from the little town of Chiloquin, thirty-five miles away.

"Show me on the map exactly where he is," said Mike, who turned out to be the head of the park's search-and-rescue department. He and David turned to an immense, well-worn, highly detailed topographic wall map that had obviously been poked by thousands of fingers and more than a few pins.

"He's here, at this little open flat at the base of the pyramid, about five miles up, where the new trail joins the old trail."

According to Lynn, it was an excellent, clear, and concise description. Except that the map showed only one trail, not two, connecting the Pacific Crest Trail with Union Peak. The trail on the map broke off to the right three miles up the PCT, not two and a half miles, in the middle of a large flat. A quick glance told David that it was not the same trail as the one he and I had just taken, mainly because the trail on the map did not follow the top of a ridge.

"What do you mean by 'new trail'?" Mike asked.

"We turned onto the Union Peak Trail at two and a half miles, not three. Art said it had to be a new trail because the Union Peak Trail used to begin at mile three, like the one on the map. He even showed me when we passed the spot where the old trail meets the new trail. That's where he is, on the new trail, not far from where the two trails meet at the far end."

"I don't know anything about a new trail," Mike said. "Are you positive that's where he is?"

David reiterated his description of my location, and Mike kept grilling him, trying to get him to change his story.

Lynn, watching all this, could see David getting frustrated. She, in turn, began growing annoyed that the dispatcher didn't seem to believe

David. Lynn is not one to quietly endure such things, especially when her children are involved.

"Have you ever been on the Union Peak Trail?" she asked Mike finally.

"No," the dispatcher admitted. "I've been on the Pacific Crest Trail past the Union Peak turnoff to the southern park boundary, but that was five years ago."

"Well, my boyfriend writes hiking books—you sell a couple of them at your visitor center. He's been on every trail in the park and on every trail in Forest Service areas adjacent to the park. He knows trails, maps, and distances like the back of his hand. And if he says there's a new trail that begins at two and a half miles, then there's a new trail that begins at two and a half miles, and you'd be incredibly stupid to send your people past the new junction sign looking for the old trail at mile three while he's up there dying."

"I guess I'd better take the young man's word for it," said the dispatcher with a smile. "You need to know, though, that that's a very bad location. They're predicting a low temperature at park headquarters tonight of 28 degrees. At seven thousand feet, where your friend is located, it could go down to 20 or lower. Not to mention that's an extremely windy spot. I hope your friend has the good sense to move off the ridgetop. I'm instructing the search-and-rescue team to dress very warmly."

Finally, all was ready. The first group of six search and rescuers departed at 5:00 p.m. with a wheelbarrow stretcher (a stretcher with one large wheel attached to the front end) and several backpacks full of first-aid equipment, including an IV apparatus. A second group of six headed out at 9:00 p.m. with the goal of meeting the first group at the junction with the Union Peak Trail (either two and a half or three miles up) and relieving them. The little green park ambulance was driven to the trailhead to await the rescuers' return. Lynn and David ate dinner when the food arrived and waited in the dispatch office listening to the rescuers radio back periodic reports on their progress.

Mother and son smiled at each other in satisfaction when the team arrived at the junction with the Union Peak Trail after two and a half miles. It turned out that nobody on the search-and-rescue team had ever been on the Union Peak Trail before, old or new.

PART 8

As I waited alone in the little ridgetop clearing propped against a stunted, windswept whitebark pine, with little else to think about, I became fixated on my own imagined timeline for the rescue. Understand that I was in a state of semi-shock and not thinking clearly. In retrospect, and in all fairness, even though the search-and-rescue team arrived well after my anticipated and unrealistic timeline, they showed up with remarkable speed. I was extremely lucky. Had they arrived only an hour after they did, I'd have been in serious trouble with respect to body heat.

Soon after David's 2:30 departure, I calculated that he would reach the trailhead at around 3:30, which meant I could expect a helicopter to land in the little clearing no earlier than 4:00 p.m. and no later than perhaps 4:30. It never occurred to me that they would never send a helicopter without first dispatching a search-and-rescue team on the ground to ascertain the seriousness of my injury and the availability of a suitable landing site. (As it turned out, the little flat where I waited was definitely not a suitable landing site because the mountain summit was too close.)

If they sent only a ground search-and-rescue team to get me (assuming that the rescuers were all in much better shape than I), I anticipated that they would arrive no earlier than 5:00 p.m. and no later than 5:30. Give or take a few minutes. Five or 5:30, I knew, was also about when the sun would probably dip behind the looming rock pyramid that dominated my view. The pyramid would then cast a shadow across the little clearing, and the ridgetop would start to get very cold very fast. It had been getting dark between 6:30 and 7:00.

"I'll give it to 5:30 before I start worrying," I told myself. "Until then, there's nothing for me to do but sit here and wait."

The location was unbelievably beautiful—a little clump of stunted trees on a grassy ridge with the Crater Lake rim to the north, the Sky Lakes Wilderness to the south, and the rock pyramid's rise beginning a couple hundred feet to the west.

My first thoughts were about how magnificent the pyramid was and how lovely a spot I'd picked for my accident. Those thoughts, of course, quickly morphed into *You couldn't have picked a better place to die*. I'd often thought that I'd rather die on a trail, in a beautiful spot, of something swift and immediate like a heart attack or a fall over a cliff than waste away slowly in bed, sick and frightened. But not just yet.

One thing that I began doing early on was watch the shadow of the mountain inch its way across the clearing toward the spot where I sat. As long as the sun was shining on me, I felt warm, comfortable, and reasonably content.

To kill time, I drank a little water, ate a granola bar, looked at the watch every few minutes, and tried to nap. As an aging ADHD-type, the boredom was excruciating.

At about 4:00 p.m., when I had predicted the helicopter would arrive, I began listening for engine noises. Sure enough, within a couple minutes I heard the growl of an aircraft far in the distance. It could have been a helicopter. I looked up and around but didn't see anything. As I listened, the sound appeared to get closer—or at least louder—and I started getting excited. The noise lasted a very long time and ended up extremely loud. But I still couldn't see where it was coming from. Then it started sounding more and more distant. And then it was gone. Over the next hour, I heard aircraft engine noises three more times, but none got as close or as loud, or lasted as long, as that first one.

By five o'clock, I no longer expected a helicopter and started listening instead for the sound of a search-and-rescue team coming up the trail. By then, my water was gone, my food was gone, and I found myself seriously pondering—I should say obsessing on—the chances of ever being rescued at all.

I calculated that the odds of David not making it back to the trailhead within a reasonable period of time at about 2 percent. I figured that Lynn would make sure I was rescued—even if she had to do it herself—or die trying, but that the rangers at park headquarters might decide it was too cold and late in the day and persuade Lynn that they should wait until morning. By morning, I was absolutely certain, I would be dead of exposure (remember that it had snowed two nights earlier). I estimated the chances of the rescuers waiting until morning at 15 percent.

All the while, the mountain shadow was moving inexorably toward the spot where I sat. Shortly after 5:00, I drifted off to sleep for a few minutes. When I woke up, I was indeed in shadow, although there was still considerable daylight left. A stiff breeze was now blowing across the open, exposed ridge. I found myself shivering slightly despite wearing both a jacket and David's sweatshirt.

With great effort, I managed to move fifteen feet, around the same clump of trees, so that I was on the sheltered side, protected from the wind by the trees instead of out on the ridgetop. The wind was coming from the south, so I moved to the north side of the tree cluster. The change in location had the added advantage of putting me closer to the trail (about ten feet away). It had the disadvantage of putting me in a very moist spot, squarely atop a small patch of snow. Despite the dampness, the spot, which smelled pleasantly of wet soil and balsam, was very comfortable and sheltered, and the snow quickly melted. I'd have positioned myself closer to the trail, or even on the trail, but the spot by the trees formed a cozy little nest that I found myself reluctant to leave.

Too reluctant, as it turned out. All I wanted to do was lie there and huddle and sleep and try to stay warm. As 5:30 came with no sign of rescuers, then 6:00, then 6:30, it grew colder and colder. The wind grew stronger and steadier, and I found myself shivering more and more. I was pretty much OK as long as I huddled in my little nook, curled up in a fetal position with my arms wrapped around me and my shoulders hunched. At those times, I only shivered a little. When I changed position or got out of my fetal ball, I would shiver violently and uncontrollably. More so, I thought, than the wind and cold warranted.

At 6:30, as I continued to huddle in my little nest, I figured the chances were now about 40 percent that I would die. Amazingly, that didn't bother me nearly as much as I would have predicted. It would merely be an extension of going to sleep, which continued to strike me as a fine idea. Not that I was happy about the idea of dying. But I was happier about the idea of dying—much happier, in fact—than I was about the idea of making an effort to save myself.

Feeling guilty about my sudden lack of ambition for self-preservation, I began thinking about people I'd read about who, in the face of death, struggled mightily to their last ounce of strength and endurance to extricate themselves. I thought about the guy who was hiking in the wilderness when a boulder fell on and pinned his hand. After three days, he cut the hand off with a dull pocketknife and hiked out.

Or the guy who was driving on a dirt road when his car caught fire and burned off 60 percent of his skin. He walked ten miles to the nearest highway to save himself.

And here I was—after spending the past sixty-two years fearing death more than anything else in life—wanting only to sleep and most likely die.

With nowhere else to turn, and with no feasible escape plan coming to mind, I began talking to God, as I have done from time to time in my life, albeit infrequently. At that point, I had not talked to God in two or three years.

"Please get me out of this," I pleaded in my thoughts. "Let the rescuers show up before I freeze to death. Or better yet, give me the gumption to save myself. Do that and I promise I will believe in you forever."

And God, in His (or Her) infinite patience and wisdom, did not answer. Or at least He did not answer just then and in a way that was immediately obvious to me.

Soon after my attempt to bargain with the Divine Creator, I found my thoughts wandering to news stories I'd read where people died of exposure or hypothermia. I thought about the two men who had been backpacking during winter in a wilderness near where I live (the Wild Rogue) a few years earlier. When they came down off the mountain to the river's edge, one of the men realized he had forgotten something, so he went back up the mountain. It started snowing and he never came back. In spring they found his body, sitting peacefully and contentedly under a tree with his hands folded in his lap.

The message was clear: Hypothermia affects your will to survive. If I was to survive, I needed to overcome that. And fast!

By 7:00, as the last glimmer of daylight faded to night, I was almost certain I was a goner. Every neuron in my body and mind cried out in exhaustion to be left alone. I was prepared to die, right then and there.

As silly as this may sound, it was my vanity that ultimately saved the day and my life. Even though I was having a terrible time mustering the energy and will to survive, one nagging thought would not go away: Were I to give up, it would ruin my long-standing (and probably little deserved) local reputation as a rugged outdoorsman.

"When they get here, if they get here, I want them to know—Lynn and David to know, my beloved daughters to know, the newspaper reporters to know—that I at least tried," I said to myself. I realized that I could never make it all the way to the trailhead by myself, but I figured that if I could somehow at least get off the ridge and down into the woods, I might have a slightly better shot at surviving the night. If I remained where I was, I would die for certain.

With a deep sigh and shivering uncontrollably, I raised myself up onto my knees and pulled my jacket sleeves over my hands. After three slow, exhausting, and laborious steps, I was on the trail.

My mind, as always, began imagining the worst possible scenario in the most minute and unpleasant detail. It flashed pictures of me inching down the path with my sleeves ripped and my hands bleeding—in agonized pain at every step until I could go no farther and dropped dead from exhaustion. In no scenario could I imagine crawling more than a half mile or so, and it all seemed miserable and impossible.

"What a waste of time," I kept telling myself. "Better to die."

"You're probably right," said my vanity. "But why don't you at least take a few steps so that when they find you, they'll at least *think* you were trying to crawl out?"

"I don't want to," I protested.

"I know, but imagine how heroic you'll look," my vanity pointed out.

"All right, all right. But just a few steps."

I crawled exactly two steps down the trail.

And a voice, not too far away, yelled, "Is anybody there? Art? Hello?"

PART 9

The rescuers wrapped me in a plastic space blanket, gave me some food (but not much, on the theory that I could very well end up in surgery before long and should have an empty stomach), tied me to a stretcher, and at 7:30 headed out. The guy who had called my name was with a party of only two, but four others showed up a few minutes later, including a very sweet and reassuring lady in a park ranger uniform who turned out to be an emergency medical technician. She took my pulse and blood pressure and asked me who I was and if I knew what day it was.

"It's the first day of the rest of my life," I replied.

I heard her radio that I seemed alert and oriented and that my vital signs were normal.

The trip back took four hours (most of which, I was later told, Lynn and David spent playing Hangman in the dispatch office and listening to the rescuers' radio reports). The ride on the stretcher was too bumpy to try to sleep, and I had to go to the bathroom the entire time (they were not about to untie me after all that work lashing me down). The rescue team bantered and made jokes, and a point person walking a few feet ahead would frequently yell out, "rock on left" or "branch on right."

Being able to look only straight up, all I could see were stars, a few branches, and a lot of blackness. I couldn't see any of the amazing vistas that had illuminated the hike in the daytime; neither, I assumed, could the rescue team.

Shortly after passing the trail junction, where we turned back onto the Pacific Crest Trail, the relief team showed up. They bantered a little less, since it was getting late, and none of them talked to me at all. At 11:30 p.m., we arrived at the trailhead where I was put into a waiting ambulance tended by two very sweet ladies. They informed me that David and Lynn had decided to wait for me at the hospital in Klamath Falls instead of riding with me so that they'd have our truck with them. I was then driven ten miles to the eastern park boundary, where we hooked up with another ambulance, from Chiloquin, which drove the final sixty miles to the hospital in Klamath Falls.

I was tearfully reunited with Lynn at 1:00 a.m. Then I was X-rayed and informed that my fibula was broken in two places. The splints were removed and replaced with a form-fitted plastic splint held on by Ace bandages. I was complimented on the splint that David and I had fabricated by both the search-and-rescue team, who had decided to leave it in place, and by the physician who set the plastic splint. I couldn't help noticing that the two sun-bleached, lichen-covered sticks that we'd used for a splint looked very forlorn and out of place in the wastebasket of the ultramodern, antiseptic-smelling hospital emergency room.

The X-rays showed that when I initially twisted the ankle, I dislocated my foot, ripping out every tendon and connector. An instant later, as I fell forward, the loose foot was driven backward into my leg, between the large tibia and the much smaller fibula. The fibula is secured to the tibia by a dense web of connective tissue, all of which I tore loose when I broke the bone.

I underwent surgery the next day. They secured foot and fibula back into place with a long titanium screw, set the broken bone with a metal plate and three smaller screws, stitched it up, and wrapped it all in a removable cast. I was told that I would probably be in a cast for six months, that it could be a year before I could hike again, and that I might never regain full motion in my ankle. As it turned out, the cast was off in twelve weeks, and Lynn and I went hiking two weeks after that. (It was a short hike, and I stepped very gingerly over any place that might possibly be slippery.)

EPILOGUE

Naturally I noticed the close timing between my attempt to save myself and the arrival of the rescue team. However, it wasn't until Lynn brought it up a couple weeks later that it occurred to me that the two events might actually be related and that God (as Lynn calls the Creator of the Universe) deliberately waited for me to take action before allowing me to be rescued.

"How would that work?" I asked.

"I don't know. Maybe God set a thousand possible outcomes in motion when you broke your leg, and because you made the choices you did, He or She allowed the one in which you were rescued to proceed."

I haven't a clue whether Lynn is right or wrong, but I do know that for some reason, as a result of the experience on Union Peak, I no longer fear death (or at least I don't fear death nearly as much). I now feel confident that when the time comes, the Creator of the Universe will be there for me and that I will be able to handle it without going to pieces.

Still, the last time Lynn and I went hiking, we carried three quarts of water, three sandwiches, four granola bars, cheese slices, a complete first-aid kit, a compass, a topographic map, hiking poles, sunscreen, insect repellent, a water filter, an extra jacket each, a space blanket, Sting-Kill swabs, a snakebite kit, Tylenol, a long-nosed lighter, steel wool (excellent tinder), and a set of walkie-talkies. We didn't use any of it, except for the water and two granola bars, but you never know when you're going to need such things.

TO VISIT

The hike: Pacific Crest Trail to Union Peak Trail, Crater Lake National Park, Oregon

Distance: Two and a half miles on the PCT to Union Peak Trail, then three more miles to the summit (one-way)

Directions: From I-5 in Medford, Oregon, follow OR 62 (Crater Lake Highway) to Crater Lake National Park. (Turn right just past the town of Union Creek to stay on OR 62.) At mile seventy-eight, a green sign pointing to the right says PACIFIC CREST TRAIL PARKING. Park there, follow the PCT southbound to the junction with the Union Peak Trail, then turn right.

ABOUT THE AUTHOR

Art Bernstein is the author of fifteen nature and hiking guides, including FalconGuides' *Hiking Oregon's Southern Cascades and Siskiyous*. An avid hiker and naturalist, he holds a master's degree in Natural Resource Management from the University of Michigan. He lives in Gold Hill, Oregon.